JAPANESE PARTICIPATION IN BRITISH INDUSTRY

THE CROOM HELM SERIES IN INTERNATIONAL BUSINESS

Academic Editor: Alan M. Rugman, Dalhousie University

Multinationals and Transfer Pricing

Alan M. Rugman and Lorraine Eden

Multinationals: The Swedish Case

Erik Hörnell and Jan-Erik Vahhe

JAPANESE PARTICIPATION IN BRITISH INDUSTRY

JOHN H. DUNNING

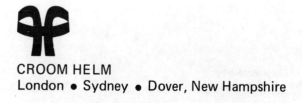

CROOM HELM
London • Sydney • Dover, New Hampshire

© John H. Dunning 1986
Croom Helm Ltd, Provident House, Burrell Row,
Beckenham, Kent BR3 1AT

Croom Helm Australia Pty Ltd, Suite 4, 6th Floor,
64-76 Kippax Street, Surry Hills, NSW 2010, Australia

British Library Cataloguing in Publication Data

Dunning, John H.
    Japanese participation in British industry:
    Trojan horse or catalyst for growth? – (Croom
    Helm series international business)
    1. Investments, Japanese – Great Britain
    2. Great Britain – Industries
    I. Title
    332.6'7352'041   HC256.6

    ISBN 0-7099-4500-0

Croom Helm Ltd, Washington Street
Dover, New Hampshire 03820, USA

Library of Congress Cataloging in Publication Data

Dunning, John H.
    Japanese participation in British industry.

    (Croom Helm series in international business)
    Bibliography: p.
    1. Corporations, Japanese—Great Britain. .
2. Investments, Japanese—Great Britain. I. Title.
II. Series.
HD2845.D86   1986   338.8'8952'041   85-28374
ISBN 0-7099-4500-0

Printed and bound in Great Britain by
Biddles Ltd, Guildford and King's Lynn

CONTENTS

LIST OF FIGURES AND TABLES

ACKNOWLEDGEMENTS

I wish, first, to acknowledge, with gratitude, the Department of Industry for permitting me to publish most of the material contained in a report prepared for them in 1984; and the Economists Advisory Group (EAG) on whose behalf I directed the research project. I should stress, however, that I alone take responsibility for what is written in this book, and that the opinions expressed represent neither those of the Department of Industry or EAG.

Second, this book could not have been completed without the co-operation of the senior management and staff of a large number of Japanese affiliates and UK firms, who gave liberally of their time and patience in completing extensive questionnaires, and allowing me to interview them. I also received much encouragement and guidance from officials at the Japanese Embassy in the UK, and from the Japanese Trade Centre (JETRO) in London.

To all those who shared in my researches, I extend my very warmest thanks; I only hope I have represented their views correctly, and that they will find something of interest and value in the pages which follow.

Finally a word of appreciation to the typists, both at EAG and the University of Reading for their contribution in preparing this book for publication.

J.H.D.

1 JAPANESE DIRECT INVESTMENT IN THE UK: THE GENERAL PICTURE

Introduction

This monograph contains the results of a field survey on Japanese manufacturing affiliates in the UK conducted for the (UK) Department of Industry between July 1983 and March 1984. It is based on data provided by all the affiliates known to be operating at 30 June 1983, supplemented by published information (e.g. official statistics, company accounts, journal articles, etc.). Information and opinions were also obtained from 20 suppliers and 12 competitors of Japanese affiliates in the UK.

The book is divided into three main parts. Part I, comprising Chapters 2 and 3, describes the extent and form of Japanese participation in UK industry and the reasons for it. Part II, which consists of Chapters 4 and 5, examines some organisational relationships between the affiliates and their parent companies; and then presents some data about the performance of the affiliates, *vis-à-vis* both their parent companies and their UK competitors. Chapters 6 to 11, which make up Part III, review some of the ways in which the Japanese presence in the UK has impinged upon the UK economy. As can be seen by the terms of reference for the study,[1] we were asked to give especial attention to the extent to which direct investment by Japanese MNEs has aided the transfer of (acceptable) Japanese management styles and technologies to the UK economy; and to identify both the incentives and obstacles to such a transfer. A final chapter speculates a little about the future prospects for Japanese participation in UK industry.

Japanese Direct Investment Worldwide and in Europe 1951-1984

As a background to the results of the field study, we set out, in Tables 1.1 and 1.2, some details on the UK's share of Japanese direct foreign investment since 1951. Table 1.1 shows that, at the end of March 1984, the UK accounted for 4% of the cumulative investment, considerably more than that of any other European country, but well below the 27.0%

1

Table 1.1: Japanese Foreign Direct Investment by Regions of the World and Countries of Europe (cumulative, April 1951 to March 1984)

	Cases	Amount (US $ million)	Percent share
North America	11,478	17,926	29.3
US	10,846	16,535	27.0
Canada	623	1,391	2.3
Latin America	3,924	10,730	17.5
Brazil	1,244	3,955	6.5
Panama	1,477	3,245	5.3
Asia	10,170	16,399	26.8
Indonesia	1,237	7,641	12.5
Hong Kong	2,180	2,287	3.9
Singapore	1,557	1,705	2.8
Korea	1,150	1,442	2.4
Middle and Near East	295	2,654	4.3
Europe	3,338	7,136	11.6
United Kingdom	895	2,448	4.0
West Germany	662	925	1.5
France	579	634	1.0
Netherlands	226	662	1.0
Belgium	222	588	1.0
Luxembourg	64	601	1.0
Switzerland	176	373	0.6
Spain	129	283	0.5
USSR	6	193	0.4
Irish Republic	52	179	0.3
Italy	121	127	0.2
Others	206	162	0.3
Africa	989	2,871	4.7
Liberia	537	2,015	3.3
Oceania	1,620	3,560	5.8
Australia	667	3,048	5.0
Total	31,814	61,276	100.0

Source: Japanese Ministry of Finance, Tokyo.

of the US. Over the final four years (1980-4), in which 48% of all the new investment since 1951 occurred, the UK's share fell to 2.1% (compared with 5.8% in the earlier period). Table 1.2 also shows some reorientation of Japanese investment towards other developed countries, and particularly North America, and away from the Middle and Near East. The geographical pattern is consistent with the findings of other scholars (e.g. Marsh, 1983)[2] who emphasise that, following the initial interest of Japanese investors in resource based sectors in developing countries (particularly in Asia and Latin America), there has been a

Table 1.2: Japanese Foreign Direct Investment, 1951-80 and 1980-84

	1951/80		1980/84		1951/84	
	$m	%	$m	%	$m	%
Developed countries						
North America	8,202	25.9	9,724	32.9	17,926	29.3
US						
Canada						
Europe	3,885	12.3	3,251	10.6	7,136	11.6
UK	1,824	5.8	624	2.2	2,448	4.0
West Germany	387	1.2	538	2.0	925	1.5
France	301	0.9	331	1.1	634	1.0
Netherlands	257	0.8	365	1.2	622	1.0
Belgium	224	0.7	364	1.2	588	1.0
Other	892	2.8	1,027	3.0	1,919	3.1
Oceania	2,077	6.6	1,483	6.0	3,560	5.8
Total	14,164	44.7	14,458	49.4	28,622	46.7
Developing countries						
Latin America	5,580	17.6	5,150	15.3	10,730	17.5
Asia	8,544	27.0	7,855	28.1	16,399	26.8
Middle East and Near East	2,101	6.6	553	1.8	2,654	4.3
Africa	1,306	4.1	1,565	5.6	2,871	4.7
Total	17,531	55.3	15,123	50.7	32,654	53.3
All countries	31,695	100.0	29,581	100.0	61,276	100.0

Note: Due to rounding up, percentages may not sum to 100.0.
Source: Japanese Ministry of Finance, Tokyo.

shift towards involvement in manufacturing and service activities in the OECD area.

Table 1.3 illustrates the changing sectoral distribution of Japanese direct investment in developed countries over recent years, and Table 1.4 presents the same distribution for Europe only in March 1984. The increase in the share of new investment directed to manufacturing industry, particularly the electrical machinery and transportation equipment sectors, is perhaps the main feature of Table 1.3. The significance of manufacturing, commercial and financial investments in Western Europe is particularly noteworthy; in March 1984, that region clearly had a comparative locational advantage for Japanese firms in the machinery, commerce, finance and insurance sectors. Oceania attracted Japanese investment mainly in mining and resource-based manufacturing activities. Japanese investment in North America (and particularly the US) is also strongly concentrated in the commercial sector, but relative to Europe and Oceania, its apparent strength lies in transport and electrical machinery and other services. Surveys by the Japan Trade

Table 1.3: Cumulative Regional and Industrial Distribution of Japan's Direct Investment in Developed Countries (% of total)

	North America As at 31.3.76	North America As at 31.3.84	Western Europe As at 31.3.76	Western Europe As at 31.3.84	Oceania[a] As at 31.3.76	Oceania[a] As at 31.3.84	Total developed areas As at 31.3.76	Total developed areas As at 31.3.84	Total world As at 31.3.76	Total world As at 31.3.84
Foodstuffs	1.4	2.3	1.3	0.8	3.8	1.7	1.6	1.8	1.8	1.4
Textiles	1.3	1.3	0.7	2.4	0.4	0.2	1.0	1.4	6.4	3.2
Wood & pulp	5.7	2.8	0.0	0.0	8.2	3.5	4.1	2.2	3.2	1.6
Chemicals	1.2	2.6	2.1	2.8	9.5	2.8	2.6	2.7	5.6	5.9
Metals	4.6	2.6	1.4	2.9	7.2	9.8	3.8	3.9	4.9	6.7
Industrial machinery	2.2	2.5	2.3	2.3	0.6	0.9	2.0	2.3	2.5	2.3
Electrical machinery	3.3	8.4	1.0	4.1	1.0	0.6	2.2	6.5	3.3	4.6
Transport equipment	0.7	4.6	0.2	2.1	3.1	6.8	0.8	4.3	2.3	3.8
Other manufacturing	0.9	1.8	1.2	2.7	0.1	2.0	0.9	2.1	2.4	2.3
Total manufacturing	21.2	29.2	10.1	20.0	34.1	28.3	19.1	27.3	32.4	31.9
Agriculture & forestry	0.7	1.3	0.0	0.0	3.3	2.5	0.8	1.2	1.3	1.2
Fishery	0.4	0.5	0.1	0.0	2.4	1.3	0.6	0.5	0.8	0.6
Mining	9.8	4.7	33.8[b]	12.0[b]	43.3	37.2	22.2	10.8	25.9	17.4
Construction	1.0	1.0	0.2	0.6	0.1	0.4	0.6	0.9	0.7	1.0
Commerce	39.7	33.6	10.3	23.3	8.8	13.1	25.8	29.0	13.9	15.7
Insurance & finance	11.1	11.8	17.0	24.1	2.8	2.4	12.0	14.0	8.2	8.1
Other services	15.0	17.2	26.4	16.7	4.8	14.5	17.6	15.0	13.3	21.2
Total non-manufacturing	77.7	70.1	87.8	76.7	65.5	71.4	79.6	71.4	64.1	65.2
Foreign branches	1.1	0.6	2.0	3.3	0.3	0.3	1.3	1.3	3.4	2.9
Total	100.0	100.0	100.0	100.0	100.0	100.0	100.0	100.0	100.0	100.0

Notes: a. Mostly Australia.
b. A high proportion of this is investment in the Middle East through the UK.
Source: Japanese Ministry of Finance, Tokyo.

Table 1.4: Industrial Structure of Japanese Direct European Investments in Europe (cumulative as of end of March 1984)

	Cases	US $m	Amount %	% of total overseas investment
Manufacturing				
Food	35	55	0.8	6.2
Textiles	98	170	2.4	8.6
Wood and pulp	1	0	0.0	0.0
Chemicals	76	199	2.8	5.5
Ferrous and non-ferrous metals	299	206	2.9	5.0
Machinery	123	164	2.3	11.4
Electrical machinery	99	294	4.1	10.4
Transport machinery	20	149	2.1	6.4
Others	114	191	2.7	13.5
All manufacturing industry	865	1,428	20.1	7.3
Non-manufacturing				
Agriculture/forestry & fisheries	7	2	0.0	0.2
Mining	9	859	12.0	8.0
Construction	16	40	0.6	6.8
Commerce	1,534	1,660	23.3	17.2
Finance and insurance	204	1,720	24.1	34.6
Business services	106	130	1.8	3.9
Transportation	10	3	0.0	0.1
Real estate	11	46	0.6	5.1
Others	228	975	13.7	19.0
All non-manufacturing	2,125	5,434	76.1	14.0
Establishment and expansion of branch offices	168	235	3.3	13.3
Property	180	38	0.5	6.4
Total	3,338	7,636	100.0	11.6

Source: Japanese Ministry of Finance, Tokyo.

Centre in New York (JETRO (US), 1981, 1984) suggest that there has been a dramatic increase in Japanese manufacturing investment in the US since the mid-1970s, and that in March 1984 there were upwards of 300 manufacturing affiliates employing over 60,000 people. Since the US is often the first preferred location of Japanese MNEs in the developed world, we shall later find it instructive to compare some of the findings of the JETRO surveys with those of our own.

Japanese Companies in the UK

By far the greater part of the involvement by Japanese companies in the UK is outside the manufacturing sector. Our own estimates (for the end of the financial year 1982/3) puts the total assets owned by Japanese MNEs in UK manufacturing industry at £163m ($264m); and capital employed (net assets) at £74m ($120m). These figures represent only about 11% and 5% of the total Japanese investment stake in the UK, but it should be noted that these data represent investment 'approved' by the Ministry of Finance and not the capital expenditure actually carried out.

Other data published by the Anglo-Japanese Economic Institute suggest that there were over 400 Japanese companies operating in the United Kingdom at the end of 1983. Table 1.5 shows that the great majority of these are concentrated in two main activities, viz (i) import/export merchanting, sales and distribution and (ii) insurance, banking and finance. According to one Japanese writer (Oba, 1983), Japanese businessmen have always had a high regard for British service industries mainly because of the belief that the British are strong where they work independently rather than as a group, and it is in the service sector (including the professions) where to quote Oba 'the creative power, individuality and devotion of Britons' is so much in evidence. The 27 manufacturing and assembling ventures include those set up and/or acquired in 1983.

Table 1.5: Number of Japanese Companies Operating in Britain — End 1983

Manufacturing & assembly		27
Service Activities		385
of which:		
Trading Houses	33	
Banking and finance	43	
Investment & securities	15	
Oil & metal trading	26	
Insurance	24	
Advertising	13	
Translating/Interpreting services	13	
Buying houses	11	
Transport-related activities	20	
Travel and tour operators	9	
Sales, distribution & other activities	187	
Total		412

Source: Anglo-Japanese Economic Institute (1984).

An earlier survey carried out by the same Institute (Anglo-Japanese Economic Institute, 1981) revealed that the 184 Japanese affiliates in the UK surveyed in January 1981, employed 9,243 people, of whom 1,219, or 13%, were Japanese expatriates. This is consistent with an estimate by Thurley and others (1981) that, in 1980, there were 10,290 personnel in Japanese firms in the UK, of which 3,876 (38%) were employed in manufacturing. At that time, there were 12 manufacturing subsidiaries, the output of which was £119.4 million and the exports £49m (or 41%).

In September 1983, an analysis of Japanese manufacturing companies in Europe was published (JETRO, 1983). Some 157 enterprises were requested to complete a questionnaire, and 117 responded. Some relevant details are set out in Tables 1.6 and 1.7. The UK is seen to account for about 13% of the employment in Japanese-owned factories in Europe, but the average capitalisation of these plants is one of the lowest in Europe. We estimate the employment in all Japanese firms in the UK by the end of 1984 had risen to about 15,000.

Most Japanese affiliates in the UK are small or very small. In 1980, of the 204 firms surveyed by Thurley and others, 99 or 48.5% employed 10 or fewer people and 166 or 81.3%, 50 or less. At that time, GEC-Hitachi, with over 2,000 employees, was the largest employer,[3] but there were 7 other manufacturing firms and 15 service affiliates which employed 101 or more. Some four-fifths of these firms first started operations in the UK after 1970.

Japanese Production in UK *vis-à-vis* Imports from Japan

In 1983, the UK imported £3,355 million of manufactured goods from Japan; this compares with an estimated sales of Japanese manufacturing affiliates in the UK of £325 million.[4] Thus, about 9% of all goods sold by Japanese firms to UK consumers were, at least, partly made in the UK. This ratio, while much higher than in preceding years, and likely to rise in the future, was considerably lower than that for other countries selling to the UK; for example, the sales of US manufacturing affiliates in the UK exceeded UK imports from the US by a 4 to 1 ratio.[5] It was very considerably lower than its counterpart in the US. Further details about the composition of the sales of manufacturing Japanese affiliates in the UK are given in Chapter 2.

Table 1.6: Number of Japanese Manufacturing Enterprises in Europe by Industrial Types and Locations

Industrial type / Country	Food processing	Textile	Chemical	Rubber	Glass/ceramics	Steel	Metal	Machinery	Electrical machinery	Transportation machinery	Precision machinery	Others	Total
UK			3					1	8		1	2	15
France	3	3							2			2	10
W. Germany	1		1					4	7		4	3	20
Italy		1	1		1					2		2	7
Netherlands			4		1		1	4			2	1	13
Belgium			4		3				3	1		2	13
Ireland		2	1		2				3		1		9
Greece			1			1			1				3
Spain			5				5		5	2		1	18
Portugal			1				1			1		1	4
Austria				1								1	2
N. Europe			1								2		3
Total	4	6	22	1	7	1	7	9	29	6	10	15	117

Source: JETRO (1983).

Table 1.7 Employment and Capital Invested in Japanese Manufacturing Affiliates in Europe, 1983

	Total employees	Average per affiliate	Total capital $000s	Average per affiliate
UK	4,737	315	22,815	1,521
France	1,912	191	31,993	3,199
W. Germany	2,991	149	56,479	2,973
Italy	2,081	297	47,970	6,852
Netherlands	1,658	128	67,410	5,185
Belgium	6,176	475	86,300	6,638
Ireland	1,623	180	27,200	3,022
Greece	1,194	398	30,250	10,083
Spain	12,663	703	200,900	11,161
Portugal	645	161	7,680	1,920
Austria	125	62	5,862	2,931
Northern Europe	66	22	3,182	1,061
	35,871	306	588,041	5,049

Source: Tables IV 3 & IV 4 (pp. 50-1) of JETRO (1983).

The Reverse Situation: UK Direct Investment in Japan

According to the Business Statistics Office of the Department of Industry, the value of the net assets owned by UK firms in Japan (excluding those in oil, insurance and banking) was £187.2m in 1981, some £136.9m less than the capital stake by Japanese companies in the UK.

Further details are set out in Table 1.8. It can be seen that until the late 1970s, UK companies invested more in Japan than Japanese companies in the UK since that time, the situation has been reversed. There are currently over 100 UK firms with direct investments in Japan.

Table 1.8: Anglo-Japanese Direct Investment Stake and Investment Flows, 1962-83

(i) Direct investment stake[a] 1962-81

£m

	UK-owned assets in Japan		Japanese-owned assets in UK	
	Total	Manufacturing	Total	Manufacturing
1962	4.0	n.a[b]	-4.0	n.a
1965	5.9	4.1	-5.6	n.a
1968	11.0	5.5	1.7	n.a
1971	15.9	n.a	13.3	n.a
1974	39.7	14.6	-18.5	n.a
1978	111.7	48.8	-23.9	n.a
1981	187.2	54.9	324.1	44.5

(ii) Investment flows (1972-83)

	Outward		Inward	
	Total	Manufacturing	Total	Manufacturing
1972	4.9	0.1	14.0	n.a
1973	7.8	0.2	17.7	n.a
1974	17.1	2.8	-22.0	n.a
1975	3.1	4.0	-42.0	n.a
1976	0.7	3.0	-15.7	n.a
1977	17.0	2.6	98.9	n.a
1978	32.0	9.7	-23.9	n.a
1979	38.9	3.0	50.9	n.a
1980	14.7	5.7	14.0	n.a
1981	17.2	1.3	173.3	n.a
1982	13.7	17.2	-62.7	n.a
1983	25.5	-13.3	190.3	n.a

Notes: a. Defined as the investing companies' share in the book value of fixed assets (net of depreciation) plus current assets less current liabilities (net of amounts to the investing company), less long-term liabilities (net of amounts owed to the investing company), less minority shareholders' interest in net assets. All sectors of industry are included except banking, insurance and oil.
b. n.a = not available.
Source: Department of Industry, Business Statistics Office M4 & MA4; Census of Overseas Assets, and Overseas Transactions, various editions.

Royalties and fees received from UK affiliates in Japan and indigenous Japanese firms, have greatly exceeded the payment made by UK firms (including the affiliates of Japanese firms) over the past decade. This strongly suggests the net flow of technology has been from the UK to Japan rather than vice versa. The relevant data are set out in Table 1.9. In 1981, receipts from related UK firms (e.g. subsidiaries and associates) in Japan amounted to £19.72m, or 35% total receipts, while payments made by related Japanese firms in the UK were £0.58m, or 27% of total payments.

Table 1.9: Anglo-Japanese Overseas Royalties and Similar Transactions, 1972-83 (excluding oil, banks and insurance companies)

	Receipts £m	Payments £m
1972	12.57	0.24
1973	16.35	0.40
1974	19.08	0.76
1975	22.33	0.45
1976	30.49	0.88
1977	37.44	0.88
1978	46.70	0.95
1979	48.59	0.92
1980	45.33	1.09
1981	54.90	2.13
1982	52.50	2.70
1983	53.00	5.10

Source: Department of Industry, Business Statistics Office, M4 & MA4 Overseas Transactions, various editions.

Notes

1. As set out in Appendix A (p. 198).
2. Details of all references cited in the text are given at the end of the book.
3. The Rank Toshiba Venture having collapsed in 1980.
4. See Chapter 2.
5. The latest data on the manufacturing sales of US affiliates in the UK (published by the US Department of Commerce) is for the year 1977. These then amounted to $26,600m compared with imports of manufactured goods from the US of $5,950m.

PART I

2 THE EXTENT AND STRUCTURE OF JAPANESE PARTICIPATION IN UK MANUFACTURING INDUSTRY

Introduction

Japanese direct investment in UK manufacturing industry is of very recent origin. The first post-World War II manufacturing affiliate – UK Fasteners Ltd – was set up in 1969 at Runcorn, Cheshire, to produce zip fasteners, and was very much the prototype of the more successful ventures which succeeded it.[1] By the middle of 1983, there were 26 UK manufacturing affiliates of Japanese companies employing 5,555 people including 142 Japanese nationals; all but three of these, viz. J2T and George Ellison and Key Med, were 50% or more owned by Japanese capital. At the same time, there were three other affiliates involved in warehousing and storage activities which, in the 1970s, had undertaken some manufacturing.[2] We also identified four manufacturing companies which at one time were partly Japanese owned, but which are now either defunct or entirely UK owned.[3] It is, perhaps, salutary to remark that, at a time when Japanese companies are lauded as an example for UK industry to emulate, the majority of the ventures set up in the early 1970s were unsuccessful.

In our study, we confine our attention to 23 of the 26 affiliates. We exclude Polychrome as it is a UK subsidiary of an American Corporation which, in 1977, was acquired by the Dai-Nippon Company of Japan. We understand from the Polychrome management that 'in no way has this acquisition affected either our US or UK operations'. In the case of Key Med, a private company supplying optical and medical equipment, the Japanese company Olympus Optical acquired a 25% equity stake in 1978, which was increased to 45% in 1984. Again there has been no direct administrative control from Japan, although the two UK owners readily admit that the thrust of their management style and philosophy and their approach to quality control and testing procedures have been greatly influenced by the Japanese. We also exclude George Ellison in which there is a 23% stake by Mitsubishi, again for the reason that the company considers this investment as akin to a portfolio rather than a direct investment.

The relevant details of Japanese involvement in British manufacturing

Table 2.1: Japanese-owned or Part-owned Enterprises Manufacturing in the United Kingdom

Name of British affiliate	Parent organisation	% Share-holding	Location in UK	Date of establishment or acquisition	Products made in UK	Employment (end 1982) Total	Japanese
GROUP 1							
Consumer and industrial electronics							
1 Sony (UK) Ltd	Sony Overseas SA (Switzerland) Sony Corporation	72 28	Bridgend, Glamorgan	1973	Colour TV (originally some audio, but ceased in 1976	923	40
2 Matsushita Electric (UK) Ltd	Matsushita Electric Co Ltd	100	Cardiff, South Wales	1976	Colour TV, audio products	461	15
3 Mitsubishi Electric (UK) Ltd	Mitsubishi Group	100	Haddington, East Lothian, Scotland	1979	Colour TV, video recorders by end 1983	228	6
4 GEC-Hitachi Television Ltd	Hitachi Ltd GEC	50[a] 50	Aberdare, Mid Glamorgan, S Wales	1979	Colour TV	1,568	5
5 Aiwa (UK) Ltd	Aiwa Co Ltd	100	Crumlin, Newport, Gwent	1980	Audio products	130	6
6 Toshiba Consumer Products UK Ltd	Toshiba	100	Plymouth, Devon	1981	Colour TV, video recorders by mid-1984; microwave ovens by mid-1985	264	7
7 Sanyo Industries (UK) Ltd	Sanyo Electric Sanyo Electric Trading Co Sanyo Marubeni (UK) Ltd Marubeni Corp	40 40 10 10	Lowestoft, Suffolk	1982	Colour TV; video recorders by end 1983	90	5
8 NEC Semiconductors (UK) Ltd	Nippon Electric Co Ltd	100	Livingston, West Lothian, Scotland	1982	Integrated circuits	64	8

No. & Company	Parent company	%	Location	Year	Product	No.	No.
9 JT2	Thorn-EMI Telefunken (Ger) JVC (Japan)	33.3 33.3 33.3	Newhaven, Sussex	1982	Video recorders	161	3
Hitachi Maxell	Hitachi Ltd		Telford, Shropshire	1984	Audio & video cassettes	170	10+
GROUP 2 **Light engineering**							
10 Nittan (UK) Ltd	Nittan Co Ltd Okura Co Ltd	69.9 30	Old Woking, Surrey	1972	Automatic fire alarm equipment	58	1
11 YKK Fasteners (UK) Ltd	Yoshida Kogyo KK	100	Runcorn, Cheshire Slough, Berkshire	1972 1984b	Zip fasteners Zip fasteners	221 Not known	18 Not known
12 Tekara Belmont Ltd	Takara Belmont Co Ltd	100	Mile End, London	1974	Assembling of hair dressing, beauty salon and dental chairs	16	3
13 NSK Bearings Europe Ltd	Nippon Seiko KK	100	Peterlee, Co Durham	1976	Bearings	224	11
14 Terasaki Europe Ltd	Terasaki (Japan)	100	Glasgow, Scotland	1978	Circuit breakers	40	–
George Ellison Ltd	Mitsubishi Electric British interests – remainder	23.3	Perry Bar, Birmingham	1915 (Mitsubishi holding acquired 1979)	Switchgear	350	–
Polychrome (Berwick) Ltd	Polychrome Corp (USA) (wholly owned by Dai-Nippon Inc)	100	Berwick-on-Tweed, Northumberland	1977	Printing plates	68	–
15 Yuasa Battery (UK) Ltd	Yuasa Battery Co	100	Ebbw Vale, Gwent, S. Wales	1981	Sealed lead-acid batteries	71	3

Table 2.1 (continued)

Name of British affiliate	Parent organisation	% Shareholding	Location in UK	Date of establishment or acquisition	Products made in UK	Employment (end 1982) Total	Japanese
Chemicals and plastics							
16 Takiron (UK) Ltd	Takiron Co Ltd Wolseley Hughes	95 5	Newport, Gwent, S. Wales	1973	PVC corrugated sheeting	51	1
17 Sekisui (UK) Ltd	Sekisui Chemical Co Ltd	100	Merthyr Tydfil, Mid-Glamorgan, S. Wales	1978	Irradiation cross-linked polyethylene foam	43	1
18 Sansetsu (UK) Ltd	Sansetsu (individual managers have invested in UK company)		Milton Keynes	1979	Plastic bubble	10	2
19 Tamura Kahen (UK) Ltd	Tamura Seisakusho Co Ltd	100	Northampton	1980	UV-cured screen printing printing inks for electronics industry	2	2
Other							
20 Merlin Aerials Ltd	Nippon Antenna Co Ltd UTC Corp (Switz)	49 51	Newbury, Berks	1975	Electrically actuated car aerials	25	2
21 Daiwa Sports Ltd	Daiwa Group	100	Wishaw, Glasgow	1978	Fishing tackle	111	3
22 Paddox Fine Worstedc	Daido Keori Co Ltd OMC Group	75 25	Huddersfield, Yorks	1978	Fine worsted suitings	42	0
23 Hoya Lens (UK) Ltd	Hoya Corp Ltd	100	Wrexham, Clwyd, Wales	1980	Ophthalmic lenses	54	4
24 Key Med Ltd	Olympus Optical	25 (45 since mid-'84)	Southend, Essex	1978	Optical and medical equipment	280	0

Notes: a. As of 31 March 1984, 100% owned by Hitachi. b. In January 1984, YKK (UK) acquired the New Zipper Company. c. An acquisition of an existing company.

industry as of December 1982 are set out in Table 2.1. In the course of our enquiries, we also visited Hitachi Maxell which commenced production of audio and video cassettes at Telford, Shropshire, in January 1984, and three UK firms which at the time were producing under licence to Japanese companies.[4] Information about these (and other non-equity ventures in which the Japanese are involved) is scattered throughout this book, but, except where specifically indicated, is not included in the statistical tables.

The Japanese affiliates identified in Table 2.1 fall neatly into two main groups. The first — Group 1 — comprises nine producers of consumer and industrial electronic products: three of these supply only colour television sets (CTVs); two CTVs and audio products; one CTVs and video recorders, one only audio products and one video recorders.[5] In June 1983, there was only one specialist integrated circuit producer — NEC Semiconductors (UK) Ltd; but some CTV set affiliates manufacture, or are about to manufacture, some of their electronic components (e.g. tubes, printed circuit boards (PCBs), etc.). Between them, Group 1 affiliates employed 3,889 at 31 December 1982, 80% of the 4,857 people employed in all manufacturing affiliates.[6] By the end of December 1983, their labour force had slightly risen to 4,200 and by 30 December 1984 to (an estimated) 5,500.[7]

In Chapters 3 and 4, we shall suggest that Group 1 affiliates display a number of common operational features and management techniques. By contrast, the second group of affiliates — Group 2 — is altogether more heterogeneous, both in type of activity and organisational style. Of the 14 affiliates in December 1982 employing 968 people, six, employing 630, were in light engineering, four, employing 106, supplied light chemical products, and four, employing 232, produced a mixed bag of products including fishing tackle, car aerials, fine worsted suitings and ophthalmic lenses. The labour force of these affiliates remained about the same throughout 1983, but increased in 1984 to around 1,200.

A slightly different breakdown of the activities of Japanese manufacturing affiliates reveals that 12, employing 4,258 people in December 1982, supply mainly consumer products and 11, employing 583, supply mainly industrial goods. But, in both sectors, the parent companies spend considerably more than the average on research and development (R & D) and are among the most technically progressive and fastest growing Japanese companies; of the 20 affiliates providing the relevant data, the *unweighted* average of their parent companies' R & D/worldwide sales ratio in the 1981/2 financial year was 3.1%, nearly twice the average for all Japanese manufacturers.[8]

Date of Establishment in the UK

Between 1969 and the end of 1984, four main phases of Japanese direct involvement in UK manufacturing may be distinguished. In the first, from 1969 to 1975, nine Japanese affiliates were set up, only one of which — Sony — was a CTV manufacturer. Two of the eight affiliates — Rembrandt and Rikadenki Mitsui — are no longer manufacturing, and four were joint ventures. In two of these latter affiliates, one or other of the major trading houses had an investment stake.

The second phase was from 1976 to 1978 when a mixed bag of ten new subsidiaries were set up. These included two affiliates — Hyfil and Ringwood Chemicals (now renamed Staveley Industries) in which there is no longer any Japanese involvement — and two — Horiba and Kubota Tractors — which are no longer manufacturing. Five of the ten were partly financed by UK capital; these included the ill-fated Rank-Toshiba venture which was wound up in 1981. The third phase of Japanese involvement was from 1979 to 1983, and represented a major penetration of the UK market by CTV, audio, and (towards the end of the period) video recorder manufacturers; and the move into industrial electronics. Some 11 new manufacturing affiliates were set up in these years; only two of these were joint ventures, one of which — GEC-Hitachi — has since become 100% Japanese owned. Like all but three of their predecessors, all were greenfield investments rather than acquisitions of established UK companies.[9]

By the end of 1983, except for their participation in the consumer electronics sector, Japanese direct investment in UK manufacturing had still not 'taken off'. However, 1984 was a watershed year in which several very large new investments were announced; and which augur a major surge forward of the Japanese presence. Details of some of these, which, if fulfilled, would more than double the employment in Japanese affiliates by early 1986, are set out in Table 2.2. Beside the well publicised Nissan venture, worthy of particular note are (1) the growing interest being shown by component manufacturers of consumer and industrial electronic assemblers, (2) the diversification of Japanese MNEs into new areas of production[10] and (3) the first major takeover of a UK firm, in an industry in which the Japanese are not known to have a comparative advantage.[11] In addition, a number of established Japanese subsidiaries are planning a major expansion in manufacturing capacity; we review some of these intentions in the final chapter.

We would also expect an increase in the number of licensing or technical assistance agreements, concluded between UK and Japanese firms,

Table 2.2: New Manufacturing Ventures in UK by Japanese Companies, 1985/6 (excluding expansion of those companies listed in Table 2.1)

Name of British affiliate	Parent organisation	% Share holding	Location in UK	Start of UK production	Products made in UK	Anticipated employment (a) Initial (b) Eventual (up to 1988)
Alps Electric Ltd	Alps Electric Co Ltd	100	Milton Keynes	1985	Video recorder parts	(a) 230 (b) 400
Brother Industries Ltd	Brother Industries Ltd	100	Wrexham	1985	Electronic typewriters	(a) 150
Dainichi-Sykes Robotics	Dainichi Kiko	76	Preston	1985[a]	Automatic manufacturing systems	(a) ? (b) 150
Iwax Ltd	Iwax Inc Ltd	100	Ballymoney, County Antrim	1985	Disposable cigarette lighters	(a) 66 (b) 116
Honda Motor Co (UK) Ltd	Honda Motor Co Ltd	100	Swindon	1986	Motor vehicles	(a) 400
Nissan Motor Man. (UK) Ltd	Nissan Motor Co Ltd	100	Washington, Tyne & Wear	1986	Motor vehicles	(a) 500 (b) 2,700
Ricoh Products UK Ltd	Ricoh Co Ltd	100	Telford, Shropshire	1985	Photocopier parts	(a) 100 (b) 170
Sumitomo Rubber	Sumitomo Corp	100	Birmingham and Washington, Tyne & Wear	1985	Rubber tyres[b]	(a) 7,000
Sharp Electronics	Sharp Corporation	100	Wrexham, Clwyd, Wales	1985	Video tape recorders	(a) 240 (b) 630
Shin-Etsu Chemical Co Ltd	Shin-Etsu, Handontai Ltd	100	Livingston, Scotland	1985	Silicon wafers	(a) ? (b) 400
Tabuchi Electric Co Ltd	Tabuchi Electric Ltd	100	Thornaby, Cleveland	1985	Transformers for CTV sets, microwave ovens, etc.	(a) 150 (b) ?
Yamasaki Ltd	Yamasaki Ltd	100	Worcester	1985	Machine tools	(a) 200 (b) ?

Notes: a. But UK company previously under licence to Dainichi Kiko. b. Sumitomo acquired Dunlop's tyre research and development activities in July 1984.

sometimes coupled with a minority equity stake. Our reading of the situation is that such deals have increased markedly in the last two or three years, particularly in the technologically more advanced UK sectors.[12] We shall return to this point later in this book.[13]

The Ownership Pattern of Japanese Affiliates

Table 2.1 reveals that 17 of the 23 Japanese affiliates were 100% owned by Japanese companies in December 1982, although in two cases, viz. Sanyo and Nittan, Japanese companies other than the parent enterprise also had an investment stake. We have seen that in the early and mid-1970s Japanese trading companies were actively involved;[14] in the late 1970s and early 1980s, all but two of the new affiliates were 100% Japanese owned. One of the exceptions, J2T, illustrates an alternative mode of entry into UK industry. Set up in 1982 to manufacture video recorders for the European market, J2T is a tripartite venture combining the technical and marketing expertise of the Victor Company (Japanese), Thorn/EMI (UK) and Telefunken (German).[15] Prior to Hitachi gaining full ownership, GEC-Hitachi represented a more traditional joint venture. Established in 1979, at the initiation of GEC and after Hitachi had withdrawn its plans to set up a 100% subsidiary in Washington, Northumberland, it was, until March 1984, the only joint venture in CTV production. A year earlier, an Anglo-Japanese venture of Rank-Toshiba came on stream at Plymouth; but this, after a promising start, was wound up in 1981. Chapter 3 examines the preference of Japanese firms for 100% equity involvement in more detail; suffice to point out here, it now tends to be the predominant vehicle in industries where (a) the technology is new and/or idiosyncratic; (b) the application of the Japanese management style is regarded as crucial for success; (c) the markets served are part of a European or global strategy; and (d) the production methods and quality control techniques are relatively labour intensive.

There is no obvious pattern of *changes* in involvement by established Japanese affiliates over the past decade, but as Table 2.2 shows, all but one of the new entrants are all opting for 100% ownership. If there has been a trend, it has been for joint ventures to be converted into fully-owned subsidiaries. Besides the Hitachi acquisition of the GEC stake in GEC-Hitachi, examples include a translation of 30% Japanese equity stake in Terasaki Europe (originally no fuse circuit breakers) into a 100% stake; a 30% involvement by Daiwa Sanko in Daiwa Sports, also into a 100% stake, and a 30% involvement by Toshiba in Rank Toshiba being replaced by a slimmed down wholly owned Toshiba operation. An example of a partial divestment is sale of 25% of the equity in Paddox Fine Worsted by Daido Keori to the OMC Group[16] in 1980. It appears, however, that the early failures of Japanese participation were mainly in joint venture enterprises; examples include Rank Toshiba, Rikadenki-Mitsui, Hyfil and Ringwood Chemicals. By contrast, YKK Fasteners, a 100% affiliate established in 1969, and Nittan (UK), which is 99.9% Japanese owned, established in 1972, have been two of the most successful Japanese affiliates.[17]

The reasons for the failures of the early ventures are varied, but an inability successfully to predict future market conditions and the incapacity or unwillingness of UK management to perform as to Japanese expectations have undoubtedly been the two most important. In the case of Rank Toshiba, the project was based on predictions about a macro-economic climate in the UK which failed to materialise. In addition, the product mix was misjudged — the plant specialised in the production of larger CTVs at a time when demand was switching to smaller sets; while the main distributors did not care for a Japanese style chassis, which, if it went wrong, required expensive servicing. Finally Rank's management ethos and organisation of work was not properly attuned to the technological requirements of the Japanese. Failure to achieve the projected rate of worldwide growth, due to the recession, was the reason given by Rikadenki-Mitsui for closing its UK plant in 1982. (Apparently it was less expensive to cut back employment in the UK than in the Japanese plant because of the latter's policy of life-time employment.) The rising value of the yen between 1977 and 1979 had a considerable adverse affect on the repayment of loans made by the Export-Import Bank in Japan to finance the development at Ringwood Chemicals (in which Hodogaya Chemicals had a 35% stake). It also meant that imports of a key raw material (a chemical feedstock) from Japan doubled in price. Add to this costs arising from more stringent environmental requirements imposed on the UK factory (the company were forced to shut down while the necessary adaptations were being made), the losses of the joint venture became so great that the Japanese sold all their interests. The failure of Hyfil was partly due to a friction of management styles and objectives between a large Japanese textile and chemical enterprise (Toray) and a small independent UK carbon fibre company (Hyfil); partly to problems arising from alleged patent restrictions; partly to the world recession for carbon fibre; and partly to the involvement of Toray in a competitive venture in France arising from alleged patent restrictions. The difficulties of GEC-Hitachi were mainly an outcome of an inappropriate (UK) management style and industrial relations being superimposed on Japanese production technology and control procedures. This case is separately reviewed in Chapter 10 of this book.

Takeovers or Greenfield Ventures

Of the 23 Japanese manufacturing affiliates operating in June 1983, all but one were established as new companies.[18] However, in five of these, although new companies were set up, existing factory premises were acquired. This has been especially the mode of entry of later arrivals in the colour TV industry, including GEC-Hitachi, which acquired GEC's plant at Hirwaun, South Wales, Sanyo which acquired a site at Lowestoft previously occupied by Pye/Philips, Mitsubishi which took over a factory which had housed the Norwegian Tanberg company, and J2T which acquired a radio factory from Thorn EMI at Newhaven. In several other instances, the location of activity was influenced by the availability of factory accommodation at the time of investment.

The only acquired firm in our survey — Paddox Fine Worsted — had been previously exporting to its new parent — the Daido Company — while the Mitsubishi interest in George Ellison, and that of Mitsui in Hyfil, were by trading companies. Olympus acquired an interest in its main UK distributing agent — Key Med — to help with its manufacturing programme. In one other case, Polychrome, the Japanese company Dai-Nippon bought out the US American parent company. Most acquisitions or partial acquisitions occurred in the early 1970s, and most have since been disbanded; all too were partial rather than full acquisitions, and supplied products outside the consumer and industrial electronics sector.

The Sumitomo acquisition of four tyre plants in Europe and a research institute in the UK from Dunlop Holdings of Dunlop for £130m (involving equity, trademarks and equipment sales), is by far the largest takeover and is quite unlike any which has preceded it. It has occurred in an industry with considerable overcapacity and affords the Japanese an entry in the European market without increasing the total output of the industry.[19]

The Location of Japanese Manufacturing Affiliates in the UK

Tables 2.2 and 2.3 reveal that, compared with UK manufacturers, Japanese affiliates are (or plan to be) strongly concentrated either in the less prosperous regions of the United Kingdom, viz. South Wales, Scotland and Northern England, or in the fast expanding cities and towns along the M4 corridor and in the South Midlands, e.g. Swindon, Milton Keynes and Telford. At the end of 1982, 14 affiliates employing 4,225 people or 87% of the total labour force, were located in areas qualifying for regional development assistance;[20] eight of these, employing 1,708, were located in Special Development Areas (SDAs) and six, employing 2,517, in Development Areas (DAs). Three affiliates, viz. Toshiba, J2T and Sanyo, which acquired established factories, were sited in coastal locations at Plymouth, Newhaven and Lowestoft. Seven of the new manufacturing ventures, identified in Table 2.2, are also scheduled to be set up in Development Areas.

Table 2.3: Location of Japanese Manufacturing Affiliates in the UK, Distribution by Employment

| | Japanese affiliates (end 1982) | | | All foreign firms (1979) | All UK firms (1979) |
	No.	Employment	%	%	%
Regions above average unemployment					
Northern England[a]	3	487	10.0	26.0	26.6
Wales	8	3,301	68.0	5.6	4.5
Scotland	4	443	9.1	10.1	9.4
Southwest England	1	264	5.4	4.5	6.9
	16	4,495	92.5	46.3	47.4
Regions of average or below average unemployment					
Midlands	2	12	0.2	12.5	16.7
Southeast England	4	260	5.4	36.5	32.9
East Anglia	1	90	1.9	4.6	3.0
	7	362	7.5	53.7	52.6
	23	4,857	100.0	100.0	100.0

Note: a. Includes North West and North East.
Source: All foreign firms and UK data: Census of Production — Summary Tables, 1979.

Of the Group 1 affiliates, all except the three companies in the previous paragraph named, are located in Wales or Scotland; earlier, Rank-Toshiba had set up in Plymouth which, at the time, was also in an 'assisted' area. As is further explained in Chapter 3, Japanese companies have been particularly responsive both to regional and other incentives, and to the persuasion of central government and local development agencies. There has also been a distinct 'follow my leader' approach to investing in the UK. In the 1970s, the success of Sony in Bridgend attracted other CTV Japanese affiliates to South Wales; while, a decade later, most of the major Japanese companies have plans to produce video recorders in the UK. In the industrial electronics sector, mid-Scotland may well develop as the preferred location for Japanese micro-chip producers, following the examples of NEC Semiconductors and Shin-Etsu Chemical, which themselves were no doubt influenced by the presence of US subsidiaries, e.g. Motorola, Wang, Digital and National Semi-Conductor. One estimate[21] (see *Financial Times*, 14 December 1983) is that Scotland will produce more than one-half of the UK's output of micro-chips by the end of 1985.

There is a less clear locational pattern of Group 2 affiliates, except that, for the smaller subsidiaries at least there has been some concentration in the Home Counties and the South Midlands — usually in towns in which development corporations have played an active promotional role. Japanese companies have followed the edicts of UK regional policy very well. The larger employers are all concentrated in the less prosperous regions or have taken over derelict factories. At the end of 1982, only one of the 23 affiliates — YKK — had more than one manufacturing plant in the UK, although in August 1983, Mitsubishi opened a second factory at Livingston and Toshiba has plans for a new microwave oven plant in Plymouth. At the same time, several affiliates had sales offices, distribution centres or warehousing activities in other locations. It is indeed a feature of Japanese companies that the manufacturing and marketing functions are often kept quite separate. In some cases, the sales office may not even be in the same country; for example, all of Mitsubishi's output from its Scottish factory is exported to West Germany (Dusseldorf). Of the other affiliates, 11 have separate sales offices in the UK, usually in or near London.

Origin and Destination of Sales

The 23 manufacturing affiliates produced or sold goods worth £235 million in 1982 (or the nearest financial year) and £325 million in 1983. In addition, either directly or through sister sales companies, they imported more than £400 million of finished goods for resale. Of the £235 million sales, £92m was accounted for by imported raw materials, components and semiprocessed goods. This means that £143m, or 61% of the total output of affiliates, was either produced in their UK factories or bought from British suppliers. This represents our best estimate of the local (UK) value added resulting from the Japanese presence in manufacturing industry; excluding the value of warehousing, distribution and marketing activities, when undertaken by non-manufacturing Japanese affiliates.[22] As will be discussed later, these ratios vary between sector, degree of product and/or market diversification, age and size of affiliate; they tend to be highest among the longer established affiliates, those producing a limited range of products, and those supplying mainly the UK market.

As far as the destination of their final output is concerned, all affiliates, except one, supply almost exclusively to the UK and European markets: the exception is Paddox Fine Worsted which sells all its woollen cloth to Japan. Total exports in 1982 were £74 million, or 31% of the output produced. Of the nine Group 1 affiliates, three exported more than 50% of their output in 1982 and the average amount exported was 29%. Of the 14 Group 2 affiliates, six exported more than 50%, and the weighted average was 43%. In the case of six of the 22 affiliates, the UK factory is the sole supplier of the European market. As regards the rest, this function is either undertaken by other European affiliates and/or by exports from Japan.

Further particulars are set out in Table 2.4. It will be seen that there is some correlation between age of affiliate and export performance. However, only in the case of three affiliates is there any kind of product or process specialisation, either between UK and Japanese, or UK and Continental European, manufacturing operations.[23] In the case of the one joint venture (which also happened to be the largest employer), the export rate was well below that for the average of the CTV sector.

Product Diversification

Twenty-one of the 23 Japanese affiliates are essentially single-product producers. In June 1983, in the case of the nine electronics affiliates, six produce only colour TV or audio products or video recorders; one produces colour TV and audio products and one colour TV and video

Table 2.4: Sales and Export Performance of Japanese Manufacturing Affiliates in the UK, 1982 (or nearest financial year)

	Total sales £m	Exports £m	% Exports to sales
1) By sector			
Group 1 affiliates	197.2	57.4	29.1
Group 2 affiliates			
Light engineering	28.5	12.4	43.5
Chemicals	5.6	2.5	44.6
Other	3.8	1.2	31.6
All Group 2 affiliates	37.9	16.1	42.5
Total	235.1	73.5	31.1
2) By age of affiliate			
Pre 1976	70.7	28.0	39.6
1976-78	39.6	15.9	30.7
1979-82	124.8	29.6	23.7
	235.1	73.5	31.1
3) By size of affiliate (Nos employed)			
1-49	8.4	3.1	36.9
50-99	13.4	7.9	61.7
100-249	73.6	31.4	42.7
250 & over	139.7	31.1	22.3
	235.1	73.5	31.1

recorders. Of the 14 Group 2 affiliates, all produce just one main product though the range of such products, e.g. spectacle lenses, fishing rods, zip fasteners, bearings, chairs and fire detection systems, is often quite extensive.

The product specialisation of Japanese affiliates is in marked contrast to the output of their parent companies. It is perhaps worth noting that 11 of the Japanese parent companies are among the top 500 non-US industrial companies listed by *Fortune*; and all save two are among the leading five producers in their sectors. Most manufacture a very wide range of products, some of which are exported to the UK. Even the older subsidiaries remain essentially uni-product; on the other hand, the degree of vertical integration has increased over the years, with the ratio of value added to sales generally increasing with age and size of affiliate. Of the 23 affiliates, eight indicated that they had plans to extend their product range between June 1983 and the end of 1985; another 12 expected to produce a larger proportion of the final product in-house.[24]

The Significance of Japanese Participation in UK Industry

Compared to that of affiliates of other foreign companies, Japanese participation in UK manufacturing industry is still minute. In 1981, the sales of Japanese affiliates were only 0.40% of all foreign-owned affiliates in the UK and 0.08% of all manufacturing firms. The corresponding figures for gross value added are 0.31% and 0.06%; and for employment 0.52% and 0.05%. Since 1981, the share of Japanese involvement has risen but, even in 1983, Japanese affiliates accounted for probably not more than £1 of every £1,000 of manufacturing sales produced in the UK. Further details are set out in Table 2.5.

Table 2.5: The Significance of Japanese Participation in UK Manufacturing Industry, 1981

	All enterprises	Foreign affiliates	Japanese affiliates
Employment (000s)	5,779.0	878.1	3.0
Sales (£ million)	163,936	31,819	127.1
Gross value added (£ million)	57,935	10,602	32.4
Gross value added per head (£)	10,027	12,355	10,917
Capital expenditure (£ million)	5,493	1,402	11.4
Capital expenditure per head	950	1,597	3,800
Average wages (£)			
Operators	5,410	6,049	4,472
Non-operators	7,229	8,091	5,957

In particular sectors, however, the contribution of Japanese affiliates is much more important. The market shares of a selection of products as identified by the affiliates are set out in Table 2.6.[25] Of the larger employers, it is seen to be most pronounced in the video and audio equipment industries, but in more specialised sectors also, e.g. zip fasteners, chairs for hairdressing salons, fire alarm equipment, spectacle lens, fishing tackle, etc., Japanese affiliates account for an even larger share. As we shall describe later,[26] this usually reflects a particular and special technological or marketing advantage possessed by Japanese firms over their UK competitors. However, in June 1983, in sectors making up 95% of UK manufacturing output there was no Japanese direct investment at all![27]

Table 2.7 compares the output of Japanese affiliates in the UK with imports of the same products from Japan. Again, the relative significance of CTV production in the UK stands out from that of other products.

Table 2.6: Estimated Share of UK Produced Output Produced by Japanese Affiliates in Selected Sectors, 1982/3

	%
Group 1 affiliates	
Colour television sets	35
Audio hi-fi equipment	15
Video recorders	100
Video and audio tapes[a]	16
Integrated circuits	10
Microwave ovens[b]	
Group 2 affiliates	
Fire alarm systems	25
Zip fasteners	50+
Ball bearings	10
Circuit breakers	20
Sealed lead acid batteries	40
Foamed plastic products	32
Air bubble cushioning materials	30
Electrically activated car aerials	25
Fishing tackle	35
Ophthalmic lenses	16
Chairs for hairdressing salons	60

Note: a. Of one Japanese firm due to start UK manufacturing in 1984 it is expected that its market share will rise to 30%.

One of the reasons for this is the voluntary restraint by Japanese TV set producers in exporting to the EEC.[28] Such a restraint does not appear to condition the export of other products — at least to the same extent; here the varying ratio of local production/imports is determined by other factors, e.g. transport costs, the need to adapt to local requirements, and the age of the affiliate's establishment.

Table 2.7: Sales of Japanese Manufacturing Affiliates in UK[a] as an Approximate Proportion of Imports from Japan, 1982/3 (selected items)

	%
Group 1 affiliates	
Colour television sets	650
Video tape recorders	20
Other telecommunication and sound equipment	10
Group 2 affiliates	
Ball bearings	60
Other engineering products	2
Photographic and optical equipment	1
Plastic materials	35
Textile yarn, fabrics	1

Note: a. Of output produced in UK. b. Expected in 1985.

In 1982, Japanese affiliates in the UK both exported and imported a higher percentage of their output than their UK counterparts. Apart from the woollen clothing firm mentioned earlier, more than 90% of exports went to the rest of the EEC; while 80% of imports originated from Japan. About 70% of the exports and 90% of imports were intra-group transactions.

The Mode of Entry

All the Japanese manufacturing affiliates had been previously selling to the UK - in most cases through their own sales outlets. Only in the cases of Toshiba and Paddox Fine Worsted was some manufacturing undertaken, and, as Chapter 3 will explain, in only two cases was a licensing agreement with a UK firm seriously contemplated as an alternative to direct investment.

Conclusions

While growing quite rapidly relative to both inward direct investment as a whole and to imports from Japan, Japanese direct investment in UK industry is still in its infancy. It is also highly concentrated in particular industrial sectors. The mode of entry has been chiefly via a greenfield investment, following previous sales and marketing involvement. Japanese affiliates are strongly located in the less prosperous regions of the UK; at the end of 1982, 68% of the employment of all manufacturing affiliates was in Wales.

In the early 1980s Japanese affiliates produced a very truncated range of products, although most of them are part of very large and diversified Japanese manufacturing firms. Some product diversification seems likely in the second half of the decade. The majority of Japanese affiliates supply the rest of Europe from their UK factories; in three of the five cases where there are other manufacturing affiliates in Europe, there is some specialisation of output and cross trading. For the most part, however, imports originate from Japan.

According to the Invest in Britain Bureau there were 16 announcements of new investment or expansion by Japanese firms in the UK in 1984. These projects heralded a further £450 million of investment, and an expected 6,192 additional jobs. By the end of 1985, the employment by Japanese manufacturing affiliates is expected to rise to around 15,000.

Notes

1. There were a few manufacturing affiliates mainly owned or partly owned by trading companies operating before the war, but we have not dealt with these in our study.

2. Viz. Horiba, Rikadenki-Mitsui and Kubota Tractors.

3. Viz. Hyfil and Rembrandt Design owned partly by Toray, Staveley Chemicals (at one time Ringwood Chemicals) owned partly by Hodogaya Chemicals, and Rank Toshiba owned partly by Toshiba. Toshiba now has its own manufacturing affiliate in the UK, but this is an entirely new company.

4. British Leyland, Dainichi Sykes Robotics and International Computers Ltd. In the spring of 1985, Dainichi Kiko of Yamanaski acquired Sykes Group's controlling 76% stake in Dainichi Sykes Robotics.

5. In the latter part of 1983 both Mitsubishi (at a new plant in Livingston) and Sanyo (in the Lowestoft factory) began assembling recorders from kits imported from Japan.

6. Further details of employment in Japanese affiliates are given in Chapter 10.

7. The figure would have been considerably higher had there not been a cutback in employment at GEC-Hitachi from 1,568 to 819.

8. For further details see Chapter 10. Also see Chapter 2 of Franko (1983) and Marsh (1983).

9. See Table 2.1 for further details.

10. It is also expected that once Nissan begins manufacturing in the UK several Japanese motor vehicle component suppliers will follow in its wake. In the US, a survey (quoted in the *Sunday Times* on 12 May 1985) has revealed that 30 Japanese motor car component affiliates are being set up in America to supply not only Japanese car assemblers, e.g. Honda, Nissan and Toyota, but US manufacturers, e.g. Chrysler, as well.

11. For an analysis of these new investments, see Dunning (1984).

12. Recent examples include Toyota's 16.5% stake in Group Lotus, Kayaba's 15% stake in TI Suspension Systems, Fujitsu's technical and marketing co-operation with ICL, and similar links between Toyobo and BP Chemicals, Fanuc with the 600 Group and a number of Japanese Companies with Rolls-Royce.

13. See Chapter 3.

14. E.g. Toray had an investment in Hyfil and Rembrandt, Mitsui in Rikadenki, Mitsui Okura in Nittan, Sumitomo in Ringwood Chemicals and CJ Itoh in Takiron.

15. Now partly owned by Thomson Brandt (France).

16. Although this had been agreed at the time of the initial investment by Daido in 1977.

17. Apart from GEC-Hitachi, the average labour force employed by 100% affiliates in December 1982 was 219 compared with 43 in joint ventures.

18. And all are incorporated in the UK; i.e. there are no Japanese branch plants in the manufacturing sector.

19. The plants acquired currently account for 15% of the Dunlop group's global output of 30,000 tons; this added to the 10,000 tons of Dunlop brand tyres already produced by Sumitomo will enable the company to supply nearly one half of all Dunlop tyres marketed.

20. As set out in Section 7 of the Industrial Development Act, 1982.

21. These include all of the other colour TV affiliates, YKK, NSK, Terasaki and Yuasa Battery.

22. See Chapter 6.

23. These include Sony and Matsushita where the Spanish affiliates produce audio sets and the German affiliates video sets for the European market. Audio

tapes are also produced by Sony in their French factory, while Hitachi has semi-conductor and video recorder plants in Frankfurt. According to the Hitachi management, had the Hirwaun plant been under full ownership of the Japanese (or at least had been operating efficiently) at the time the company was contemplating video production, South Wales would have been the chosen location.

24. See Chapter 12.

25. In some cases the categories have been broadened to avoid identifying particular companies.

26. See Chapter 3.

27. One of the few Japanese CTV set manufacturers not manufacturing in the UK is JVC. Negotiations to acquire the former Decca plant at Bridgenorth from Racal came to nothing; in fact the plant was acquired by a Taiwanese company — Tatung.

28. Again this situation seems likely to change in the later 1980s.

3 THE REASONS FOR JAPANESE PARTICIPATION IN UK MANUFACTURING INDUSTRY

The Analytical Framework

The literature on international production, i.e. production financed by foreign direct investment,[1] suggests that firms with headquarters in one country will set up and/or expand value adding activities outside their national boundaries whenever

(a) they perceive that, due to their nationality of ownership or degree of multinationality, they possess some kind of competitive advantage over indigenous firms (actual or potential) in the host country;

(b) they find it economic to exploit these advantages themselves, i.e. to internalise their use, rather than sell the right so to do to host country firms, via an arms length transaction (e.g. a technical service agreement or management contract);

(c) they believe that it is in their global interests to produce at least part of the value added from a foreign rather than a home location.

The literature further identifies these advantages and some of these are set out in Table 3.1. Attention is especially drawn to the distinction between asset (or production) and common governance (or transaction cost minimising ownership advantages). From the perspective of a potential recipient country, the more a foreign firm possesses ownership advantages over its own firms, the more imperfect the market is for the transfer of these intangible assets between the exporting and importing country, and the more the foreign firm finds it attractive to deploy these assets to produce goods in the host rather than in the home (or indeed in another foreign) country, the more inward direct investment is likely to take place.

It is also now widely accepted that the extent and juxtaposition of these ownership (O), internalisation (I) and location (L) advantages vary accordingly to industry, country and firm specific circumstances, and that these in turn may vary over time. Again, some illustrations are set out in Table 3.2. *Inter alia* this framework suggests that individual countries may have distinctive types of ownership advantages and

Table 3.1: The Eclectic Theory of International Production

1. *Ownership Specific Advantages* (of enterprises of one nationality (or affiliates of same) over those of another)
    (a) Property right and/or intangible asset advantages
        Product innovations, production management, organisational and marketing systems, innovatory capacity; non-codifiable knowledge; 'bank' of human capital experience; marketing, finance, knowhow, etc.
    (b) Advantages of common governance
        (i) Which those branch plants of established enterprises may enjoy over *de novo* firms. Those due mainly to size and established position of enterprise, e.g. economies of scope and specialisation; monopoly power, better resource capacity and usage. Exclusive or favoured access to inputs, e.g. labour, natural resources, finance, information. Ability to obtain inputs on favoured terms (due e.g. to size or monopsonistic influence). Exclusive or favoured access to product markets. Access to resources of parent company at marginal cost. Economies of joint supply (not only in production, but in purchasing, marketing, finance, etc., arrangements).
        (ii) Which specifically arise because of multinationality. Multinationality enhances above advantages by offering wider opportunities. More favoured access to and/or better knowledge about international markets, e.g. for information, finance, labour, etc. Ability to take advantage of geographical differences in factor endowments, markets. Ability to diversify or reduce risks, e.g. in different currency areas, and/or political scenarios.

2. *Internalisation Incentive Advantages* (i.e. to protect against or exploit market failure)
    Avoidance of search and negotiating costs.
    To avoid costs of enforcing property rights.
    Buyer uncertainty (about nature and value of inputs (e.g. technology) being sold).
    Where market does not permit price discrimination.
    Need of seller to protect quality of products.
    To capture economies of interdependent activities (see (b) above).
    To compensate for absence of future markets.
    To avoid or exploit government intervention (e.g. quotas, tariffs, price controls, tax differences, etc.).
    To control supplies and conditions of sale of inputs (including technology).
    To control market outlets (including those which might be used by competitors).
    To be able to engage in practices, e.g. cross-subsidisation, predatory pricing, etc., as a competitive (or anti-competitive) strategy.

3. *Location Specific Variables* (these may favour home or host countries)
    Spatial distribution of inputs and markets.
    Input prices, quality and productivity, e.g. labour, energy, materials, components, semi finished goods.
    Transport and communications costs.
    Investment incentives and disincentives (including performance requirements, etc.).
    Artificial barriers to trade in goods.
    Infrastructure provisions (commercial, legal, educational, transportation).
    Psychic distance (language, cultural, business, customs, etc., differences).
    Economies of centralisation of R & D production and marketing.

Table 3.2: Some Illustrations of how OLI Characteristics May Vary According to Country, Industry and Firm Specific Considerations

OLI	Structural variables	Country (home-host)	Industry	Firm
Ownership		factor endowments (e.g. resources and skilled labour) and market size and character. Government policy towards innovation, protection of proprietary rights, competition and industrial structure, government controls on inward direct investment	degree of product or process technological intensity; nature of product innovations; extent of product differentiation; production economies (e.g. if there are economies of scale); importance of favoured access to inputs and/or markets	size, extent of production, process or market diversification; extent to which enterprise is innovative, or marketing-oriented, or values security and/or stability, e.g. in sources of inputs, markets, etc.; extent to which there are economies of joint production
Internalisation		government intervention and extent to which policies encourage MNEs to internalise transactions, e.g. transfer pricing; government policy towards mergers; differences in market structures between countries, e.g. with respect to transaction costs, enforcement of contracts, buyer uncertainty, etc.; adequacy of technological, educational, communications, etc., infrastructure in host countries and ability to absorb contractual resource transfers	extent to which vertical or horizontal integration is possible/ desirable, e.g. need to control sourcing of inputs or markets, extent to which internalising advantages can be captured in contractual agreements (cf. early and later stages of product cycle); use made of ownership advantages; cf. IBM with Unilever type operation; extent to which local firms have complementary advantage to those of foreign firms; extent to which opportunities for output specialisation and international division of labour exist	organisational and control procedures of enterprise; attitudes to growth and diversification (e.g. the boundaries of a firm's activities); attitudes toward subcontracting-contractual ventures, e.g. licensing, franchising, technical assistance agreements, etc.; extent to which control procedures can be built into contractual agreements

| Location | physical and psychic distance between countries; government intervention (tariffs, quotas, taxes, assistance to foreign investors or to own MNEs, e.g. Japanese government's financial aid to Japanese firms investing in South East Asian labour intensive industries | origin and distribution of immobile resources; transport costs of intermediate and final goods products; industry specific tariff and non-tariff barriers; nature of competition between firms in industry; can functions of activities of industry be split? Significance of "sensitive" locational variables, e.g. tax incentives, energy and labour costs | management strategy towards foreign involvement; age and experience of foreign involvement; (position of enterprise in product cycle, etc.); psychic distance variables (culture, language, legal and commercial framework); attitudes towards centralisation of certain functions, e.g. R & D; regional office and market allocation, etc.; geographical structure of asset portfolio and attitude to risk diversification |

differently evaluate the best modality, viz. exports, foreign direct investment and licensing,[2] of exploiting them; and that different firms (quite
apart from their nationality) may view the same set of investment
opportunities in a different way, according, for example, to their size,
the attitude to risk taking, the existing geographical distribution of
their investments[3] and (their perception of) the actions of their competitors.[4]

In the context of our present study, we wish to identify and, as far
as possible evaluate, the ownership advantages of Japanese affiliates in
the UK; their reasons for choosing to internalise these advantages rather
than to license the rights so to do to UK firms; and their locational
preferences for the UK as a production base rather than their home
country, or indeed another European country.

The Ownership Advantages of Japanese MNEs

All Japanese manufacturing affiliates were requested to assess, on a
scale 1-5, the perceived significance of a number of competitive advantages commonly ascribed to multinational enterprises (MNEs) *vis-
à-vis* their uninational counterparts. Table 3.3 sets out the average of
the scores for each advantage, as indicated by our two main groups
of affiliates. The conclusion of this exercise is that the 24 Japanese
firms[5] perceive their main advantages to be four-fold: (1) product
quality and reliability which embraces quality control and testing procedures of both outside purchases and in-house activity; (2) a flexible manufacturing and work system; (3) an ability to foster both
management and worker commitment; and (4) favoured access to the
supply of intermediate products. In a few cases, a near unique product
is supplied, e.g. UV-cured screen printing ink, electrically activated car
aerials, uncoated bubble packaging, etc. In others, the advantage is
contained in proprietary machinery, product design, materials formulae
or production processes; or in speedier and more reliable delivery dates,
quality standards, adaptation of product to consumer needs, marketing
methods, good industrial relations (especially in Group 1 affiliates),
Japanese government regulations,[6] favoured access to R & D, etc. Yet
*it is perhaps the way in which these various advantages are packaged
together to achieve a holistic set of goals acceptable to the management
and workforce alike, which most marks off Japanese affiliates from
their UK competitors.*

The quotations from various affiliates in the consumer electronics

Table 3.3: Competitive (Ownership) Advantages of Japanese Firms' Manufacturing Affiliates, as Perceived by Management of Affiliates[a]

	Group 1	Group 2			Total
	Eng	Chem	Other	All	
(1) Advantages based on privileged possession of particular assets					
(a) Product related variables					
1 Nature of product	3.2	3.8	3.5	3.5	3.6	3.4
2 Patent protection	2.3	3.0	2.3	1.3	2.1	2.3
3 Product quality & reliability[b]	4.7	5.0	4.5	4.8	4.7	4.7
4 Product price	3.1	3.2	4.0	2.8	3.3	3.2
5 Keeping to delivery dates	3.6	4.6	3.5	3.8	4.0	3.8
6 After sales servicing	2.3	3.8	2.0	2.5	2.6	2.6
7 Advertising	1.6	2.0	1.5	1.3	1.6	1.6
8 Marketing methods	2.5	2.8	1.5	1.8	2.0	2.2
9 Product adaptation	1.9	3.0	1.3	2.3	2.2	2.0
(b) Production related variables					
1 Process technology	4.0	4.0	4.8	3.0	3.9	4.0
2 Work organisation	4.3	3.5	2.3	3.3	3.0	3.4
3 Industrial relations	3.7	3.0	2.3	2.8	2.7	3.0
4 Materials usage	2.1	2.5	2.8	1.8	2.3	2.2
5 Incentive schemes	1.2	1.8	1.8	1.5	1.7	1.5
6 Management philosophy	4.3	3.3	2.8	3.0	2.9	3.5
7 Quality of inputs	4.2	2.4	1.3	1.3	1.5	2.7
(2) Common governance (transaction cost minimising) advantages					
1 More dynamic entrepreneurship	2.3	2.8	2.5	2.5	2.6	2.4
2 Favoured access to parent's inputs	2.1	3.3	1.3	3.0	2.5	2.3
3 Favoured access to R & D	3.5	3.0	4.3	3.3	3.5	3.5
4 Favoured access to parent's admin. services	2.2	1.5	2.2	2.0	1.9	2.0
5 Economies of scale[a]	2.0	2.0	1.5	1.8	1.8	1.9
6 Product diversification	1.5	2.3	1.8	1.8	1.8	1.7
7 Market diversification	1.6	2.3	1.5	1.3	1.7	1.7
8 Favoured access to markets	1.5	1.0	1.0	2.0	1.2	1.4

Notes: a. Companies were asked to indicate each variable on a scale 1-5. 1 indicates no significance and 4/5 of greatest significance.
b. Part of which reflect efficiency of quality control and inspection procedures of the parent company.

sector testify to what is now a well acknowledged story of Japanese success.

As far as product quality is concerned we are established as a standard of comparison in the market (a colour TV producer).

In the organisation of work, we achieve the maximum flexibility of personnel by avoiding all job demarcation (a colour TV producer).

Our management philosophy stresses individual contribution and a good working environment. At the same time, we keep our work force fully informed of our goals and allow them to participate in decision making, even though the final decisions are taken by management (a colour TV producer).

One other conclusion to be drawn from Table 3.3 is that, apart from drawing upon their parent companies' R & D, and, in the case of some Group 2 affiliates, favoured access to inputs, Japanese affiliates do not acknowledge any substantial advantages of being part of a common governance of multinational activities. It is possible, of course, that the parent organisation might have a different perception on this issue,[7] but we suspect the main reason to be that the great majority of Japanese affiliates are single-product firms and usually the only one of their kind in Europe.

However, in spite of many specific examples, at the end of the day it would seem that if there is a single ownership advantage of Japanese firms, it is their recognition of the ingredients of success and their ability to promote this goal by encouraging the best out of both machines and people, and co-ordinating quality control at different stages of the production chain. This in itself is a common governance advantage, but while the advantage *per se* might reflect the affiliate's parentage, its application is essentially an intra-plant rather than an intra-firm kind. As has been suggested, it is rarely the basic product which is unique; rather the adaptations and refinements to that product, the attention to detail and the consistency of its quality; these, in turn, reflect a careful appraisal of market needs and the belief that these needs should be met as completely as possible. Often, too, there is nothing unusual in the technology of production;[8] although, for the most part, Japanese manufacturing processes are far more flexible than their US or European counterparts (Tsurumi, 1984). What seems now generally accepted and is certainly confirmed by our study, is that the quality of many kinds of components is generally higher in Japan than in the UK; and it is as much in this area as in the assembling of these components, that one might expect to see the most marked impact of Japanese participation in UK industry.

The recognition of customer needs and the determination to meet them is one thing; the ability to do so rests on the efficient management of resources. In particular, there is accumulating evidence that the Japanese have shown an ability to get the best out of their UK workforce (Trevor, 1983). Whether this reflects a combination of circumstances to do with the type and motivation of the workforce recruited – it has for example, already been observed that a large proportion of Japanese affiliates are located in areas of above average unemployment, and employ non-unionised labour – or something uniquely Japanese in the methods of organising work, we are not sure. But, as Chapter 10 will show, although their personnel philosophy is different, with a much greater emphasis being placed on team co-operation, there is nothing particularly distinctive in the industrial relations policy of Japanese affiliates. Superficially, this is reflected in a somewhat regimented and paternalistic ethos, but it is more than this; indeed, it starts and finishes with the involvement of all grades of labour in the company's ideals and objectives, and the responsibility assigned to individual workers for their part in achieving these ideals and objectives. As one consumer electronics affiliate put it:

The quest for quality extends to all areas of our organisation and not just production, and the acceptance of all workers to this quest is vital to our success.

and another – and more generally –

If Japanese companies do have an edge over British companies it is in their ability to get their workers to work together as a group and for them to recognise that the customer is still 'king'. The British are strong when they work independently, and where the qualities of creativity, imagination, individuality and initiative are at a premium. Hence the success of the British in the professions, finance and the arts, while the Japanese excel in those parts of manufacturing industry, the success of which depends on a dedicated loyal and hardworking labour force, seeking to achieve the goals of the team rather than that of a particular individual.

The sense of a family partnership and the avoidance of adverse industrial relations, while not special to Japanese affiliates, is as unusual in the UK as it is commonplace in Japan. While there may be other ways of achieving high productivity, an enthusiastic acceptance of common goals is undoubtedly one of the most positive contributions to it.

The kind of ownership advantages just identified appear to be most pronounced in assembling, consumer goods industries and those in which employees, both individually and collectively, may have a decisive influence on the quality of output. In the continuous processing, capital intensive sectors, producing intermediate producer goods, although the quality of end product remains a dominant ownership advantage, there is a difference of emphasis on process related variables.[9] For example, in several affiliates visited in this group, there appeared to be a distinct absence of the Japanese management style in organising work, even though the attention given cost minimisation and quality control was no less evident. Since more inputs were standard raw materials, or purchased in spot markets, the emphasis on quality of outside purchases was much less in Group 2 affiliates.[10] This point is further taken up in Chapter 6. But our strong impression is that while, in some instances, the ownership advantages of Japanese firms in the UK may be traced to a particular product or process technology — which themselves may reflect the distinctive needs of the Japanese economy[11] — for the most part they are likely to rest in the ability to supply a product of consistent and reliable (though not necessarily the highest) quality, at competitive prices; this, in turn, implies high productivity, not only through mechanisation, but through well trained, well motivated and co-operative labour, as measured by high quality throughput per employee.

In the course of interviews, Japanese affiliates were asked their perception of the extent to which the advantages which their parent companies had over their indigenous competitors could be transmitted to a UK culture. The almost universal answer was that the great majority — including the attainment of quality standards — were transferrable, but there was a residual (not easily quantifiable) which could not be. This residual reflected the basic differences in attitude to work and leisure by Japanese and UK workers. In Japan, it was alleged, employees always put work first and leisure and their domestic life second; in the UK it was the reverse. Moreover, as a matter of pride and keeping face with his employers and fellow workers, the Japanese employee would always be more strongly motivated to give of his best, irrespective of monetary incentives.[12] It is possible, of course, this might change should the Japanese culture become more Westernised, but for the foreseeable future, our best guess is that this makes for a productivity gap of around 10%.[13]

To what extent are the ownership advantages of Japanese companies likely to be eroded over time? The views of Sony are typical of those expressed.

> The specific advantage of the 'Triniton' colour television must lessen with time; it follows then that to retain our competitive position, maximum benefits must be gained from new technologies.

Several other Japanese firms[14] also indicated that their initial product or process advantages had been partly competed away since their arrival in the UK. On the other hand, it was perceived that as Japanese affiliates increased their output in the UK and elsewhere in Europe, a new generation of products or processes would be introduced from Japan, while the synergistic benefits arising from being part of a geographically diversified MNE would become more important.

At a more general level, if and when UK competitors are persuaded to adopt Japanese style attitudes and management policies, the productivity gap will narrow. Already the 'shake-out' in many sectors of UK manufacturing industry is forcing this to happen without the Japanese presence in this country; the 220% productivity improvement in British Leyland between 1978 and 1983 is a case in point. But in the consumer electronics industry, the dramatic turnround in the fortunes of Thorn/ EMI and other UK based manufacturers is put quite specifically at the door of competition from Japanese firms.[15] And several component suppliers assert that their productivity has been raised by their dealings with these same affiliates.[16]

On the other hand, because of their research intensity, size, product strategy and growing geographical diversification, and because of their somewhat different objectives – with more emphasis on quality control and customisation – one might expect Japanese MNEs to generate new ownership advantages. Up to now, for example, because of their comparatively low profile as international producers, they have managed to recoup only a few of the advantages of multinationalisation enjoyed by their European and US counterparts: one suspects such economies of international specialisation of products and markets may become much more important in the 1980s and 1990s. To compete effectively, (European) firms may need to rationalise, merge or collaborate, in much the same way as they did when faced with competition from US affiliates in the 1950s and 1960s.[17]

The Attractions of the UK as a Location for Production

The Motives for Coming to the UK

Why should Japanese firms choose the UK as a production base (to exploit their ownership advantages) rather than (a) Japan and (b) other parts of Europe?

In all cases but one, the initial *raison d'être* for investing in Europe[18] was primarily to supply either the local (in this case the UK) or the EEC market. Only in the case of Paddox Worsted was the investment made to take advantage of local resources for export — after processing — back to Japan. Even in 1982, 31% of the output of Japanese manufacturing affiliates was sold in Europe; and only in two cases was there any kind of product or process division of labour either between Japanese parent and the UK affiliate or between the UK and other Japanese affiliates in Europe.

Table 3.4 sets out the main motives indicated by 24[19] Japanese affiliates for investment in the UK. Each affiliate was asked to assign a figure of 0-5 indicating the importance of the particular variable identified. It can be seen that the most important single reason given was to secure a foothold for supplying goods to the EEC. This was particularly noticeable in the case of Group 1, viz. the electronics firms. In 8 of the 10 firms,[20] this motive was ranked 5 and in the other two, 4 and 3 respectively. It is not surprising then that this group of firms exported on average 29% of their output of £197m in 1982, and 91% of this to the rest of the EEC. It is particularly noteworthy that, apart from Sony, the more recently established Japanese affiliates recorded the best export performances, and stated that they looked on the UK as a production base for the whole of the EEC (and, occasionally, for other markets as well). Yet, none of Group 1 affiliates were part of any regional product or process specialisation; indeed, the total recurrent imports from other EEC countries in 1982 amounted to only about £6m, and almost all of this took the form of components or raw materials.

It also appears that where the UK was initially chosen because it offered one of the largest domestic markets in Europe for Japanese exports (the most recent example being that of video recorders), its share of European sales has fallen over time; and that, increasingly, Japanese firms are viewing Western Europe as a single market. This has the important implication that supply (e.g. cost) and strategic factors are more likely to influence the locational choice of Japanese investors than the size or growth of domestic markets; and that for Group 1 firms, at least, the UK has been (and is being) chosen as a site for production either

Table 3.4: Main Motives for Japanese Companies in Establishing Manufacturing Affiliates in the UK

		Group 1	Group 2				Total
			Eng	Chem	Other	All	
1	Primarily to supply UK market	2.9	3.5	4.8	3.8	3.9	3.5
2	As a point of entry into the EEC	4.8	3.4	2.5	1.5	2.6	3.6
3	To supply Japanese market with products	0.2	0.0	0.0	1.2	0.4	0.3
4	As a means of gaining access to UK intangible assets or other resources	1.5	1.0	1.0	1.0	1.0	1.2
5	As part of an integrated European or worldwide product mandate	3.5	2.8	2.0	0.5	2.2	2.8
6	To promote exports from the parent or other Japanese companies	1.8	2.0	0.8	2.3	1.5	1.6
7	To service other Japanese companies in the UK and/or Europe	1.3	0.0	0.8	0.8	0.5	0.8

Note: Companies were asked to indicate significance of each variable as scale 0 to 5, 0 indicated no significance, 5 of greatest significance.

because of its (perceived) favourable costs, and/or because of agglomerative or other benefits offered by it.[21]

In answer to the question 'Has this strategy changed over the years since producing in the UK?', the only two firms which replied 'Yes' explained that while they had initially set up in the UK to supply the local market, in the last two or three years their product and marketing mandate had been geared more to Continental customers.

The views expressed by one longer established CTV producer sum up those of this group: 'Our original motive was to be close to the UK market; now [September 1983] we are taking the best advantage of EEC membership.' It is finally worth mentioning that the later arrivals in the industrial electronics sector, e.g. NEC Semi-Conductors and Shin Etsui, emphasise the point that micro electronic components are high value added products, incur low transport costs and engage in automated methods of production; and that all these factors favour the centralisation of production. This having been said however, these, and most CTV and video set producers, would probably not be manufacturing in Europe at all — at least, not at this point of time — were it not for the trade imbalances between Japan and the EEC, the imposition of various tariff and non-tariff restrictions, e.g. country of origin require-ments, placed upon various consumer electronic goods, and intergovern-ment agreements with respect to e.g. videos and micro electronics. We shall return to this point later.

In Group 2 sectors, the motives for investment were rather more mixed. In four of the six light engineering firms, the attraction of the European market was ranked the highest importance; in the other two — YKK and Tekara — there are other manufacturing subsidiaries in Europe, and the UK plants are designed to service the UK market. Three of the chemical and all the 'other' affiliates (and particularly the latter) ranked the UK market as more important than the EEC market. One exception was a petrochemicals affiliate. In the words of the Managing Director

Looking back, not being a member of the EEC would certainly have affected our company's decision where to manufacture in Europe. No question at all. If we contracted out our parent would have second thoughts about this country. We have a big plant, but if the UK decided to come out, it would undoubtedly be looked on un-favourably. We would not have the backing of future investment.

Five of Group 2 affiliates (as well as 5 of Group 1 affiliates) con-sidered the promotion of exports from their parent company or other Japanese companies important enough to warrant a 3 or 4 (on the scale 1-5); in two cases (two also in the case of Group 1 affiliates) the same rating was given to 'servicing other Japanese companies in the UK or Europe'.

The need to by-pass enforced or voluntary import restrictions ap-peared less significant for Group 2 affiliates; in the case of an ophthal-mic lens company, speed of delivery was considered a vital factor, and for a smoke detector and a zip fastener company there was the need to adapt to local market requirements.

Group 2 affiliates exported, on average, 43% of their output of £38m in 1982, 86% of which was to the rest of the EEC. Excluding the affili-ate that exported all its output to Japan, the relevant export percentages were 41% and 87%. Five of the 14 firms indicated that had moved increas-ingly into the European market since they started producing in the UK. In all, three light engineering and two chemical considered that they now operated a fairly integrated European marketing strategy, though none admitted to any kind of division of labour between their European plants or between their Japanese parent and UK affiliate. Indeed, in 1982 imports of Group 2 affiliates from Europe amounted to less than £½m.

In summary, it appears that, to date, most of Japanese affiliates in the UK are not part of an integrated product or marketing strategy in Europe.[22] Indeed, only 6 of the 23 affiliates had other production affiliates elsewhere in Europe, and only in one was there a substantial amount (over £1m) of intra-firm trade. This is a very different situation from that of US MNE activity, and reflects both the very early stage of Japanese investment in Europe and the fact that most Japanese affiliates are single product, and centralise their plant capacity to capture the economies of large-scale production.

The Specific Reasons for Choosing the UK Compared with Japan

We now turn to consider the more specific reasons why Japanese affiliates chose the UK as a production base relative to (a) Japan and (b) the 'next best' European location. We asked each affiliate to rank on a scale −5 to +5 the importance of a group of factors commonly thought to influence the location of manufacturing activity. We divided these variables into 5 groups.

(a) impediments to trade in goods, e.g. transport costs, tariff and non-tariff barriers;

(b) production (including intra-firm communication) costs;

(c) differences in the Japanese or European cf UK environment (including language, custom, commercial regulations, etc.);

(d) government policy towards fdi, including investment incentives, regional development grants, selective financial assistance, tax rebates, procurement policies;

(e) other, including the need to adapt to local customer requirements and action (or likely action) on part of competitors.

Our main findings are set out in Table 3.5. Of the factors favouring a UK rather than a Japanese location, those overwhelmingly regarded most important by Group 1 and 2 affiliates were various forms of trade barriers and the falling value of the £ in relation to the yen; however, non-tariff obstacles (import quotas, etc.) were far more important in

Table 3.5: Factors Influencing Choice of Location by Japanese Firms
(i) UK Compared with Japan (ii) UK Compared with Next Best European Location

	Group 1 affiliates (i)	Group 1 affiliates (ii)	Group 2 affiliates (i)	Group 2 affiliates (ii)	All affiliates (i)	All affiliates (ii)
(1) Transport costs & trade barriers	+1.5	+0.2	+1.5	+0.4	+1.5	+0.4
(a) Transport costs from main suppliers	-2.1	-0.1	0.0	0.0	-0.9	-0.1
(b) Transport costs of finished goods to customers	+1.8	+0.2	+3.4	+1.3	+2.8	+1.3
(c) Import duties and/or controls	+3.2	+0.2	+2.6	-0.2	+2.9	+0.0
(d) Non-tariff barriers	+3.6	+0.3	+0.6	+0.2	+1.9	+0.3
(e) Absence of trade barriers	+0.8	+0.6	+1.3	+0.5	+1.3	+0.5
(2) Production costs	-1.2	+0.5	-0.5	+0.3	-0.8	+0.4
(a) Operative wage rates	+0.0	+1.4	+0.6	+1.0	+0.3	+1.3
(b) Other wages and salaries	+0.7	+1.3	-0.3	+1.3	+0.1	+1.3
(c) Rent and rates	+0.1	+0.5	+0.3	+0.5	+0.2	+0.5
(d) Co-ordination costs between parent and affiliate	-3.0	+0.6	-0.1	+0.2	-1.7	-0.4
(e) Industrial relations and productivity	-2.1	-0.3	-1.8	-0.7	-1.9	-1.5
(f) Energy costs	+0.0	-0.4	-0.3	-0.2	-0.3	-0.3
(g) Component supply availability & price	-3.9	+0.4	-0.8	0.0	-2.1	+0.2
(3) Environmental factors	-1.2	+1.8	-0.8	+1.3	-1.0	+1.5
(a) Differences in legal and commercial system	-1.4	+1.3	-0.8	+1.0	-1.0	+1.1
(b) Dealing with UK suppliers, government, etc.	-1.7	+1.6	+0.1	+0.9	-0.7	+1.2
(c) Language	-3.6	+4.3	-3.1	+4.6	-3.3	+4.5
(d) Housing, educational facilities	+0.0	+1.7	0.0	+0.8	0.0	+1.1

(e) Airport *et al.* communication facilities	+0.1	+1.1	+0.1	+0.3	+0.1	+0.6
(f) Cultural	−2.4	−2.9	−1.4	+2.1	−1.8	+2.3
(g) Technological and educational infrastructure	−1.5	−0.2	−0.5	−0.4	−0.9	−0.3
(4) Government policy affecting FDI	+1.2	+0.8	+0.9	+0.6	+1.0	+0.7
(a) Taxes	−0.1	0.0	−0.4	−0.7	−0.3	−0.4
(b) Procurement policies	+0.0	+0.1	+0.3	+0.5	+0.2	+0.3
(c) Incentives	+2.3	+1.5	+0.9	+0.5	+1.4	+0.9
(d) FDI policies	+1.0	+1.0	+1.3	+1.4	+1.2	+1.3
(e) Exchange rates	+2.9	+1.5	+2.6	+1.4	+2.7	+1.4
(5) Other	+0.9	+1.3	+1.1	0.7	+1.0	+0.9
(a) Need to adapt to customer requirements (and speed of delivery)	+1.0	+1.0	+2.4	+1.0	+1.9	+1.0
(b) Need to be near other affiliates	+1.0	+1.7	+0.6	+1.2	+0.7	+1.4
(c) Action (or likely action) on part of competitors	+3.1	+1.3	+1.0	+0.8	+2.0	+0.9
(d) Access to technology, information or finance	−1.6	+0.9	+0.3	−0.3	−0.6	+0.2

Note: Affiliates were asked to assess importance of factors on a scale 1-5 and to assign a + where location favours the UK, and − where location favours Japan or 'next best' European location.

the case of Group 1 affiliates, while transport costs of finished goods to the final customer were more relevant for Group 2 (and particularly chemical) affiliates. The only other locational advantage of the UK was seen to be its proximity to customers, both to provide speedy delivery (especially identified by one firm producing chemical materials, and another producing spectacle lenses) or to adapt to their specialised needs (mentioned by a zip fastener and a spectacle lens affiliate). As a form of competitive strategy, our findings lend some support to the hypothesis that firms take account of the behaviour of their competitors when considering whether to engage in or expand their foreign direct investment; and that many practise a 'follow my leader strategy'.[23] This was especially noticeable in the CTV sector in the late 1970s and is becoming so in the video recorder and micro-chip sectors in the 1980s; and parallels a similar bunching by US affiliates in the UK pharmaceutical sector in the late 1960s and in the semiconductor sector in the early 1970s, described by Lake (1976).

By contrast, the main obstacles of the UK as a location compared with Japan are undoubtedly environmental. These are partly initial 'entry' barriers; once established, a Japanese affiliate is unlikely to encounter additional obstacles; indeed, through learning and experience, these disadvantages are likely to fall. Of the barriers, language was assigned by far the highest score, with cultural considerations (including unfamiliarity of UK workers with the Japanese work ethic), and UK suppliers unable to meet Japanese delivery needs not far behind. It is perhaps worth observing that these obstacles were felt to be the most important among firms whose success rested on communicating the Japanese management style and quality needs to workers and suppliers (i.e. Group 1 affiliates) and those which had most recently set up in the UK.

As far as production costs were concerned, it appears that UK wage rates and salaries compare quite favourably with those in Japan;[24] however, labour productivity is lower in the UK, and many (perhaps the majority in value terms) inputs (particularly those bought by Group 1 firms) are either not available or cost a good deal more in the UK than in Japan (even allowing for the additional transport costs).[25] Partly the lower costs reflect the economies of scale enjoyed by Japanese producers; and partly their higher efficiency. Scale economies in production — be they in assembling or continuous processing operations — also favour centralisation of production in Europe: as the output of the affiliates increases, so the difference between Japanese and UK productivity might be expected to fall.[26]

We conclude, then, that much of the initial impetus of Japanese participation in the UK has been prompted by barriers to the export of goods from Japan and the desire to minimise trade friction between Europe and Japan. However, there is a lot of casual evidence to suggest that, over the last five years or so, both the environment and production costs have moved strongly in the UK's favour. This is partly reflected in the £/yen exchange rate (which depreciated by 33% between January 1977 and December 1982); but it also appears that neither the environmental barriers, nor labour-related problems in the UK, have been as serious as the Japanese had been led to believe. For a variety of reasons, the real cost of Japanese labour has risen sharply in the last five years, while the ability of both UK suppliers and Japanese affiliates to produce a product of a comparable standard to that of its Japanese equivalent has improved.

In answer to the question 'Which factors have favoured and which have disfavoured the UK relative to Japan in the years 1978-1982?', there was fairly general unanimity that the appreciation of the yen and higher labour productivity in the UK had enhanced the prospects for further Japanese investment. Other points in favour of the UK were technological infrastructure, good investment incentives;[27] low corporation taxes, the increased need for customised products and the liking of the policies of the present government. In all, there were 27 mentions of factors making for more favourable conditions and nine factors disfavouring the UK. Of the latter, energy costs were cited three times and industrial relations twice (five other firms mentioned this as a plus factor); also pinpointed were rent and rates and relative material prices.

On the other hand, there is little doubt that Japanese affiliates have had to overcome a variety of difficulties of operating in the UK. Some of these, such as problems of labour management and industrial relations, are dealt with in Chapter 10. Others, such as different social and legal systems, safety and health regulations, the global recession and the EEC's country of origin requirements, are common to most European countries; indeed, if anything, the problems are less inhibiting in the UK than elsewhere (see next section).

Reasons for Choosing the UK Rather than Another European Country

Given the reasons for wishing to supply the UK or European market from a European rather than a Japanese production base, why should the UK be the preferred location?

Of the 20 affiliates able to identify their next most preferred European location to the UK, 13 gave Germany, five either the Netherlands or Belgium (but near to the German border), and two Ireland. Of the nine Group 1 affiliates, all would have chosen Germany.

It would seem that the main variables influencing the choice of European base were (and probably still are — at least for newcomers):

(i)   language and cultural considerations;
(ii)   political stability;
(iii)   size of market and technological infrastructure, including research and development capacity;
(iv)   labour quality and industrial relations,
(v)   availability of good management,
(vi)   communications;
(vii)   location of competitors.

Trade barriers were broadly comparable among the larger EEC countries, with the possible exception of non-tariff barriers being greater in France.

As can be seen from Table 3.5, the UK comes out very well compared with other European locations for all environmental variables, apart from technological and educational infrastructure, and especially so on language and cultural grounds. It scores over all European countries, except Germany, on size of markets and on some production costs, e.g. wage rates and salaries. However, it loses out on industrial relations and labour productivity, and the availability of supplies and price of some raw materials (e.g. PVC, feedstock and funnel glass) and parts (e.g. electronic components). All of the affiliates questioned asserted that, in most of the above respects, the advantage had swung in the UK's favour since 1978. The UK also scored on housing, educational and leisure provisions and on air and road communication facilities.

There are some variations in the locational perceptions of Japanese MNEs between industrial sectors. This is confirmed by the differences in the distribution of Japanese (and other) affiliates within Europe.[28] It seems that in the high technology, capital intensive sectors, where (a) a sophisticated and highly trained work force is required, yet (b) where the need for regular verbal communication between workers and managers, and between the affiliate and its suppliers, is relatively less vital to the success of a company, Germany has the edge over the UK — or at least it did so up to around 1980. However, in the more labour intensive sectors, and where the advantages of the Japanese rest more on management style, work organisation and quality of inputs, the UK is preferred. Hence the concentration of CTV manufacturing in the UK, while industrial machinery companies favour Germany.

The Japanese affiliates seem to have widely different views on what, if anything, the UK government might do to encourage more direct investment from Japan. Several suggestions, e.g. the reduction of energy costs, the improvement of investment incentives or grants, the containment of inflation, and the discouragement of unrealistic wage settlements, might equally have been voiced by UK firms. The ones rather more specific to foreign ownership are (i) the assistance of UK suppliers of Japanese firms with capital equipment to improve their quality control and inspection procedures and (ii) the resistance of any protectionist moves by other member countries of the EEC, such as the imposition of more stringent country of origin rules on goods (partly) produced in the UK.

The conclusion of this section is that, like their US predecessors in the 1950s, Japanese firms were initially prompted to set up manufacturing affiliates in Europe to overcome barriers to exports from Japan, rather than for any aggressive reasons. More recently, however, Japanese MNEs have been viewing a European production base more positively as part of their long-term international strategy. Nevertheless, differences in comparative wage levels, culture and in language, and uncertainties as to how far Japanese management styles, organisation procedures and work ethic could be transferred into a European environment, have kept direct investment much less than might have been expected had, for example, US MNEs been faced with a similar situation.

Within Europe, the UK and Germany are the two most favoured locations for Japanese manufacturers. The eastern boundaries of the Netherlands and Belgium are also liked. The UK is seen to have a particular advantage in that it offers the Japanese a more familiar and congenial working and cultural environment. In recent years, the UK has lost some of its unfavourable industrial relations image, and inflation has been better contained. This general improvement in the international competitive position of the UK augurs well for Japanese participation in the 1980s.[29]

Much of what has been written is consistent with the findings of the JETRO survey of Japanese Manufacturing Companies in Europe (JETRO, 1983). The relevant paragraph of their report which deals with the advantage offered by the major European countries may be quoted in full.

It is very risky to judge the character of each European country since the number of samples was small and there was imbalance in the distribution of the respondents from country to country. But relatively many of the corporations surveyed pointed out the merits of each nation as follows: West Germany and the Netherlands are more favourable in the procurement of raw materials and parts; the United Kingdom and Spain in the quality of labour force; Belgium and Spain in the influence of trade unions; and Belgium, the United Kingdom, Italy, the Netherlands and Spain in the availability of industrial parks. As for preferential treatment, Belgium and the United Kingdom were chosen as the best by seven respondents, respectively, West Germany, Ireland and Spain by five and Italy by three.

The Choice of Location Within the UK

All but three of the Japanese affiliates took a great deal of guidance from the UK Department of Industry about the location of their activities in the UK; and in some cases – and particularly where existing premises were vacant[30] – the Department was directly instrumental in the site chosen. Japanese companies also indicated a very positive response to incentives – particularly investment grants.

For a variety of reasons – not least the efforts of the Development Corporation for Wales (now Winvest) – it is not surprising there has been some concentration of Japanese affiliates in Wales. Undoubtedly the pioneering venture by Sony at Bridgend in 1973, led to the later siting of companies like Mitsubishi (National Panasonic), Aiwa, Takiron, Sekisui and Yuasa Battery in South Wales. On the other hand, particular circumstances such as the availability of the appropriate factory premises at the right time explains the choice of GEC-Hitachi at Hirwaun of Merlin Aerials at Newbury, Nittan at Woking, Tamura Kaken at Northampton, Sanyo at Lowestoft, Toshiba at Plymouth, JV2 at Newhaven and Teraka Belmont in London.

The availability of young semi-trained and well motivated female labour and the excellent communication facilities along the M4 also had a lot to do with the choice of South Wales by the consumer electronics companies; while the (perceived) greater technical competence of the Scottish engineering workers, of good educational facilities and the presence of similar US and UK companies most certainly encouraged both NEC Semiconductors and Shin-Etsu to set up new manufacturing units in Livingston. Outside the less prosperous regions, Japanese affiliates, and particularly those in Group 2, tend to prefer new or expanding towns on or adjacent to main highways, e.g. Sansetsu and Alps Electric at Milton Keynes and Hitachi Maxell and Ricoh Products at Telford; again each of these affiliates mentioned the efforts made by the local development corporation to attract them. One affiliate – Paddox Fine Worsted

— chose its location at the centre of the high grade woollen cloth industry.

The Role of Regional and other Government Incentives

We have observed that 14 of the 23 Japanese affiliates covered by our survey have qualified for regional development assistance;[31] from their balance sheets, we estimate that they have benefited from about £4m of such grants.

To what extent have these grants influenced the amount, type and location of investment undertaken by Japanese affiliates? Our impression, strongly confirmed by the CTV affiliates, is that, in their initial decision of *whether* to set up a manufacturing facility in Europe, grants are *not* of crucial significance. In the words of one affiliate: 'It is company policy that we should assess the viability of all investment projects on purely commercial grounds excluding all government incentives.' At the same time, the amount of the investment, the speed at which a manufacturing facility is built up and where it is located is, at least marginally, affected by such grants. One engineering affiliate also mentioned that the level of grants also affected the rate at which it replaced machinery and equipment, and therefore its ability to keep up with its competitors. This is clearly likely to be most relevant in the rapidly innovating sectors and those in which additional assurance of the good faith of the UK economy is needed. It is perhaps not surprising that those Japanese affiliates making losses preferred grants or interest free loans to any form of tax relief; and that, given a choice, the majority of firms would opt for grants rather than investment or depreciation allowances.

None of the Japanese affiliates indicated they had taken advantage of government assistance for research and development, or innovation-linked investment schemes; nor did they consider such incentives were likely to influence the extent to which they engaged in innovating activities in the UK.

It is perhaps worth observing that the JETRO study referred to earlier (JETRO, 1983), found that, in relation to other factors influencing the choice of location of Japanese affiliates in the UK, incentives were ranked 1st or 2nd more frequently; and that the UK was ranked 1st or 2nd on account of this factor more often than other countries in Europe. Belgium, West Germany and Spain were also fairly highly rated.

Finally, mention might be made of a survey by Hood and Young (1983), which *inter alia* dealt with the question of regional incentives affecting the investing decision of US and Continental based MNEs in the UK. The broad conclusion was that while such incentives exercised only a modest influence on the *initial* decision to invest, more than one-third of some 87 affiliates which had undertaken some *expansionary* investment since 1977 in assisted areas asserted that, because of regional development grants (RDGs) the scale of investment was larger than would otherwise have been the case. Of the other dimensions studied, RDGs etc. were claimed to have had an effect on capital intensity in 28% of the relevant firms and on process technology in 20% of the applicable sample. Overall, the authors state: 'The alleged impact of regional incentives is far from insignificant'.[32] Of the various types of project which RDGs might have influenced, those involving additional equipment expenditure were most frequently mentioned. Lastly there is some evidence to suggest that a minority of firms (between 5 and 10%) thought their technology had been changed 'in a major way' by regional incentives.[33]

In another study on Japanese involvement in the consumer electronics industry (Brech and Sharp, 1984), the authors estimate that the total value of discretionary assistance, from which seven Japanese affiliates have benefited, is £1.9m, or 7% of their total capital investment. Including an allowance for Regional Development Grants at the rate of 20-22%, the direct total assistance has averaged 27-29%. The total number of jobs estimated by Brech and Sharp to have been created by these firms is about 1,620; so assistance works out at £4,730 per head. Our own estimate would put the per employee assistance lower than this (around £3,000); but, as already indicated, we believe that not many of the jobs would have been created in any case.

The report also found that 36 of the sample 100 companies operating in assisted areas considered that incentives were a factor 'of significance' in influencing decisions on investment projects over the next three years; 44 companies denied any influence from incentives, while the remaining 20 companies had new investments in the pipeline. The amount of government assistance so far given pales into insignificance when the Nissan venture is considered; between 1985 and 1987 up to £35 million of financial incentives are likely to be provided by the UK government.

The Foreign Direct Investment v Licensing Decision

Given the ownership advantages of Japanese firms described in the previous section, and the reasons why it may be preferable to locate production based upon these advantages in the UK, why should Japanese firms prefer to ·internalise' the advantages rather than sell or lease the property rights to UK firms?

The kernel of the fdi v licence decisions (using the term license to embrace all forms of non-equity participation)[34] rests in the extent to which the return for a specific proprietary asset, or group of assets, can be fully captured through a market transaction where uncertainty (= uninsurable risk) arises, either for the buyer as to the nature and value of the knowledge being transferred, or for each party on the capacity and willingness of the other to fulfil and abide by the terms of contract. Markets may also fail because they cannot capture the benefits and costs external to a specific transaction, which again may be appropriated by one of the participating parties when that transaction is internalised. Finally, firms may wish to internalise transactions which otherwise may operate to their disadvantage through the actions of governments.

Earlier in this chapter we identified some market failures. For our purposes we consider three groups of variables which might influence the equity[35] v non-equity route of Japanese involvement in the UK. These are

(i) The nature of the market associated with the sale of the right to the use of specific property rights possessed by Japanese companies.

(ii) The extent to which the internalised transfer or use of these assets generate either benefits to the affiliate or to the parent organisation, e.g. arising from the common governance and co-ordination of activities with or between it and the parent company in the UK operation.

(iii) The extent to which the UK environment is conducive towards one modality or another. For example, in some countries fdi may be outlawed by government decree. In others, the technological or social infrastructure may be inadequate to justify an equity investment.[36] Perceived differences of government policies, e.g. with respect to taxation of corporate profits or uncertainty about exchange rates, may tempt firms to internalise certain transactions to protect themselves against, or even exploit, e.g. by way of transfer prices, what is, to them, another form of market failure. On the other hand, unfamiliarity with domestic laws, commercial practices, customs, lack of knowledge about suppliers and difficulties in breaking into an existing market might encourage a potential investor to prefer a licensing (or at least a joint venture) arrangement to that of a fully owned affiliate.

Table 3.6 sets out the perception of 23 affiliates as to the importance of the variables in influencing why they chose to invest in the UK rather than license UK firms.

Taking first Group 1 affiliates, the most important reason, making for foreign direct investment (fdi), is the perception that, to protect one of the main ownership advantages, viz. standards of quality, it is necessary to control the way resources are used. This is further confirmed by the high score (3.7) given to the need for a Japanese management style which was thought easier to achieve with full equity ownership. One of the reasons for preferring fdi is that certain types of knowledge, techniques or philosophy are tacit or non-codifiable.[37] This is certainly the case when organising work, in communicating ideas, in promoting good labour relations, and in introducing new management styles, and was a major consideration in Nissan's preference for a 100% owned greenfield venture in the UK.[38]

Some Group 1 firms — particularly those in the industrial electronics and video sectors - argue that because their production processes are idiosyncratic, flexible and involve team organisation, they need to maintain close supervision over them, while there is some suggestion that firms do not believe that licensing will fully protect themselves against the infringement of property rights. In a few cases, the difficulty of finding an appropriate licensee was the predominant factor.[38]

Group 1 affiliates also attached some significance to synergistic variables; equity investment was preferred because it was felt that the benefits of joint production of separate activities or economies of scope could be better captured by the MNE when the transactions were internalised. Among such variables identified were the freedom to take advantage of product, market or process diversity and the flexibility to pursue global objectives (awarded a score of 4 or 5 by 6 of 9 firms); but more generally, and especially by the longer established affiliates and ones which exported through independent sales affiliates, of being part of a large and diversified multinational organisation. It is these kinds of multinationality-associated benefits, which are less easily exploitable through licensing,[39] that are likely to become more important in the future as Japanese firms increase their participation in Europe.

Neither Group 1 nor Group 2 affiliates considered environmental variables to be an important influence in their choice of involvement. Only one (in a somewhat depressed sector) mentioned that, had the

Table 3.6: The Reasons for Preferring an Equity Investment Rather than a Licensing Arrangement in the UK

	Group 1	Group 2				Total
	Eng	Chem	Other	All		
(a) To do with market imperfections (for a particular asset)						
1 Difficulty of locating an appropriate licensee	2.9	3.4	2.3	3.3	3.0	2.9
2 Difficulty of guaranteeing quality control (including that of components)	4.2	4.0	3.3	3.3	3.5	3.8
3 Difficulty of enforcing patent or trade mark rights	3.0	3.0	4.0	1.8	2.9	3.0
4 Unable to negotiate a satisfactory price for '0' advantage	3.1	2.3	3.3	2.5	2.5	2.8
5 Difficulty of ensuring speedy or reliable delivery dates from UK firm	2.2	3.0	1.8	2.3	2.5	2.4
6 Unable to ensure Japanese work style/management philosophy	3.7	2.3	2.5	1.5	2.1	2.8
7 Uncertainty about prices	2.1	1.3	1.5	1.0	1.3	1.6
8 Speed of introducing innovations	3.5	1.5	1.8	1.3	1.5	2.4
(b) To do with synergistic relationships						
1 Unable to capture full economies of scope and organisational synergy via licensing	3.1	2.5	2.3	2.8	2.6	2.9
2 Need to maintain full product, process or market flexibility	3.7	3.3	3.0	2.3	2.8	3.3
3 Need to control distribution outlets	3.1	3.0	2.0	2.8	2.3	2.8
(c) To do with environmental variables						
1 Wishes of home government	1.8	1.0	1.0	1.0	1.0	1.3
2 Wishes of host government	1.9	1.8	1.3	1.0	1.3	1.5
3 To avoid (or exploit) host government intervention and/or take advantage of transfer price manipulation	1.7	1.3	1.3	1.3	1.3	1.4
(d) To do with firm specific considerations						
1 Company policy to prefer 100% equity ownership	3.6	3.6	2.5	3.0	3.0	3.2

Note: Companies were asked to indicate significance of each variable on a scale 1-5, 1 indicates no significance and 5 of greatest significance.

parent company been able to persuade a local (UK) firm to put up some of the equity investment, it would have preferred a joint venture operation. Another (in a high technology sector) indicated that both the Japanese and the UK governments had encouraged a 100% involvement by the parent company. While three companies (all producing consumer electronics) opined (by a score of 3) this choice of modality as being influenced by the desire to accommodate host government (and in one case, home government) wishes, the rest discounted the relevance of this factor.

The reasons for Group 2 firms preferring an equity interest were rather different and more disparate. To begin with, they appear to be less decisive in their choice, e.g. no one factor scored on average more than 3.5. While quality control was again the most frequently cited variable, four firms ranked the fear of patent infringement or the dissipation of codifiable knowledge as the most important reason; these included two chemical and two light engineering affiliates. And, as Table 3.6 shows, this group of firms attached less significance to synergistic economies and Japanese management styles; this suggests that their ownership advantages were contained in particular intangible assets, and that the know-how involved was more easily codifiable. However, because these assets were thought to be of vital competitive importance, firms were reluctant to externalise their use.

Only one of 23 firms saw any likelihood of their form of involvement in the UK changing in the foreseeable future. In all except one of Group 1 affiliates, it was company policy to prefer 100% ventures. Since most firms saw a closer integration of their European affiliates as part of a global strategy of their parent companies in the 1980s, the need for centralisation of decision-taking was thought likely to become more rather than less pronounced; the one exception mentioned by an executive of one CTV affiliate was that, in his opinion, there was less need for Japanese style quality control procedures than ten years ago.

Group 2 firms were generally more relaxed about their ownership structure and, in four cases, the possibility of a joint venture or selling out to a UK producer was envisaged. However, more generally, since several of the affiliates opined that they were likely to increase their vertical integration (rather than their external purchases) in the UK this would point to the continued preference for 100% control.

Taking all Japanese affiliates, of the 14 possible reasons cited for changing the nature of the involvement, 11 worked in favour of equity investment and three against.[40]

Conclusions

In explaining the pattern of Japanese participation in UK manufacturing industry, it is convenient to consider two groups of affiliates. The first, which mainly comprise those in the electronics sector,[41] possess a group of ownership advantages embodying the uniqueness of Japanese production systems, a distinctive managerial philosophy and an ability to extract the maximum co-operation from their workforce and the best quality of inputs from their suppliers. Up to this point, at least, the Japanese companies believe these advantages can be better transferred to the UK within their organisation rather than by licensing arrangements with UK firms. The reasons for locating in Europe are chiefly to overcome natural and artificial barriers to trade; and in the UK, rather than on the Continent for language and cultural reasons.

In the second group of affiliates, the competitive advantages tend to be rather more individualistic and specific, e.g. to do with product content and equipment or process know-how; and these are internalised because the Japanese parent companies regard them as too important to risk their possible dissipation through licensing. From a locational viewpoint, since a larger proportion of the output is sold to the UK market and is often quite costly to transport and/or where customisation or speed of delivery are important, the main reasons for preferring the UK to Japan or another European base are to do with differences in production and transport costs rather than artificial barriers imposed by governments.

In all sectors it would seem that the pressures to establish a European base are increasing; and that, because of the improvement in its competitive position, the UK is in a particularly good position to attract further participation by Japanese MNEs. It would also appear that the new investors of the mid-1980s[42] prefer a 100% involvement; at the same time, in some of the high technology and/or specialised sectors of UK industry, minority ventures and contractual agreements are also on the increase. It could also be that in sectors which the Japanese feel they need a European presence, yet in which they do not have a pronounced international advantage (e.g. pharmaceuticals), their mode of entry might be via a merger with, or partial take-over of – established UK companies.

Notes

1. As summarised in Caves (1982), Buckley & Casson (1985). See also

Dunning (1981), (1983) and (1985). Teece (1983 and 1985).

2. We use licensing as a generic word covering all forms of non-equity contractual relationships between firms of different nationalities.

3. Reference here may be made to the portfolio theory of foreign direct investment described in Rugman (1979), and also that which emphasises the imperfection of capital and foreign exchange markets (Aliber, 1971).

4. It being argued by some economists, e.g. Knickerbocker (1973), that oligopolists adopt a 'follow my leader' policy towards foreign direct investment (fdi). The product cycle theory of fdi (Vernon, 1966, 1979) also lays great emphasis on the oligopolistic strategy of firms.

5. Including in this instance, Hitachi Maxell, which began production in the UK in 1984.

6. In the case of smoke detector equipment, for example, the Japanese government insists upon exceptionally high product standards.

7. Particularly in respect of marketing activities; for as mentioned in Chapter 2 most manufacturing affiliates in the UK do not themselves market their output in Europe.

8. With the exception perhaps of some chemical firms in our sample.

9. For example, organisation of work and industrial relations, management philosophy and quality of inputs scored 4.3 and 3.7, 4.3 and 4.2 for Group 1 firms and 3.0 and 2.7, 3.0 and 1.8 in Group 2 affiliates.

10. A good case is fire extinguishers.

11. As set out in Franko (1983) pp. 37-8. For example, a large proportion of Japanese innovations in the postwar period have been devoted to raw material and energy conservation and the saving of space; *inter alia* these have resulted in important advances in automobile and colour TV design, and in micro-circuits.

12. In the words of one Scottish affiliate, 'The UK nature does not comprehend the Japanese philosophy of "company comes first" and constant hard work'.

13. See Chapter 5.

14. Including those producing plastic sheeting, fire detection equipment, ophthalmic lenses, zip fasteners and bearings.

15. See Chapter 9 for further details.

16. See Chapters 6 and 7.

17. This question is further explored in Chapter 12.

18. Again, as perceived by the Chief Executive of the subsidiaries, most of whom, as it turned out, were involved in the original decision to set up a UK affiliate.

19. Including Hitachi Maxell which is scheduled to produce video cassettes at Telford in 1984.

20. Including Hitachi Maxell.

21. Such as the presence of other Japanese affiliates, facilities for Japanese personnel and their families, etc.

22. But may well be the 'beach-head' which leads to such a strategy. We suspect if we were writing this study in the late 1980s this statement would no longer be true!

23. See particularly the thesis of Knickerbocker (1973).

24. At the then current exchange rate, in June 1983 the average wages of workers in manufacturing industry were 10% higher in Japan than in the UK.

25. For further details see Chapter 6.

26. Some details on the comparative productivity of Japanese affiliates and their parent companies are set out in Chapter 5.

27. As set out, for example, in literature produced by the Invest in Britain Bureau.

28. For example, the Netherlands and Germany are particular favourites for machinery investment, the UK for electrical investment, Italy and Belgium for chemical investment and France for metals investment.

29. The future of Japanese investment is discussed in Chapter 12.

30. E.g. in the case of Mitsubishi which took over the CTV factory of Tandberg in Haddington, and Sanyo which acquired the plant of Philips-Pye at Lowestoft.

31. And six of those about to start manufacturing operations in the UK (as listed in Table 2.2).

32. Op. cit., p. 176.

33. Hood & Young, op. cit., p. 178.

34. Such as management contracts, technical service agreements, turnkey operations, franchising, sub-contracting, etc.

35. Equity includes both 100% and majority owned Japanese affiliates.

36. As explored in Chapter 5 of Dunning (1981).

37. For an analysis of the transactional difficulties in the international transfer of technology, see Teece (1981), (1983).

38. One of the reasons for locating the plant in Washington is that Nissan believed it could gain acceptance of Japanese work practices more easily by workers that had little experience of motor-car production, i.e. greenfield workers (!) than by those with inherited traditions.

39. Simply because there are no markets for them except when they are sold as a package of transactions.

40. The former included, more rapid innovation, increasing need to control after sales servicing, more vertical integration, more product or process rationalisation in Europe, need for more flexibility of management, and likely growth of synergistic advantages. Amongst the latter cited were greater competition among suppliers and better quality of components, and more experience and greater acceptance of Japanese management philosophy.

41. And in the future, those in the motor vehicles assembling sector as well.

42. As listed in Table 2.2.

PART II

4 MANAGEMENT AND CONTROL STRUCTURES IN JAPANESE AFFILIATES

Introduction

Before considering some ways in which Japanese manufacturing affiliates have impacted on the UK economy, we outline some ways in which they are perceived to behave differently from their UK competitors. Chapter 3 has identified a number of ownership advantages specific of Japanese MNEs, the transfer of which to the UK via foreign direct investment may be reasonably presumed to have had some distinctive consequences. This chapter will explore the extent to which the various management functions performed by Japanese affiliates are influenced by Japanese thinking and philosophy; and how far decisions taken about resource allocation in the UK are directed or guided by their parent companies. Chapter 5 will then discuss the ways in which the resources transferred and the control over their use affects the performance and structure of production within Japanese affiliates; and Chapters 6 to 9 the extent to which other UK suppliers, competitors and customers have been (or may have been) affected by the presence of these affiliates. Chapter 10 will focus on labour-related issues.

An Economic Theory of Management and Control of Foreign Affiliates

Why should the management of Japanese affiliates not be given full autonomy in decision-taking? Economic theory[1] suggests there may be three main reasons. First, the objectives of the affiliate — as a self-contained profit centre — may not always accord with that of the firm of which it is part; this conflict will normally only arise if there are costs or benefits arising from decisions taken by, or on behalf of, the affiliate which are external to that affiliate, but internal to the rest of the organisation. Second, the price of management or management-related services may be higher in the host than in the home country; third, for one reason or another, the technical competence of local management may not warrant the delegation of decision-taking authority.

Using the framework of the eclectic paradigm set out in the previous chapter, the first and third reasons suggest that the choice between centralisation and autonomy within an organisation may be likened to that between the internal-external route of transferring 'O' specific advantages. The greater the 'O' advantages of an MNE which stem from common governance of geographically dispersed but interrelated activities, and the more the asset-specific 'O' advantages are idiosyncratic, uncodifiable, costly to transmit and likely to be dissipated through, e.g. labour turnover or lack of quality control, the more likely that either the top management of the affiliate will be filled by nationals of the home country, or decisions will be most closely guided or controlled by management in parent companies. The second reason for not decentralising decision-taking is a locational one: where the (marginal) cost of decision taking is less in the home country than in the host country, then such decisions are unlikely to be delegated. Quite apart from economies of scale in decision-taking, management, and management support costs may vary across boundaries. In some cases, management may need to be close to the market and decisions customised to local requirements; in others, it mayneed to be close to the main centre of the activity. Thus while the management of industrial relations may be localised, the management of innovatory activities may be centralised.

Using this framework, and in the light of the OLI advantages identified in the previous chapter, it should not be difficult to predict the extent to which decision-taking in Japan is controlled by their parent companies. Because of the idiosyncratic nature of Japanese management and the fact its success often rests on successful face-to-face contact with those it wishes to influence and because the price of management real services is (or was in 1982) no higher in Japan than in the UK, one might predict a fairly close surveillance of the activities of Japanese affiliates would be exercised by their parent companies. At the same time, since *prima facie* the affiliates are essentially one-product firms and not part of a European network of activities, it might be felt that there are few advantages of common governance, and thus decisions more delegated. However, in our field research, we gained the strong impression that the parent companies of Japanese affiliates regarded their UK investments as a first stage in a consciously planned, long-term regional strategy and it was in this light that they allocated their decision-taking responsibilities. Moreover, because a substantial part of inputs of the affiliates were purchased from Japan and most of their exports are sold to other parts of the same operation, there were additional reasons for centralised control.

We would then suggest that the combination of these factors makes for fairly strong control over decision-taking in Japanese affiliates; in this respect there are both similarities and differences to the control exercised over US subsidiaries 30 years ago,[3] but, overall, we believe that these subsidiaries had more autonomy in decision-taking than their modern Japanese counterparts.

We now turn to discuss the results of our field research. There seems little doubt that, in the 1960s and 1970s most Japanese industrialists perceived various weaknesses in British management, which, as they set up subsidiaries in the UK made them reluctant to delegate decision-making responsibilities. Foremost among these were (i) amateurism in top management and particularly a lack of technological expertise, cf. that possessed by the average Japanese firm, (ii) conservatism and/or inertia in introducing new management techniques; (iii) lack of entrepreneurship and dynamism in meeting the challenge of new overseas markets; (iv) the indulgent treatment of labour unions by UK management; (v) the failure to develop advance basic research into marketable products; (vi) the particular lack of attention given to both production management and to procurement policy as a means of ensuring adequate quality control of intermediate and end products.[4]

Since the mid-1970s, the Japanese have gained a new respect for UK management, not least as a result of the experiences of Japanese manufacturing companies in Britain (Oba, 1983). Nevertheless, for the most part, the management of these affiliates remains closely controlled and monitored from Japan.

Management Styles

To what extent are the main functional areas of management affected by Japanese techniques and philosophy? Table 4.1 sets out the perception of affiliates on this question. The Chief Executive of each affiliate was asked to indicate whether the operational areas or tasks listed followed (a) strongly, (b) partly or (c) not at all those practised by its parent organisation.[5] In assigning a figure of 3 for strongly, 2 for partly and 1 for not at all, we arrived at the numbers set out in the table.

Even discounting for the inevitable differences in interpretation and subjectivity of the responses, the picture presented is quite clear. In product composition and range, production methods, work organisation, research and development, accounting and financial procedures and the markets to be served, the Japanese influence is a decisive one;

Table 4.1: Extent to which Management Functions in Japanese
Affiliates are Influenced by Japanese Philosophy and Methods

	Group 1	Group 2 Engineering	Chemical	Other	All	Total
Product range	2.3	2.7	2.3	1.8	2.3	2.3
Production methods and work organisation	2.7	2.9	2.7	1.5	2.4	2.6
Marketing methods	1.8	1.4	1.0	1.3	1.3	1.5
Markets serviced	2.6	2.2	3.0	1.8	2.3	2.4
Sourcing methods	1.9	1.6	1.7	1.0	1.4	1.5
Origin of sourcing	2.0	1.8	1.3	2.0	1.8	1.9
Accounting and finance	2.2	2.6	1.7	1.5	2.0	2.1
Industrial relations	1.9	1.5	1.7	1.0	1.3	1.6
Wages and incentives	1.3	1.3	2.0	2.3	1.5	1.4
Research and development	2.7	2.4	2.0	2.3	2.2	2.4
Capital expenditure	2.5	2.4	2.0	2.0	2.2	2.3
Overall company philosophy	2.8	2.4	2.3	2.3	2.3	2.5

Note: when function is perceived to be strongly influenced by Japanese methods
or philosophy a figure of 3 was assigned; when it was moderately influenced a
figure of 2 was assigned; and when it was weakly influenced a figure of 1 was
assigned.

in the origin and methods of purchasing inputs and capital investment
it is a moderate one; while in marketing methods, industrial relations
and wage payments, it is insignificant.[6]

There is, however, some variation in the responses of Group 1 and
Group 2 companies. In general, Group 1 affiliates appear to be more
closely influenced by Japanese methods than Group 2 affiliates (the
overall average score of the former group was 2.2 and of the latter 1.9)
with 'other' Group 2 affiliates being affected the least; the differences
appear to be more marked in marketing and sourcing methods, in
overall company philosophy, and, in the case of 'other' Group 2 affiliates, in production techniques and work organisation. Such differences
mainly reflect the nature of competitive or ownership advantages of
the Japanese parent companies and the extent to which they can be
economically implemented by their affiliates. As we have suggested,
the more the advantages rest on economies of common governance or
are new and idiosyncratic, and the more the cost of management
services favour the home country, the more the Japanese influence is
likely to be demonstrated.[7]

But how far are decisions about these functions centralised? Each affiliate was asked to indicate the extent to which all decisions of substance had to have approval from the parent company, where the affiliate was required to consult the parent company before making a decision, and where the affiliate could take the decision without reference to the parent company. We assigned a figure of 3 for the first situation, 2 for the second and 1 for the third. The results are set out in Table 4.2. As might be expected, the areas where decisions are strongly regulated are those where the Japanese philosophy and technical assistance is most marked. However, the key areas of centralised governance

Table 4.2: Extent to which Japanese Parent Companies Control or Influence Decision-taking in their UK Manufacturing Affiliates

	Group 1 Engineering	Group 2 Chemical	Other	All	Total
Product range	2.7	2.8	2.7	2.0	2.5	2.6
Production methods and work organisation	2.2	2.8	3.0	1.3	2.3	2.3
Marketing methods	1.8	1.4	1.0	1.3	1.3	1.5
Markets serviced	2.3	2.3	3.0	1.8	2.4	1.8
Sourcing methods	1.8	1.4	1.3	1.0	1.3	1.5
Origin of sourcing	1.4	1.6	1.3	1.8	1.6	1.5
Accounting and finance	2.0	2.2	1.7	1.5	1.8	1.9
Industrial relations	1.2	1.2	1.3	1.0	1.2	1.2
Wages and incentives	1.1	1.2	1.7	1.3	1.3	1.2
Research and development	2.3	2.8	3.0	2.5	2.8	2.6
Capital expenditure	2.1	2.0	3.0	2.0	2.3	2.2
Overall company philosophy	2.4	1.6	2.3	1.8	1.8	2.1

Note: When decision-taking in the affiliate is perceived to be strongly controlled in the Japanese parent company a figure of 3 was assigned. A figure of 2 was assigned where consultation with the parent company was normally required and a figure of 1 indicates the subsidiary has complete autonomy in decision-making.

are clearly those of product range and research and development, followed fairly closely by production technology, capital expenditure,[8] and overall company philosophy. Direction from Japan appears to be least in labour related matters (though in some respects we believe this to be misleading as the Japanese, through the organisation of work and their management philosophy, exercise a great deal of influence over the environment within which labour operates) and purchasing procedures. But again, where the overall management philosophy is firmly Japanese oriented, as in Group 1 firms, control or guidance exerted by the parent company is much stronger.

Those functions in which the Japanese philosophy and/or control is most apparent are also those in which Japanese expatriates are most likely to be in charge. In only two companies – Teraski Europe and Paddox Fine Worsted – were there no Japanese employed at the end of 1982; in a few affiliates, 10 or more were employed. In the 23 affiliates in our survey, the number of Japanese nationals employed was 142, or 2.9% of all employees. The great majority of these were in senior managerial, technical or professional positions. In 20 of the affiliates,[9] the managing director of the UK factory was Japanese.[10]

In the case of J2T, the managing directorship rotated between a Japanese, UK and German national. Of the other functional areas, a Japanese expatriate was in charge of accounting and financial matters in nine affiliates; this is, perhaps, the function in which there is the most regular communication between head office and the affiliate, and where knowledge of the Japanese language and way of doing things is most desirable. In production and/or work organisation, there was a Japanese director or factory manager in nine; in all other areas the total number of Japanese in charge was only seven. However, in some consumer electronics and smaller Group 2 affiliates, the managing director had oversight of the purchasing department; and, although, except in two cases, the personnel managers were British, personnel policy was largely subjugated to the overall managerial and work philosophy of the parent company, e.g. with respect to unionisation, worker involvement in decision-making, incentives and discipline.[11]

It would seem that the extent to which Japanese expatriates are in charge of the department functions is broadly the same for the rest of Europe. In the case of 117 manufacturing subsidiaries surveyed by JETRO (1983), the managing director (or president) was a Japanese national in 59% cases; the respective percentages for other departments were 33% in accounting finance (a lower figure than in the case of UK affiliates); 55% in production or management and only 33% in personnel.

All of the affiliates questioned asserted that the Japanese management ethic and style could be more easily imported into the UK via a greenfield rather than an acquired investment; indeed this was the most frequent reason given for the preference of the former modality. Such sentiments as 'everything is new', 'no inherited problems', 'easier to introduce our ideas' were very widely expressed. One CTV affiliate company elaborated:

A new company is able to establish and enforce its operating philosophy from day one and select employees who are willing to accept the ground rules. To engineer change is far more difficult in the case of an acquisition as employee attitudes have been established by history or experience.

Another commented:

> A greenfield environment is recognised as a new venture without custom and practice hangovers. The company profile can be planned to fit in with the global strategic requirements and industry requirements.

Indeed, when asked to identify the main obstacles in introducing Japanese style practices into the UK, the answers were, uniformly, 'tradition' and 'different perceptions of the value of achievement.[12] In the field of work organisation the former was typified by the 'one man one job' philosophy. In Japanese affiliates, such task demarcation is the exception rather than the rule; indeed a willingness and capability of a worker to switch jobs is expected of all factory employees. With respect to individual achievement, and in the words of one Japanese company:

> The UK reward system is very much oriented towards individual achievement: Japanese management style is much more designed to promote team and group objectives.

The differing attitude to work, and the role of the individual and team co-operation, cropped up widely in our discussions with Japanese affiliates, as indeed it has in other surveys of Japanese companies in the UK.[13] We shall consider it in more detail in our chapter on labour-related issues.[14]

Some observations on particular functional areas may now be briefly summarised.

Product Range

We have seen that, by and large, Japanese affiliates produce only one main product in the UK, though sometimes (e.g the case of colour TVs) the range of models may be wider than that of their parent companies. Rather more product diversification is contemplated in the 1980s, particularly by Group 1 affiliates.[15] Major decisions of this kind are usually centralised.

In a few cases, the product produced in Japan and the UK is an identical one, but more often than not, some specific customisation is required for the UK and European market. This may be a minor modification to do with different electrical systems or safety standards, or a fairly major one to do with materials availability, product design and for customer needs, e.g. teletext, view data and remote control in the case of CTV sets. Usually the modifications are suggested by the local management and approved by the parent company, although quite often the relevant research, development and design is done in Japan.

Production Processes

The main differences in the production processes of Japanese affiliates *vis-à-vis* their parent companies relate to (a) range and (b) volume of final output. Chapter 5 will explore these issues in more detail, but the average Japanese affiliate is both less vertically integrated and produces a much smaller output than its parent company in Japan. Apart from these differences, the one most noted by Japanese affiliates relates to inspection, testing and quality control procedures. Whereas in Japan it is normal for each worker, or group of workers, at each stage of the production process, to be responsible for their own procedures, in the UK they tend to be undertaken by a separate group of workers at the end of the production chain. The Japanese way is being introduced into most affiliates, but the full implementation of quality circles is still limited to one or two consumer electronics companies.

More generally, during the last two decades, Japanese manufacturers have directed far more attention to production management so as to produce, on time, reliable, low cost, defect-free products, which is where Japanese affiliates believe their main competitive edge lies. By contrast, all too frequently, it appears that US and European manufacturers, in the belief that they had solved the problems of production and stock control in the 1950s and 1960s, focused their managerial interest on questions related to distribution, packaging, advertising and product differentiation. The desire, by Japanese parent companies, to control production strategy and inventories in UK affiliates is very much dictated by the belief that, to be successful in European manufacturing, the Japanese approach and philosophy must be emulated.[16]

Management and Organisation

The aim of Japanese affiliates, for example as typified by Sony, is to obtain an 'optimum blend of British and Japanese approaches'. The responsibility for this usually rests with the managing director; in every case except one, the managing director – both Japanese or British – spent some time (usually 2-3 months) in Japan being inculcated with the philosophy of the parent company. In several cases, the parent company initially sent management experts to the UK to provide training guidance. However, not all affiliates adopt a Japanese management style. One chemical company commented that 'We have no reason to enforce the Japanese style of management'. Another said 'We follow Japanese management methods, but not because they are Japanese; after all, they are common sense aren't they?'

Industrial Relations

Chapter 10 deals with this issue in more detail. Japanese companies are completely inexperienced in dealing with craft or trade unions. On the other hand, their UK affiliates do not appear to have had too much difficulty in insisting that there should be no unions or that there should be only one union.[17] Although most affiliates asserted that their parent company neither guides nor directs decisions on labour-related matters, it is quite clear that in a variety of ways, and mostly to do with work practices, the behaviour and attitudes of UK workers are often strongly affected by Japanese management philosophy. Certainly, there is more open communication and exchange of ideas between management and workers; at the same time, Japanese firms translate a good deal of their paternalistic and filial style to their UK affiliates. Moreover, although wages at least of factory workers, are largely autonomously determined, the Japanese dislike for monetary incentives, which are common in UK owned firms, may well explain why there are so few such schemes operating in Japanese affiliates, particularly Group 1 affiliates. To the Japanese management, loyalty to the company remains the only impulse worth promoting; in return for such loyalty, the company recognises its responsibilities to train, compensate and promote the work interest and career paths of its employees.

Purchasing Procedures

The great majority of the affiliates indicated that, in their perception, procurement standards in the UK were generally well below those in Japan,[18] while contract procedures were less well defined; and that they needed to be both 'patient' and 'persevering' to get the quality and consistency of their UK purchases up to Japanese levels. With few exceptions, the standards expected of UK suppliers were similar to those of Japanese suppliers; and frequently permission had to be sought from the Japanese parent company prior to a major purchase in the

UK. It also appeared that the knowledge and advice passed on to UK subcontractors was generally more detailed than that in Japan. Special equipment and tooling was often provided by the affiliate for the supplier; and, as like as not, the affiliate did its own costing of the components required. There is no question that the inability of Japanese affiliates to get some raw or processed materials, components and parts, and semi-finished goods from UK (or European) suppliers at the right quality and price[19] is one important reason why such a high proportion of their inputs still come from Japan. But, in part, this begs the question, as in the case of many Group 1 affiliates, it is the design of the product which determines the specification of the components; and this, more often than not, is controlled by the Japanese parent companies. Again we explore these points further in later chapters.

Marketing and Distribution

We have already indicated that most Japanese manufacturing affiliates do not do their own marketing. Those that did were fairly unanimous in claiming that salesmen in Japan tend to be more customer oriented than in the UK, have more pride in getting orders, and are prepared to work harder and longer hours. It was further asserted that they spend more time outside their offices visiting customers and potential customers than their UK counterparts. Gradually the Japanese philosophy is being introduced into the UK — especially, it seems, in Group 2 affiliates.

It should be noted that some colour TV affiliates asserted that their parent company encouraged competition among their European offshoots and that this sometimes led to sets being imported from the Continent. Were it not for country of origin requirements, imports from the Far East, e.g. Singapore, might be considerably greater.

The destination of markets was largely directed from Japan, though increasingly it seems that UK affiliates are being delegated the responsibility for European and Middle Eastern markets. There appeared to be little distinctive about the marketing or distribution practices of Japanese affiliates, but, in pricing, they tended to be tougher than their indigenous competitors.

The Board of Directors of Japanese Affiliates

Another indicator of the extent to which decision-taking in foreign affiliates might be controlled or influenced by their parent companies is the structure and composition of the formers' board of directors. We obtained such information from 20 of the 23 affiliates.

In 14 of the affiliates, the majority of directors were either Japanese nominees of the parent company or a Japanese trading company, or other Japanese nationals (usually the managing director) of the affiliate. The Board of seven affiliates consisted entirely of Japanese nationals. In three affiliates, UK and Japanese nationals were equally represented: in three cases — GEC-Hitachi, J2T and Paddox Fine Worsted — the majority of directors were British. Of the 107 directors of all Japanese affiliates, 81 (76%) were Japanese nationals but 62 of these were 'absentee' directors i.e. not resident in the UK. Since their additional 20% stake in Key-Med, Olympus Optical has been represented by one Japanese national on the former's board.

In the middle of 1983, in all but four cases, the chairman of the board of directors was a Japanese. Most usually, the Japanese nominees were the president or one of the vice-presidents of the parent company; in a few cases, the production manager and/or chief accountant of the affiliate were also members of the board. But clearly such a substantial majority of representatives of the parent companies on the board of affiliates suggests that there is a good deal of direct control or influence from Japan.

Typically, the UK board meets once or twice a year; but day-to-day planning and co-ordination are usually delegated to an advisory committee (or committees) on which there is a majority of non-director (and often worker) representation. In addition, regular (mostly weekly) meetings are held between line management and employees in which company strategy and performance are discussed.

Other meetings, embracing production, quality control and industrial relations matters, are also normally held each week.[20]

In general, the chief executives of Japanese affiliates asserted that they were given a good deal of autonomy to make the adaptations required in organisation and management styles to suit the UK environment. On all major matters, e.g. the introduction of a new product range, or a sizeable capital investment, the parent company would require to be consulted, but as long as the quality of the final product was acceptable (by Japanese standards) the affiliate was free to take the final decision.

Regional Offices

Only 3 of the 22 affiliates – NEC Semiconductors, Sansetu and Sekisui – had a European regional office, and in the two former cases the function of that office is a purely marketing and/or price fixing one. In Sekisui's case, the total European operation is organised by a Swiss affiliate, although its prime responsibility remained to its parent company in Japan.

A European Comparison

The JETRO survey on Japanese companies in Europe (JETRO, 1983) suggested that Japanese managerial practices have been more widely introduced into UK affiliates than those in other parts of Europe. This is especially the case with most labour-related practices. Japanese affiliates in Spain, France and Italy seem to adopt mainly local management practices; while even in Germany, where Japanese production methods and control techniques are widely assimilated there has been apparently little attempt to change traditional working conditions or personnel methods.

An American Perspective

In 1981, JETRO (US) undertook a survey on Japanese direct investment in US manufacturing industry. The survey identified some 238 Japanese affiliates, with a labour force of 45,000, the vast majority of whom were American. Among the conclusions about management and decision-taking within these affiliates the following may be highlighted:[21]

(i) Of 161 firms providing data, there were a total of 790 directors, 433 or 55% of which were Japanese nationals (cf. 76% in our survey).

(ii) In 121 or 51% of these firms, the Japanese equity participation was 10% (cf. 74% in our survey).

(iii) In 70% of manufacturing affiliates (cf. 87% in our survey) the chief executive was a Japanese national. Of the total labour force, Japanese expatriates accounted for 25% (cf. 2.9% in our survey).

(iv) With respect to the division of management responsibilities, it was common for Americans to be in charge of production, industrial relations and wages negotiations, and marketing; while Japanese expatriates to have ultimate decision-making responsibility, liaison with the Japanese parent company and finance and accounting. In addition, Japanese nationals are frequently in charge of production technology. Most of these were employed in a supervisory capacity, particularly in finance, production and technology. In March 1984 of some 876 personnel identified as occupying management positions in Japanese affiliates,[22] 75% were Japanese.

(v) Most Japanese affiliates follow the US 'top-down' pattern of decision-making rather than the collective pattern, based on concensus, favoured by the Japanese. The former pattern was particularly noteable in four categories of affiliates (a) those which originated through mergers with, or purchase of established US firms, (b) combined ventures with US firms, in which Americans held management leadership, (c) fims with few employees and where a good understanding existed with management and labour, and (d) fully fledged affiliates of Japanese parent companies in which US nationals occupied the position of president or general manager, and were allowed to determine management methods.

(vi) Japanese affiliates in the US make much more use of meetings between top management and employees than is normal in American industry. The meetings may take various forms but 'what stands out among them all is an emphasis on mutual understanding and group identification'.[23]

(vii) Another survey conducted by JETRO (US) (1982), provided some evidence of a trend towards the localisation of management practices and a transfer of authority from Japanese headquarters to their US affiliates. Specific measures mentioned included (a) giving factory supervisors greater power to hire and fire employees, (b) greater emphasis on the training of foremen to give them total authority over their sphere of responsibilities, (c) successful employment of a US senior vice-president to unify the command structure for American employees, (d) changing the product line manager from a Japanese expatriate to an American and putting the Japanese in the position of an advisor.[24]

Conclusions

There is no single management style practised by Japanese affiliates in the UK; nor, with one exception, is it possible to generalise about the Japanese influence on the product or production strategy of these same affiliates. The one exception — which is an important one as it pervades company philosophy from the sourcing of inputs and labour recruitment through to after sales servicing — is quality control. The interesting question, however, is the extent to which Japanese style management and organisational methods are necessary to attain this objective. The answer appears to be that in Group 1 affiliates it is; but in Group 2 affiliates it may or may not be; much seems to depend on the extent to which the determinants of such control rest with human beings or machines. The greater the influence of the former — at any stage of the production process — the more it would seem that Japanese parent companies want to exert influence and/or control. Otherwise the extent of Japanese involvement in the decision-taking process seems to depend on (a) the availability and quality of local (UK) technical competence and (b) the extent to which it is possible to exploit economies of synergy between the affiliate and the rest of the organisation of which it is part. For the present, this latter reason for control would appear less pervasive in Japanese affiliates than in some of their more integrated US and European counterparts; but there is some suggestion that it might play a more important role in the future. It is this, together with the projected growth in their vertical integration and product range, which suggests to us that the control or influence exerted by the parent company, far from diminishing is likely to increase in the future.[25]

Notes

1. Which views the allocation of decision-taking primarily according to whether or not it advances the economic objectives of the firm.

2. See particularly the contents of Table 3.1, which may well be applied to local and centralised decision-taking; and expatriate and UK nationals in charge of local decision-taking.

3. As detailed in Dunning (1985). For a comparative analysis of US affiliates in the UK in 1950s and Japanese affiliates in 1980s, see Dunning (1985).

4. At the same time the Japanese also acknowledged there were excellently managed firms in the UK economy, Oba (1983).

5. The affiliates were left to interpret these terms in their own way. Some guidance, however, was given at the time of interview to ensure reasonable consistency.

6. It may be questioned whether the answers received about marketing methods are very meaningful as about one-half of Japanese manufacturing affiliates do not do any marketing. This function is performed by separate marketing.

companies. From interviews with two of these companies, there is some suggestion that selling techniques are, at least, partly influenced by Japanese practice.

With respect to labour recruitment, there is a moderate Japanese influence as far as the type of employee who is favoured. (See Chapter 10 for further details.)

7. For example, the four companies which operated a co-ordinated European production and marketing strategy among their European affiliates tended to centralise decision-taking rather more than the rest; those which serviced only the UK market were the least controlled in their decision-taking.

8. The minimum amount for expenditure allowed before permission to be sought varies from zero to £100,000.

9. Twenty-two as of December 1984 as the managing director of Hitachi and Hitachi Maxell are both Japanese nationals. The new managing director of the Nissan Motor Manufacturing Co. (UK) Ltd is also Japanese.

10. Most of these affiliates expected that within 3-5 years the managing director would be British. However, three indicated it was Japanese policy for the senior executive to be a Japanese national, while another two thought it would be a 'long time' before a UK/or European took over this position. In the case of Sony, while the managing director of UK operations is British, the director in charge of the Bridgend factory is Japanese.

11. See Chapter 10.

12. Apart from one Group 2 affiliate that answered 'None' and another which replied 'we do not attempt to introduce Japanese management methods into the UK as we do not believe they would work'.

13. See especially those of Trevor (1983), European Company Services (1983), Marsh (1983), and JETRO (1982).

14. See Chapter 10.

15. The most obvious example is the production of video recorders by the CTV companies; Toshiba has also announced its intention to manufacture micro ovens in the UK.

16. A similar view is expressed by Hayes (1982).

17. This happened when Toshiba was set up following the demise of Rank Toshiba in which there were seven unions. In GEC's Hitachi there were six unions; these have been replaced by one. Nissan also has agreed to negotiate with one union.

18. See Chapter 6 for more details.

19. The two go together. Sometimes the UK supplier may be able to supply at the right quality but not the right price and vice versa.

20. See also Chapter 10.

21. Further details are contained in JETRO (US) (1981), pp. 34-42.

22. JETRO (US) (1984).

23. JETRO (US) (1981), p. 41.

24. JETRO (US) (1982), p. 9. In general, we sense this is the way the localisation of decision-taking may proceed within UK affiliates, i.e. that Japanese expatriates now employed in a decision-taking capacity will gradually assume a more advisory role.

25. There is, for example, no evidence to suggest that, except perhaps in the area of production techniques, Japanese control and influence is any less in the older than in the younger established subsidiaries.

5 THE PERFORMANCE OF JAPANESE MANUFACTURING AFFILIATES

Introduction

This chapter summarises some features about the performance of Japanese manufacturing affiliates, and attempts to identify some of the differences between this performance and that of (a) the nearest equivalent plants of their parent and (b) their UK competitors. We would emphasise at the outset that we did not pursue this question in any depth, and many (indeed most) affiliates did not possess the information to enable these comparisons to be rigorously made; neither was it within our brief to approach the parent companies of the affiliates, nor indeed their UK competitors, for more details. Nevertheless, from the data provided, it is possible to derive a number of impressions and pointers, and indeed, offer some tentative conclusions.

Affiliate and Parent Company Productivity and Costs

International productivity comparisons are fraught with all sorts of difficulties and it is tempting to eschew this issue altogether. That we chose not to do so is because we hoped to gain some new insights into the reason for differences in the performance of foreign affiliates and their domestic counterparts. It is perhaps worth observing that, unlike their US counterparts 30 years ago,[1] the Japanese do not appear to make detailed productivity comparisons between their UK manufacturing subsidiaries and parent companies (or between their manufacturing affiliates).[2] There are various reasons for this, foremost among which is that most production units are so new, small and truncated by Japanese standards, and often product modifications are quite substantial, that there are doubts as to the usefulness of any such comparisons.

However, most affiliates set standards of performance for their manufacturing operations, which they monitor and/or update frequently. To give two examples: one CTV affiliate takes as its starting point for assessing its direct labour productivity that of the nearest equivalent Japanese factory, but then makes various adjustments to allow for differences in production methods and worker experience in the two plants, and product modifications; another CTV affiliate concentrates its attention on minimising faults in the assembly process, mainly by (a) automation, (b) labour training and (c) improving the quality of components. Since its establishment in the UK in 1977, it has improved its output of CTV TV sets per direct worker per day from 0.48 to 2.09, and reduced its fault index (a somewhat complicated formula) from 200 to 25 (in Japan it is 15).

Group 1 Affiliates

Turning first to Group 1 affiliates, of the seven colour TV companies providing data, the average volume of CTV sets produced in a UK factory was 12% of that of the nearest equivalent factory[3] in Japan. Since there are substantial economies of scale in TV production, it is reasonable to hypothesise that volume-associated differences may be an important determinant of Anglo-Japanese productivity differentials. Second, in four of the six CTV affiliates, the degree of vertical integration is less than in Japan;[4] in one it is about the same; and in three (Sony, Mitsubishi and Hitachi) it is more.[5] Since labour productivity varies considerably between stages of production of a CTV set,[6] overall differences in productivity might partly reflect differences in the stages of production undertaken. Thirdly, apart from Sony and Mitsubishi, at the end of 1982, all the other Japanese colour TV plants had been manufacturing for three years or less, and were very much in the initial stages of their learning cycle. Moreover, in all affiliates but one, the proportion of (existing) plant capacity utilised was under 80% in 1982, and in three cases it was under 60%. It is, perhaps, not surprising that each of the CTV affiliates expected to increase its productivity over the period 1983/7, and all indicated that, at the end of 1982, in spite of noticeable improvements in productivity since their establishment, they had still not reached the output per head for which they were aiming. Four of the six estimated that their labour productivity would rise by 5% if output were doubled and 7-8% if it were trebled; the fifth put the likely percentage increases at 10 and 15%, and the sixth at 2 and 5% respectively.

Notwithstanding their relatively small volumes of output, the range of CTV sets produced by Japanese affiliates was generally at least as extensive as that of their parent companies. Size of screen is one example — 90% of the sets sold in Japan are 20 inches or below; in Europe the corresponding proportion is 45%; but additional items such as remote control, teletext and facilities for satellite and cable tele-

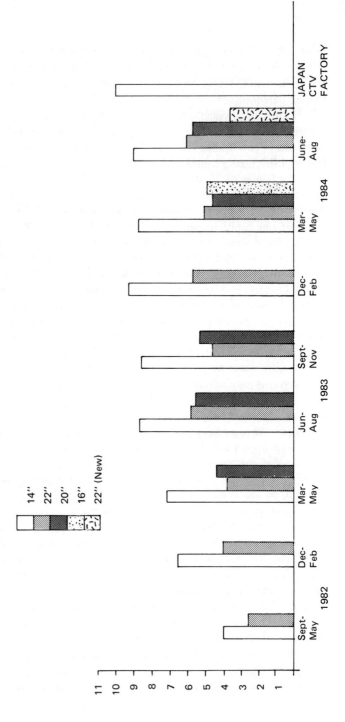

Figure 5.1: CTV Productivity in a UK Affiliate and its Japanese Parent Company (sets/days/person)

vision, are as yet relatively unexploited in Japan, and these, together with a variety of UK or European electrical and safety requirements, involve the affiliates in production and switching costs not incurred by their parent plants.

Estimates of physical labour productivity of factory workers[7] in Japanese affiliates, relative to that of their parent plants, in respect of the one or two leading CTV sets produced in the UK, averaged out at 75% in 1982, along a range from 40% to 100%, with four companies recording figures of 75-80%. The oldest established and second largest affiliate asserted its labour productivity was 'equal to that in its Japanese and US plants'. Figure 5.1 presents details in respect of one model of one fairly recently established CTV factory. This reveals a gradual improvement in productivity since the initial start up in production; and that by June 1984, productivity was not far short of that of the main Japanese plant. Affiliates with the highest degree of vertical integration in the UK recorded the highest productivity differentials; the 'learning' effect seemed only to be important in the case of one company, which reported that 'in order to get our quality right we have consciously set out productivity targets in the initial phase of production lower than we would like'.[8]

The reasons suggested for these differences fall into five groups:

(i) *The scale effect*: in all cases, the affiliates asserted their production processes were less mechanised or automated than in Japan (e.g. printed circuit board assembly in one plant was 90% automated in Japan and 80% in the UK). Machines were also generally faster and more flexible in Japan; and quality control and testing procedures were less comprehensive than in Japan. At least three CTV affiliates specifically make allowance for the scale affect in calculating their productivity; the average discount being 3.5%.

One affiliate observed its productivity had been improved as a result of the reduction of components requiring assembly on its printed circuit board (PCB). In 1977, some 878 components were needed; by 1982 only 521, and by 1985 (an estimated) 425. *Inter alia* this reduced the time of chassis assembly from 308 minutes per set in 1977 to 180 minutes in 1982.

(ii) *The product modification effect*: as already described modifications required to be made to UK and/or European CTVs reduced the sets per man produced — probably by about 5%. One affiliate built such an effect into its performance evaluation; this varied from 2 to 5%of direct labour productivity.

(iii) *The labour effect*: there was general agreement that UK plants required more management and supervisory time to keep work standards to the corresponding levels of the Japanese. Labour attitudes in the UK were less conducive to the highest levels of productivity; an estimated 5-10% of working time being lost in the UK through a more casual approach and less attention to detail by UK employees.[9] On the other hand, once trained, the technical competence of UK labour was thought to be as good as, if not better than, the Japanese.[10] Rejection rates of work undertaken in-house compared favourably with Japanese standards (see Fig. 5.1). Absenteeism and labour turnover rates in UK plants were both consistently above those in Japan.

(iv) *The age or learning effect*: while only in the case of Sony and Matsushita had the labour force no previous experience of manufacturing CTV sets, in all subsidiaries the introduction of Japanese management and work styles has taken some time to bear fruit. This has been particularly noticeable in the institution of performance feedback systems, which are intended to indicate the quality performance of individual assembly workers; it is also linked to the methods of rewarding good workmanship.[11]

(v) *The environment effect*: several affiliates claimed that supply instabilities and reject rates for components were well above acceptable Japanese standards; while delivery timings were longer and less reliable in the UK. Some examples of differences in component reliability quoted at a business seminar in 1973 are reproduced in Table 5.1. On the other hand, the reject rates of Japanese affiliates are considerably less than that of their UK competitors and are improving over time (see Table 5.2). Several Group 1 affiliates also contended that, because of less frequent, more irregular and lengthier deliveries, they had to carry additional stocks of materials and components.[12]

Of the above effects (ii), (iii) and (v) may be regarded as genuine or 'unavoidable' reasons for Anglo-Japanese productivity differences. Our best guess is that, on average, they account for about two-fifths of the total productivity differences (i.e. about 10%). We also believe, because of differences in human motivation, and an unwillingness or inability of UK suppliers to meet the quality standards of their Japanese customers,[13] there is a residual gap of around 5% which is unlikely

Table 5.1: Component Reliability in the Electronics Industry (1982)

Type of component	First time reliable (%)
Capacitors	76
EHT units	41
Resistors	40
Interfaced circuits	32
Diodes	30
Transistors	25
Tuners	17
Transformers	6

Source: *Business Survival: Learning from the Japanese*, ACM Executive Services, 1983. The above data would appear to be based on information provided by two large Japanese CTV companies in the UK.

Table 5.2: Reject Rates of Selected Parts and Components Bought by one CTV Affiliate from UK Suppliers

Parts	Quantity ordered			Reject %		
	Sept '82-Feb '83	May '83-July '83	Oct '83-Dec '83	Sept '82-Feb '83	May '83-July '83	Oct '83-Dec '83
26″ Front panel	—	486	780	—	5.1	56.0
22″ TV stand	45,834	10,760	4,373	9.7	11.9	39.9
16″ Escutcheon	—	—	1,911	—	—	32.0
22″ Din cover	—	10,760	7,683	—	2.7	31.1
20″ Front panel	—	6,062	2,968	—	5.6	18.3
14″ Escutcheon	11,476	10,316	10,810	12.4	10.5	10.5
26″ Escutcheon	—	486	557	—	12.3	11.4
20″ Escutcheon	—	6,062	8,351	—	22.9	11.0
22″ Escutcheon	14,943	10,760	6,325	18.9	7.5	7.9
Instruction book	—	—	36,908	—	—	5.7
14″ Control box	—	—	1,500	—	—	5.4
14″ Carton case	11,796	10,316	20,623	27.5	4.1	5.4
16″ Control box	—	—	1,521	—	—	4.8
16″ Carton case	—	—	1,513	—	—	4.3

to be closed.

The single industrial electronics affiliate recorded productivity levels well below the average for its Japanese parent company in 1973. The two main reasons given by the affiliate, set up in 1981, were (1) high start up costs and inexperience of UK operations, and (2) less automation in the Scottish plant.

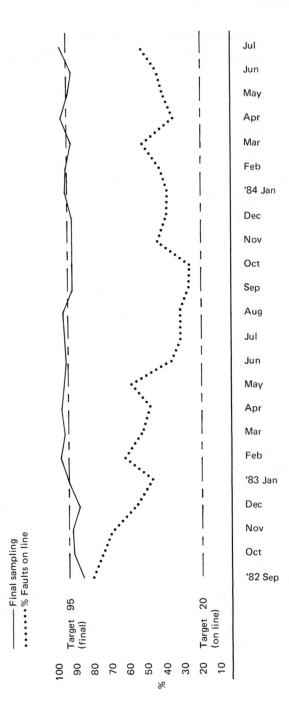

Figure 5.2: Quality Control in One Japanese CTV Affiliate (Final Sampling and % Faults On Line)

Group 2 Affiliates

Turning to Group 2 affiliates, the productivity differential between Japanese affiliates and their parent companies is rather less. In 1982 (or the nearest financial year), for the ten affiliates providing data it averaged 90 and ranged from 70 (Japanese productivity = 100). One chemical affiliate — Sekisui Plastics — estimated that its performance was now equal to that of its Japanese plants and better than its US and Dutch factories. Eight of the eleven affiliates believed their productivity to be 10% or less below their Japanese counterparts. The reason mentioned as for these differences, weighted (by the affiliates) by a score of 1 to 5 — 5 indicating of greatest significance — were as follows:

(i) *Scale related*
    Economies of size of output favour Japan   3.6
    More automation/more specialised, high speed or
        sophisticated machinery in Japan   3.3

(ii) *Product related*
    Adaptations to production in UK   1.1
    More product variety in UK   1.3

(iii) *Labour related*
    Better industrial relations, less union trouble
      in Japan   1.3
    Better timekeeping, less absenteeism, lower
      labour turnover in Japan   1.5
    Better job concentration in Japan   2.4
    Better work system, team co-operation,
      job flexibility in Japan   2.9
    More manual dexterity in Japan   −1.0[14]

(iv) *Age related*
    Lack of experience in operating UK plant   1.5[15]

(v) *Environment related*
    Quality of components higher and more consistent
      (making for less material wastage and rejects)
      in Japan   2.0

In general, although the absolute size of Group 2 affiliates is smaller than those of Group 1, the output of their UK plants relative to their Japanese factories is larger: in 1982 it averaged 27% and ranged from 5% to 75%. Yet, of all the reasons for Anglo-Japanese productivity differences, those related to size seem to be the most significant. This is particularly the case with the four chemical affiliates, but it was iden-

tified as so by eight of the ten affiliates. Sometimes the higher volume
in Japan enables the use of higher capacity; sometimes of faster or more
accurate machines; sometimes of more specialised equipment. One
company thought 80% of its productivity differences were due to
differences in machine capacity and utilisation, and 20% to differences
in labour motivation. Another noted that while, in the parent plant,
the operator looked after 12 spindles, in the UK he looked after only
four.

Although differences in labour attitudes and efficiency were not
thought to be as marked as in Group 1 affiliates (or as important in
influencing overall productivity), they were mentioned by most firms in
one way or another. As regards attitude to work, one UK purchasing
manager summed it up as follows:

> I believe the attitude of Japanese and UK workers is fundamentally
> different. The UK workers need wages to live; they have to work.
> In Japan, work is duty and once one has chosen ones company one
> has a lifetime loyalty to it.

Another, as quoted in a report by European Company Services Ltd
(1983), commented:

> There is a basic difference in attitude; in Japan people want to learn
> and do something constantly better. Here most people don't have
> the same attitude to work.

Several affiliates also stressed the team spirit of the Japanese, and
asserted that the individualism of the UK worker militated against the
acceptance of certain work practices. However, rather than try to force
UK workers into the Japanese mould, this particular managing director
(who was Japanese) preferred to adapt the process of production to
take advantage of this trait; as a result, so it was asserted, productivity
had risen.

A further example of the individualism of the UK worker was given
by a Japanese executive of a chemical affiliate who claimed that
training costs were greater in the UK as the UK worker 'will not do
anything he is told without knowing why he is required to do it'.

Lower labour absenteeism, better timekeeping, less time-wasting
(e.g. by chatting at the workplace) was cited by about half of Group 2
affiliates; but, except in two instances – one chemical and one
'other' company – none of these were an important cause of Anglo-

Japanese productivity differences. Far more frequently mentioned were attitudinal factors, small in themselves but symptomatic of wider differences between the behavioural stance of Japanese and UK workers. Almost universally, in Group 1 and Group 2 affiliates, the relative untidyness and casual air of UK workers was criticised, and coupled with this, the belief that the cleaning of machines, work benches, etc., was not the job of a factory operative. The careless use of equipment and social facilities was also a frequent complaint. The traditional tea-break was the seemingly ineradicable bugbear of one Northern factory.[16] On the other hand, poor industrial relations or difficulties with unions were very rarely cited as inhibiting factors.

Chapter 10 will deal with labour-related issues in more detail. Suffice to mention at this point that when asked to indicate their degree of satisfaction with (a) the quality and (b) the motivation of UK labour and management, all affiliates ranked the former rather higher than the latter; and while 71% of affiliates assigned a score 4 or 5 (on a scale of 1-5 indicating degrees of satisfaction) to quality of labour or management, only 50% gave such a score for worker motivation.[17]

Perhaps more to the point, in almost every case, the Japanese parent company appears to have been pleasantly surprised by employee quality and attitudes in the UK. This may be partly due to the bad (UK) press given to industrial relations in the 1970s; and partly to the efforts made by the Japanese to nurture the loyalty and commitment of UK workers. Certainly, as Trevor (1983) has described at some length, the supervisory and leadership style of Japanese managers in UK affiliates has, for the most part, been readily accepted by British employees.

Since we did not interview the Japanese parent companies, it is difficult to pronounce upon the comparative efficiency of the management of UK and Japanese plants. Certainly in all cases but two, the Japanese philosophy towards production permeated the UK affiliate, whether or not a Japanese national was in charge. And, as we have seen in several functional areas, e.g. finance and accounting, the Japanese influence and control is very strong indeed. There was some feeling that UK production and quality control engineers and factory managers were not as well trained or motivated as their Japanese counterparts, and that UK purchasing managers were less demanding of their suppliers. On the other hand, UK personnel managers were very highly esteemed. Indeed, several companies appeared surprised and gratified that UK personnel managers were so much in tune with the Japanese way of dealing with people, and enthusiastically embraced most of the work practices introduced from Japan.[18]

We conclude this section by reproducing a chart (Figure 5.3), adapted from one earlier published by ACM (1983). This demonstrates the interaction between a number of factors identified as contributing to Anglo-Japanese productivity differences. In particular it emphasises the role of operator throughout the production chain; and the need to avoid wasteful inspection procedures by continuously monitoring work quality.[19] The Japanese are not satisfied unless they produce a perfect product and they try and inculcate this way of thinking into their workforce.

Comparative Costs in UK and Japanese Plants

In explaining the locational preferences of Japanese companies and evaluating the relative competitiveness of the UK and Japanese economies, production costs rather than labour productivity[20] are the relevant measure of performance. We asked two sets of questions. The first was the average or unit *ex factory* costs of the UK plant compared with the c.i.f. cost of an equivalent product exported from Japan; the second was to compare manufacturing costs in the two countries. Let us look at these for each of our two groups of affiliates.

Group 1 Affiliates

Given a UK *ex factory* cost as 100, the average estimated imported cost for the main product(s) produced by the nine Japanese consumer and industrial electronics companies in the UK was 100.2 in the 1982/3 financial year. In two cases, costs were put at above 100.0; in the rest below, but in no case was it less than 90.

How are these figures reconcilable with a productivity differential in favour of the Japanese factories of about 25%?[21] The answer mainly lies in the freight costs of, and import duties on, Japanese imports. Assuming the same volume of output[22] were produced in Japan as in the UK, then transfer costs from Japan to the UK averaged 15-20% for Group 1 affiliates. Though there were additional co-ordination costs of running a UK subsidiary,[23] these were more than compensated by lower administrative, marketing and other overhead costs.[24]

There were other non-production costs which also varied between Japan and the UK. Inventory costs were universally higher in the UK, due to less reliable or frequent deliveries and higher rejection rates.[25] There was generally more (10-25%) materials wastage in UK factories –

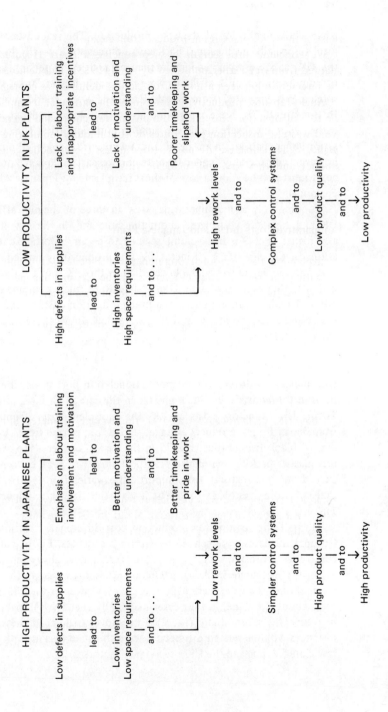

Figure 5.3: The Production Circle: British and Japanese Plants

HIGH PRODUCTIVITY IN JAPANESE PLANTS

Emphasis on labour training
involvement and motivation

lead to

Better motivation and
understanding

and to

Better timekeeping and
pride in work

Low defects in supplies

lead to

Low inventories
Low space requirements

and to . . .

Low rework levels

and to

Simpler control systems

and to

High product quality

and to

High productivity

LOW PRODUCTIVITY IN UK PLANTS

Lack of labour training
and inappropriate incentives

lead to

Lack of motivation and
understanding

and to

Poorer timekeeping and
slipshod work

High defects in supplies

lead to

High inventories
High space requirements

and to . . .

High rework levels

and to

Complex control systems

and to

Low product quality

and to

Low productivity

particularly in the initial stages of production. The real costs of technical (especially engineering) back up resources were usually higher in the UK, as were repair and maintenance facilities. Material prices for the inputs of Group 1 affiliates were marginally less in Japan; though some items imported from South East Asia were considerably less. In the late 1970s, wage rates were about 15% lower in Japan; in the early 1980s they were about the same in both countries. The compensation of expatriate managerial and technical Japanese labour was, however, considerably higher than its counterpart in Japan;[26] to these costs must also be added those of short-term visits by Japanese advisory personnel.

Looking only at manufacturing costs, in three of the nine affiliates, UK and Japanese costs were about the same and, in the rest, marginally higher (5-24%). But volume seemed to be an important consideration. In the case of 16-20 inch CTV sets produced by one company, unit costs in Japan were 10% lower than in the UK, but for the 22-26 inch sets they were the same. Due mainly to its smaller volume of output and higher learning costs, the unit production costs of the industrial electronics subsidiary in 1983, were 35% above those of its Japanese parent.

Group 2 Affiliates

Due mainly to differences in international transport costs, the variations in total costs were much greater in the case of Group 2 affiliates. Taking UK ex-factory costs as 100, the equivalent costs of importing from Japan for 14 products averaged 111.8, but ranged from 50 in the case of blank fishing rods, and 75 in the case of car aerials to over 200 for plastic packing materials. Transport cost (by sea) in two cases exceed one half of total costs. Import duties varied from 2-20%. Nevertheless, in the case of six products, it was still cheaper to import from Japan.

Most of the reasons for production cost differences mentioned by Group 1 affiliates were echoed by Group 2 affiliates. But raw material costs were more important, and these were almost always cheaper in Japan (or elsewhere in Asia), excluding transport costs. In two cases, production costs were marginally (i.e. 5-24%) lower in the UK, in two cases about the same, in four cases marginally (i.e. 5-24%) higher, and in four cases substantially (i.e. 25% or above) higher. In these latter instances, volume-related differences were the main reason, with higher raw materials costs in the UK a secondary factor.

Productivity in Japanese Affiliates Compared with their UK Competitors

Again most of our evidence on this question is impressionistic; nevertheless, there was a reasonable consensus of opinion among the Japanese affiliates visited.

Group 1 Affiliates

Compared to an 'average' UK competitor — be it an indigenous producer or non-Japanese foreign affiliate — four of the eight affiliates providing data perceived their output/employee ratio to be 10% or more above, and one of these 'probably' 50% above; three thought it to be about the same (+9 to -9%) and one 'probably' 10%-24% below. In one case it was asserted there were no UK competitors. The subsidiaries with the average or lower productivity put this down to low output volumes, lack of production experience in the UK, and 'a variety of factors, not least problems on the industrial relations front'. These latter subsidiaries were then performing well below the standards of their 'best' competitors; indeed, interestingly, only one firm thought it was doing better than its best competitor; while four thought they were 'about the same'.

There is also some evidence that when Japanese companies acquire UK TV factories they do better than their predecessors. Within a year of the start of its operations at Lowestoft, Sanyo was producing 500 TV sets monthly per worker compared to 286 per worker when Phillips owned it.[27] In 1983, Toshiba's labour productivity at Plymouth was twice that of the late 1970s when the plant was a joint Rank Toshiba venture.

More detailed empirical studies by researchers at the London School of Economics (Reitsperger (1982),[28] Trevor (1983)) confirm that Japanese affiliates in the CTV sector considerably outperform their other foreign and UK counterparts. The reasons are basically to do with the ownership advantages of the Japanese set out in Chapter 3, viz. better use of factory space, technically superior production methods, less material wastage and lower inventories, more efficient work organisation, and clearly defined lines of responsibility, more rigorous quality control and testing procedures, better labour utilisation and motivation, and the benefits of being part of a larger organisation, e.g. lower administrative overheads, more favoured access to inputs, markets, subsidised R & D, etc.

Few of these reasons are readily quantifiable. One which is concerns rejection of components from UK suppliers. According to Reitsperger (1982), rejects traceable to human error in Japanese managed CTV companies in the UK were one-tenth of those in British managed companies. Within 18 months of starting an operation, typically achieved reject levels dropped to one-eighth of those in UK companies. One year after Toshiba began manufacturing, it was achieving a 95-98% success rate in its first-time testing of CTV sets produced (in each of four stages); at the time of the Rank Toshiba joint venture the corresponding success rate was nearer 50%.

Group 2 Affiliates

Perceptions of comparative productivity of Group 2 affiliates were broadly comparable with those of Group 1 affiliates. Six of the eleven affiliates providing data put their productivity against their average UK competitor at between 10 and 49% more; and one at 50% more. Three others thought their productivity around the average at +9 to -9%. Compared with their 'best' competitor, two subsidiaries thought their productivity was 10-49% above and two 10-49% below; all other affiliates thought their productivity was around the average.

Of the major points favouring Japanese affiliates, lower administrative costs, less materials wastage, better machine efficiency, less absenteeism, more flexible manufacturing systems and work deployment, more rigorous quality control and testing procedures and better industrial relations were all cited, but, from the information provided, it was not possible to assign an order of importance to these.[29] At the same time, some Japanese affiliates considered they lost out *vis-à-vis* their competitors, through lack of experience and lower output volumes.

Trends in Labour Productivity and Costs

All except one of the affiliates thought that their labour productivity relative to that of their Japanese plants had increased over the last five years or since they first started manufacturing in the UK, whichever was more recent. Several affiliates referred to considerable improvements of 25% or above and one a doubling of productivity between 1979 and 1982. Seventeen of the 22 affiliates expected productivity to rise in the period 1983/7, mainly as a result of more automated assembly methods, lower rejects of bought out components, higher output volumes, increased operator experience and better in-house quality control.

Some 12 of the 20 affiliates providing data estimated that, assuming constant rates of exchange, their production costs *vis-à-vis* those in their Japanese factories, would be about the same in 1987 as in 1982. The balance expected a relative fall in their UK production costs. By 1987, only one firm thought its unit production costs in the UK would be substantially above those in Japan; most believed they would be about the same, viz. in the range –4 to +4%.

Conclusions

There is no reason to suppose that, given similar volumes and product structure, the labour productivity of Japanese manufacturing affiliates in the UK should not be within 5-10% of that of their parent companies. This residual, which seems likely to remain for the foreseeable future, may be put down to a more dedicated work ethic, a more meticulous attention to detail and a greater quality consciousness on the part of employees, not only of their parent companies, but of Japanese suppliers, *vis-à-vis* their UK equivalents.

Even in 1982, the productivity gap between affiliates and parent companies was less than is commonly supposed, and exceeded that which many Japanese parent companies had expected. This suggests that there has been some success in the transference of Japanese technology, management styles and work methods to the UK.

In spite of these productivity differences making for a Japanese location, transport costs and import duties raise the landed price of Japanese manufacturers above that of the production costs of Japanese affiliates in the UK; and this situation seems likely to continue in the foreseeable future. Indeed, if the £ continues to depreciate relative to the yen, while the productivity of Japanese affiliates rises relative to that of their companies, the cost advantage will increasingly favour UK production.

According to the executives of the plants visited, Japanese affiliates recorded productivity levels at least 10% above the average for their UK competitors in 60% of cases; and only in two cases was productivity thought to be more than 10% below that of their competitors. In the majority of instances, it would seem that a Japanese affiliate is the leader of its particular sector in the UK, although in a few cases, due to smaller volumes, lack of experience, and industrial relations problems, this is not so.

We would make one final point. From the data collected and

opinions of those interviewed, we are fully persuaded that the main reasons for differences in Anglo-Japanese performances is not that the Japanese possess a secret formula for success, but UK industry has not applied well known and tried principles of management as it should have; and has paid insufficient attention to purchasing standards, inventory control, production management and employee motivation as keys to success. If the presence of Japanese affiliates in the UK has done anything, it has been to demonstrate that there is no Japanese technological, marketing or managerial miracle, or even a major cultural gap; and that much of the philosophy and strategic management of Japanese firms can be successfully transferred to a UK environment. This is not to argue that British industry could be as productive as Japanese industry overnight; there are many obstacles to achieving this, but these are more to do with inappropriate institutions, unhelpful work attitudes and a tradition of adversary industrial relations, than with differences in the technical and commercial competence of British managers, or the innate ability of British workers.

Notes

1. See especially Chapter V of Dunning (1958).
2. Only four of the 22 affiliates visited indicated that such comparisons are regularly made.
3. Usually, CTV sets in Japan were produced in more than one factory; we asked for details in respect of the 'nearest equivalent factory', e.g. in terms of volume, production methods, product range, etc.
4. As measured, for example, by value added to sales ratio, and the number of separate processes engaged in.
5. For example, about half of the employment at Sony's Bridgend factory is devoted to component production, which accounts for about one-half its value added of CTV set production. For the nearest equivalent Japanese factory, the ratios would be 20% and 80%. The average value added/sales ratios of the other Japanese TV affiliates in the UK is 23%.
6. For example, the labour productivity of tube manufacturing is about three times that of the assembly of TV sets; on the other hand, the production of chassis is highly labour intensive.
7. All employed in factory, inclusive of factory, but not non-factory supervisory labour.
8. Some published data on productivity levels include the statement by Sony management that their productivity and quality levels at their Bridgend plant approaches that of their Japanese and San Diego factories. The productivity at Toshiba has increased from 150 sets per worker per year (when the factory was jointly owned with Rank) to 330 sets; this compares with 360-370 sets per worker per year in Japan. Hitachi is planning for a doubling in labour productivity in 1985 compared with that in 1982. By the spring of 1983, one year after it purchased its CTV plant from Phillips, Sanyo was producing 500 TV sets

monthly per worker, compared to 286 TV sets monthly per worker when Philips owned it (Oba, 1983).

9. As typified by the views of one executive 'Japanese people have a different view about work intensity; they are 100% for the company – and the company comes first. You don't get that intensity here. Your UK worker is altogether more relaxed.'

10. For example, it was asserted that UK female workers are more ambi-dextrous than their Japanese equivalents.

11. Another method of evaluating productivity is 'first time' passes through testing or quality control stations. In Toshiba there are four such stages and the final percentage of the passes is a multiple of each of the four stages. In 1983, this percentage averaged 90-95% compared with 98-99% in the parent company and 50-55% in the days of Rank-Toshiba.

12. One affiliate claimed that its normal stock of components averaged 1-2 months compared with 2-3 days in Japan.

13. Sometimes the unwillingness may be for good economic reasons. See Chapters 6 and 7 for examples.

14. I.e. productivity favours UK plant.

15. Two or above for most recently established plants.

16. Quoted in European Company Services Ltd (1983).

17. Interestingly for management, motivation scored marginally higher than quality, but, overall, the differences in the scoring of factory workers, other workers and management were insignificant. For further details see Chapter 10.

18. At the same time, labour matters were not regarded as the exclusive province of the personnel department. In the factory, the production manager was no less responsible for the work conditions and welfare of his operatives.

19. Honda are said to employ only 1 inspector per 200 operators in their Japanese plants. Ratios in comparable UK plants in 1983 were 1 to 10 or even 1 to 7. On the other hand, the Japanese employ two to three times as many produc-tion and industrial enforcers (in proportion to the total labour force) as do the British.

20. Labour productivity is, of course, only a partial input measure; and a higher labour productivity may be more than offset by a lower capital productivity. If anything, however, we believe that relative capital productivity (measured by output/net fixed assets) favours the Japanese plant.

21. See previous section, 'Affiliate and Parent Company Productivity and Costs'

22. Of the leading product in the UK and in Japan.

23. Few affiliates were able to give precise data; but for those which did the co-ordination costs varied between 3 and 6% of total costs.

24. These averaged 5-10% of total costs less in the affiliates than the parent companies; these figures *excluded* any payments made by affiliates for overhead services supplied.

25. One established colour TV affiliate quoted rejection rates in the UK of 5-6 per 1,000, while in Japan they were 5-6 per one million.

26. Upwards of twice as much.

27. Quoted in a speech by Mr S. Oba and first published in *Nikkei Business*, 18.4.83.

28. In a paper presented by W. Reitsperger to the Annual Conference of the European Institute of International Business in December 1982, the following output of CTV sets per production worker man-day were made for 1980: UK owned company 0.65; a US subsidiary 1.2; two Japanese firms also obtained superior productivity and quality results in the US.

29. From more general data culled at the time of interview with the Japanese affiliates, we would put quality control measures, better equipment, more efficient and flexible work processes, and more co-operative and better motivated labour as the top four considerations.

PART III

6 THE IMPACT OF JAPANESE MANUFACTURING AFFILIATES ON THEIR UK SUPPLIERS – PART ONE

Introduction

We now consider some of the consequences of the activities of Japanese manufacturing affiliates on their UK suppliers and subconstractors. In particular, we wish to identify, and where possible evaluate, the distinctive characteristics and impact of Japanese sourcing requirements and methods. In this chapter we first detail the extent to which Japanese affiliates buy inputs, e.g. materials, components, parts and semi-finished goods, from UK firms; second, we examine the factors influencing their choice as to (a) whether to make in-house or buy out and (b) if the latter, whether to buy from UK or foreign sources; and third we analyse the perceptions of the affiliates as to the ways in which they believe they have impinged upon the structure, conduct and performance of their suppliers. The next chapter tackles the latter question from the perspective of the UK suppliers.

How Much Do Affiliates Buy From UK Suppliers?

In 1982 (or the nearest financial year), some 68% of the £235m sales generated by the 23 Japanese manufacturing affiliates in the UK represented purchases from other firms for further production.[1] The *weighted* average of the reliance on outside suppliers for Group 1 affiliates was 76% and ranged from 68 to 86%; that of Group 2 affiliates was 50% and ranged from 22 to 78%.

Of the £161m of outside purchases, about £93m represented imports – very largely from Japan – and £68m procurements from UK firms. Two of the 23 affiliates bought nothing from UK suppliers in 1982 and three imported nothing. For the rest, the ratio of internal to all sourcing varied from 20 to 60% in Group 1 affiliates around a mean 49%; and from 5 to 80% in Group 2 around a mean of 37%.

Both the 'make or buy' and the'import or buy locally' options varied according to sector and age of affiliate. The 'other' and light engineering affiliates recorded the highest value added/sales ratio (45%

and 46%) while, with two exceptions, the CTV affiliates had the lowest ratio. The CTV affiliates also imported a larger than average proportion of their inputs; by contrast, three of the chemical affiliates bought more from their UK suppliers than from their foreign suppliers.

In general, as might be expected, the propensity to engage in outside sourcing was negatively related to the age of the affiliate. Taking just two groups by date of establishment in the UK, viz. those set up between 1972 and 1978 and those set up between 1979 and 1982, the respective proportions of outside sourcing to total sales in 1982 were 66% and 72%. Equally, if not more significant, were the difference between the two groups in their propensity to buy from UK sources. For the two age groups, the ratios were 35% and 31% in 1982.[2] Data on the two of the oldest Group 2 subsidiaries and one of the oldest Group 1 subsidiaries, reveal the following pattern of purchases (see Table 6.1).

Table 6.1: Purchasing Patterns of Three Japanese Affiliates, 1972-82

| | Two Group 2 affiliates | | | One Group 1 affiliate | |
	1972	1977	1982	1977	1982
UK sourced	2.5	30.0	46.0	10.0	60.0
Imported	97.5	70.0	54.0	90.0	40.0
All purchases as % of total sales	100.0	100.0	100.0	100.0	100.0
	87.0	64.0	50.0	75.0	65.0

In the CTV and video recorder industries, it is usual practice for a newly established affiliate first to import kits or parts from its Japanese parent company, and to produce for itself, or subcontract to UK suppliers, bulky, relatively standardised and low technology components and parts; these include the non-electronic parts of a TV set, e.g. cabinets, escutcheons, TV stands, backcovers and packaging materials. Next, production or sourcing of the more standardised electronic components, e.g. printed circuit boards (PCBs) and tubes is switched from Japan to the UK (or Europe) and finally (if at all, and this very much depends on the influence UK component suppliers can exert on chassis design (which incorporates the integrated circuitry)) that of the most sophisticated electronic components, e.g. diodes, electrolytic capacitors and semiconductors. Of the Japanese CTV affiliates, only Sony and GEC-Hitachi have reached the third stage; moreover, the former is one of the few TV companies that manufactures and assembles its own tube in both Japan and the UK. The later arrivals, apart from Sanyo which only began UK production in 1982, now buy out most of their non-electrical component supplies in the UK, some of their TV tubes (mainly from Mullards) and a few of their electrical components. Sanyo is currently importing 80% of its needs, but is beginning to buy in some of its electrical components from UK suppliers.

The 'make in-house or buy out' decision is mainly determined by the relative production and transaction costs of the alternatives. Where the market for the particular intermediary product is near perfect, then, as long as it is cheaper to buy out than make in-house, the output will be subcontracted; where there are high transaction costs[3] it will be internalised. More often than not, where production is internalised in the Japanese factory, the choice open to the affiliate is whether to import from that factory or make it in the UK plant; where in Japan the product is externally purchased, then the probability is that it will be bought out in the UK.

However, there are exceptions to this general rule. Much depends on the reasons for the make or buy decision. If it is based purely on production costs, then, where the internal v. external costs vary between countries due, e.g. to differences in volume produced by the parent of the affiliate, so the proportion bought externally may vary. Where the reasons are more to do with the economies (or diseconomies) of vertical integration, then, when these vary between countries, the decision to make or buy is more likely to be similar in the parent plant and the affiliate.

Our general impression is that for Group 1 affiliates, the extent of vertical integration between companies of the same size and product structure is broadly the same; the major exception is the preference of Sony to produce its own 'Triniton' tube. In these affiliates, there appeared to be a direct substitution between the import internally and make internally choice; and the import externally (though often via their parent companies) and make externally choice. In Group 2 affiliates, a higher proportion of imported inputs were internal and we gained the strong impression that, if for cost reasons, e.g. a change in the exchange rate, it became uneconomic to continue these imports, then the inputs would be made within the affiliate, rather than bought on the open market.

The great majority – between 80% and 100% – of UK electronics and light engineering components are bought on contract or long-term agreement and to the specifications of the purchaser. By contrast, the rest of Group 2 affiliates purchased their inputs mostly from the spot market. Each of the chemical and two of the 'other' affiliates bought all of their UK inputs on the open market. As a general observation, the most pronounced impact of Japanese affiliates on the UK suppliers has been in the assembling and fabricating rather than in the continuous processing sectors.[4]

In 1982, all but 10% of the recurrent imports of materials and components of Group 1 affiliates came from Japan; the balance originated from other parts of the EEC. Of the total imports, 85% were intra-group; and frequently the Japanese parent acted as purchasing agent on behalf of the affiliate in Japan. With the exception of one 'other company', Group 2 affiliates imported, on average, the same proportion of their inputs from Japan as Group 1 affiliates. However, only in one case did an affiliate import anything from Europe; while two bought parts and accessories from Korea, Taiwan and Thailand. The average proportion of intra-group transactions was 73%, and in eight cases all imports from Japan were purchased directly from the parent company.

Taken as a whole, then, in 1982, 90% of all recurrent imports of items for further manufacturing in Japanese affiliates were imported from Japan and 84% were bought either from their parent companies or sister affiliates. There is some suggestion there has been a marginal shift of import sourcing away from Japan to Europe, and, with it, a small decline in intra-group transactions.[5]

It might be tempting to conclude from the picture just painted that Japanese parent companies strongly control the sourcing policies of their UK affiliates. Chapter 4 suggested that this is by no means the case. To recapitulate, of all affiliates, just over one half asserted that their parent companies had little or no *direct influence* on the origin of their purchases, and only one-fifth believed that there was a decisive influence; the corresponding proportions for *control* over the decision of 'where to source' were three-fifths and one-tenth. The majority of affiliates also denied that their parent company exerted any centralised or integrated purchasing strategy; but in eight cases (just under 40%) such a strategy was pursued. Of these latter affiliates, four were colour TV and two light engineering companies with other manufacturing interests in Europe.

However, notwithstanding questions of influence and control, parent companies do assist their affiliates to obtain Japanese sourced inputs. For example, of the fully owned Japanese electronics companies set up in the UK since 1976, at least one half of all their recurrent inputs (excluding finished goods) are bought by their parent company and shipped by them – often in kit form – from Japan. We have said that the importation of kits is usually the first stage of any manufacturing operation; for example, at the end of 1983, the two producers of video recorders — J2T and Mitsubishi — imported their kits from their parent companies, which did all the Japanese purchasing for them. Among the benefits claimed from internalising these transactions are the better volume discounts the parent company can get than could the affiliate if it dealt directly with the Japanese supplier;[7] and the saving on transport costs by containerisation of kits saves on transport costs.

In the case of Group 2 affiliates, the story is different. While one light engineering and one chemical company relied upon its parent company to purchase all of its recurrent imports from Japan, and another chemical company for one half of its imports of raw materials,[8] the rest bought their inputs quite independently of their Japanese parents.

The Import or Make (or Buy) Locally Decision

Of the reasons influencing the location of purchases, product availability, product quality and price (which includes transport costs) were the most frequently cited, with length and/or reliability and delivery times being vital in the case of three affiliates. Other considerations, e.g. after sales servicing, were not generally considered to be significant.

Product availability, of course, is a very wide term and is subject to many different interpretations. Often the marginal costs of exporting items from Japan were less than the unit costs of supplying from a new plant in the UK. Particularly this was the case where there were costly tooling costs, e.g. strips for PCBs.[9] Most Japanese affiliates attempted to emulate (or better) the quality standards of their parent companies, and that, while preferring to source their inputs from UK or EEC firms, they would not do so unless these standards were met. Moreover, the final decision on whether the quality of a component was acceptable was frequently taken by the parent company.[10]

Again, the question of quality availability appeared to be a more important determinant of sourcing policy for Group 1 than for Group 2 affiliates. In the words of one colour TV affiliate

> In deciding where to buy our components from, quality availability is the key factor, together with continuity of supply. The fact that we do not buy more components from the EEC reflects our inability to persuade suppliers to provide us with components at the right

quality and competitive price.

This same affiliate (and others) also asserted that, were it not for voluntary export restraints by Japanese firms (e.g. of CTV tubes), and country of origin regulations imposed by the EEC, a larger quantity of inputs would be imported from Japan.[11] At the same time, as the micro-electronics industry develops in Europe, one might expect the quality of its output to improve and unit costs to fall, thus reducing imports from Japan. And certainly, the recent fall in the value of the £ relative to the yen has encouraged affiliates to develop European sources.

We have reported that, in the early 1980s, there was some switch by Group 1 affiliates in their input sourcing from Japan to the UK; almost unanimously, the main reasons given for this were the improved availability and quality of the items supplied by UK firms; only one firm thought the situation had deteriorated.[12]

On the other hand, one long established CTV affiliate asserted that for some of the more sophisticated electrical goods (and, in its case, funnel glass) Continental European rather than UK suppliers were replacing Japanese suppliers. In the words of a purchasing manager

> we always prefer to buy from UK sources, but all too frequently, we can get a better deal from European suppliers.

At the same time, since the products manufactured by Japanese affiliates are primarily based on Japanese specifications and with the local market foremost in mind, it is not surprising that many of the parts can only be supplied by Japanese sources; this 'inbuilt' home country preference is exacerbated by the difficulty, claimed by some UK component suppliers (particularly in the electronics industry), of breaking into the Japanese market. As one UK supplier put it

> Our principal cause of frustration in dealing with Japanese affiliates is our lack of visibility of, or access to, their parent companies' markets for own components. The Japanese domestic suppliers therefore have significant advantages during the design phase to refine specifications, while access to volume markets enables them to price more competitively on a worldwide basis.

Group 2 affiliates saw more obstacles in importing from Japan. On the other hand, because of the time and cost of shipment for bulky items and the need to avoid possible disruptions, e.g. dock strikes, a UK location was often preferred. Almost universally, the decision to import rested on price and quality criteria, though in the case of one chemical affiliate, the choice was more between producing in-house in Japan or in the UK, rather than from where outside purchases were sourced. This is because the particular ownership advantage of the Japanese company was so idiosyncratic and/or highly valued that they would not be prepared to risk licensing it to foreign suppliers; usually, however, such knowledge related to a production process which generated economies of scale, or required a particular expertise that could not be economically transplanted to the UK affiliates.

It is perhaps worth emphasising that the local (=UK) value added component of the Japanese manufacturing presence in the UK may be increased in three ways, (i) by extending the range of products produced, (ii) by undertaking a larger proportion of production in-house in substitute for imports, and (iii) by buying out a larger proportion of inputs from UK rather than foreign firms. As will be seen in Chapter 12, which speculates a little about the future, most Group 1 affiliates expect to increase their contribution to value added in the UK by a combination of (i), (ii) and (iii); by contrast most Group 2 affiliates – and especially the chemical affiliates – see their growth as a combination of (i) and (ii). Much depends on the policy of the parent company towards its own external sourcing. In 1983, the parent companies of Group 1 affiliates were considerably less vertically integrated relative to those of Group 2. The suggestion is then that, *ceteris paribus*, the 'internal' growth potential of the latter group of affiliates is greater than that of the former.

In summary, in Group 1 affiliates, EEC regulations, voluntary trade constraints and the PAL agreement each combine to exert some influence on the sourcing of inputs and the extents of in-house activity; but perhaps more important is the availability, quality and price on inputs in Europe and the capacity and experience of the affiliates. While most Japanese subsidiaries stated that they tried to be good corporate citizens by buying from Britain (or at least European sources), and in some cases did so in spite of a price differential favouring Japan, the greater part of CTV electronic components (apart from the tube) are still imported from Japan. There is a strong suggestion, from companies such as Sony, Matsushita and Hitachi, that over time, the in-house value added component of total sales will gradually increase; and, depending on (a) the extent to which Japanese affiliates, by themselves, or in conjunction with Japanese component suppliers, can come up with a European designed CTV chassis and (b) the efficiency of the UK component supplying industry, so will the percentage of bought out inputs sourced locally. This process may of course be hastened by the investment of Japanese component suppliers in the UK. Examples include NEC and Shin-Etsu (in microchips), Alps Electric (in video recorder parts) and Tabucki (transformers for electrical products). While the latter determinants appear relevant to the Group 2 affiliates (particularly those in light engineering) the capability of such affiliates to produce the range of goods of their parent companies seems to be a more important influence on the 'import v. make locally' choice; and here questions of scale of production are particularly relevant.[13]

On the role played by UK government policy in influencing the sourcing of components, there was some feeling by CTV affiliates that in the mid-1970s there was some pressure to source locally, but this was thought minor compared with the provisions of the PAL licensing agreement, which stipulates minimum local content requirements, and voluntary import restrictions. In any case, Japanese companies are only too aware of their responsibilities to the local community, both because they are used to working closely with their own governments and because they are conscious that, if they are to translate their work methods to the UK, they must 'go the extra mile' in accommodating to local preferences (and prejudices!). Other evidence supports this impression[14] and confirms that, at least in more recent years, one of the main contributions of UK public authorities (both central and local) has been to advise on the names of possible suppliers.

The Impact of Japanese Affiliates on their Suppliers

At the end of 1982, of the 23 Japanese manufacturing affiliates, two bought nothing from their UK suppliers (nor had attempted to do so) and six others, including the chemical affiliates, purchased only on the spot market. These firms produced goods worth 15% of the sales of all affiliates. While these latter six firms expressed an opinion on the quality and price of their supplies – and particularly on the length and reliability of delivery times – only one claimed to have affected these capabilities. The remarks which follow then relate to the remaining 15 Japanese affiliates, including seven Group 1, all the light engineering affiliates and two 'other' affiliates in Group 2. As these are all wholly or partly assembling or fabricating firms, we shall deal with them as a single group.

All affiliates were asked to give data about the way in which they negotiated contracts with their suppliers. The following represents a typical sequence of events.

In seeking to buy an item in the UK, a Japanese affiliate will normally contact up to five firms for quotations. In most cases, in seeking such bids, the affiliate will supply each firm with detailed specifications and samples of the product it requires. On the basis of the quotations tendered, and work specimens provided, it then chooses (often with the guidance of its parent company) one, or possibly two, firms with which to continue discussions and negotiate over contract terms.[15]

Here immediately there appears to be a difference between the styles and practices of Japanese and UK firms. One CTV affiliate claimed that when it first contacted potential suppliers in the mid-1970s, the practice of providing specifications was the exception rather than the rule. Certainly the idea of a purchaser visiting a supplier's factory and requiring detailed costing of its price was unheard of.

Once a contract is awarded, the interest of Japanese affiliates in the supplier's operations intensifies, the nature of which is perhaps best expressed by one supplier of integrated circuits:

We get more help from the Japanese in terms of technical help, drawings and the like. Unlike most UK firms at least, they see us as an extension of their own factory: therefore it is essential we have mutual understanding of their requirements. If we have any problems, they will send specialists to help or advise us and do everything they can to enable us to be a successful supplier.

The close bonds between customer and supplier – a kind of internalisation, but without equity participation, and not too dissimilar to the attitude of Japanese firms to their employees – is a fundamental part of production strategy in Japan.[16] All the Japanese affiliates try and emulate this practice by building up lasting relations with their main UK suppliers. However, in return they expect a total acceptance and adherence to their requirements and standards. Nowhere is this more clearly seen than in quality control, inspection and testing procedures.

By contrast, in most of UK industry, the relationship between contractor and supplier tends to be more distant – and in some cases is more adversary than co-operative. In their purchasing practices, most Japanese affiliates, and all in Group 1, follow a zero deficit concept, and reject rates are measured in parts per million (PPM). We shall discuss this scheme later; but its underlying philosophy is simply an extension of the goals which the Japanese company sets itself and its workers, via quality circles and other inspection procedures. Japanese companies will go to extraordinary lengths to 'get things right'; and they expect the same dedication to perfection from their suppliers. Sometimes this may result in unrealistically high standards or tolerance being required; and certainly there have been cases of UK suppliers being unwilling to meet Japanese specifications for genuine economic reasons. But in the experience of others, unwillingness is often a cloak for inability, complacency, laziness or ignorance, and the presence of Japanese affiliates in the UK is having a dramatic effect on some sections of UK industry.

Japanese expectations of price and delivery times from their suppliers reflect the same philosophy. Though adherence to standards was ranked the most significant difference between Japanese affiliates and other UK customers by UK suppliers in our survey, the insistence on delivery dates being kept came a close second. Again the concept of 'Kanfan' or 'just in time' deliveries is widely practised in Japan, with some major motor vehicle and consumer electronics companies keeping some stocks down to a day's requirement; hence their total reliance on their suppliers to adhere to tight and punctual schedules.

While the purchasing requirements of Japanese firms are not always more demanding than their UK counterparts – much seems to depend on the item being bought – where they are, the technical assistance given to their suppliers is often very considerable indeed. Besides providing detailed specifications, drawings, samples and prototypes, Japanese firms may, and do, give advice on plant layout, machinery, tooling, training of operatives, production methods, testing and quality control procedures; and help their suppliers to get in touch with their opposite numbers in Japan. We quote just three examples.

In our demand for printed circuit boards, we pass on all information about developments in production techniques and equipment and assist in imports of materials and equipment (a CTV affiliate).

Our procedure is to approach 3 or 4 companies to provide us samples of their work from the specification and specimens supplied by our Japanese parent company. We then choose the best of these and work with that company to iron out any difficulties. In the case of one of our suppliers, the product failed to come up to standard so the company visited Japan to sort it out. Unfortunately, it has still not been able to solve all the technical problems and in the meantime we are importing the product from Japan (a consumer electronics affiliate).

In our search for a supplier of fibre mats we asked three firms to produce samples and quote for us. We selected one firm but it took 5-6 sets of samples before the Japanese parent company finally approved the quality. Even then, in spite of a 20% transport and 9% tariff duty, the Japanese product was cheaper, but in the last two years the depreciation of the £ has made the UK supplier competitive (a light engineering affiliate).

Sometimes the interest of the Japanese affiliate in its supplier goes well beyond the product being produced; they appear no less interested in its management strategy and the way the plant is run. This may extend even to the cleanliness of work benches. One firm found that unacceptable small scratches on its components were due to the way in which its supplier's operators handled the components, and to dirt on the benches. In the opinion of one CTV affiliate

It's not so much that suppliers do not know what they have to do to satisfy our standards; but they they do not pay enough attention to ensuring these standards are met.

To us, supplier commitment is all-important. We visit suppliers not only to assess their viability, in terms of their ability to supply, but also to evaluate their attitude to their customers. We always attempt to be supportive rather than destructive, but this does not mean we are not critical where necessary.

The assistance by Japanese companies may extend to the provision of tools and equipment; a good example is the loan of moulding tools to plastics suppliers.

This interest is a continuing one. If reject levels become unacceptable, engineers and/or technical personnel from the Japanese affiliates – or even the Japanese parent company – will visit the suppliers to advise on production processes and inspection and quality control procedures. In the case of one CTV subsidiary, its engineers spent a week with its suppliers devising a completely new quality control system. In some cases, affiliates may arrange (and even financally assist) its suppliers to visit its own or Japanese suppliers.[18] But this will not help it get over another problem also cited by Japanese affiliates, viz. the failure of suppliers (or transport companies) to deliver on time or even the right quantities demanded; this unreliability causing the company to hold additional stocks.[19]

It is worth emphasising at this point that the Japanese parent company is frequently involved in the testing of UK supplied components. In about one in three cases, all components and parts have to be sent back to Japan for functional testing (e.g. with respect to temperature and pressure); this is especially the case where the UK affiliate does not have the necessary inspection facilities. It is also the case (much to the complaint of suppliers) that, if as a result of a sample inspection of Japanese customers, an unsatisfactory item is found, the whole consignment is rejected.

Not in all cases is the Japanese parent company brought into the picture. Sometimes it is reluctant to intervene; sometimes it wishes to encourage its affiliate to stand on its own feet. But in every case, there is no compromise on the standards expected.

Opinions seem to be mixed as to whether the failure of UK companies to meet the specifications of Japanese affiliates is due to incapacity or unwillingness. UK purchasing managers tend to incline as much to the second view as the first. One light engineering affiliate argues that its main UK plastics supplier could do anything the Japanese required, but that they were 'amazed at the quality asked for' and had seen 'nothing like this before'. But the tooling costs involved were too great for it to bear unless other companies were prepared to raise their standards; and in this case they were not. This is why Japanese firms often provide tools and mouldings to their suppliers and make a special effort to build up a lasting and trusting bond with them.

Another aspect of the purchasing policy of Japanese affiliates – and one unfamiliar and generally disliked by many suppliers – is their frequent insistence for a detailed cost breakdown of parts and components. For major purchases, the Japanese will often cost the items themselves and, when in doubt about a quotation, require further explanation, or even suggest ways in which they believe costs could be reduced.

One noticeable difference between the structure of the supplying industries in Japan and the UK was mentioned by several Group 1 affiliates. Generally speaking, in Japan, the suppliers tend to be smaller, less influential and more customer or product specialised than in the UK; in consequence, the bargaining power of the purchaser is greater. Moreover, the contact between supplier and customer is that much closer, with their respective functions sometimes overlapping.[20] Because they have a more diversified product and structure, UK suppliers are not as anxious to accommodate the specific needs of Japanese affiliates – particularly the smaller ones.[21] This, together with uncertainties over delivery times, often leads Japanese affiliates to engage in dual sourcing – a practice discouraged in Japan. This may change as more Japanese companies set up in the UK; and some of the larger electrical suppliers, such as Mullard and Plessey, are making a special effort to adjust to Japanese procurement policies. In the sample of UK suppliers we visited, the readiness to accommodate Japanese standards was directly correlated with the size and proportion of their total output supplied to Japanese affiliates. Which way the causation runs is not clear, but there are some quite spectacular success stories of UK suppliers rising to the Japanese challenge, taking advantage of the advice given by their customers, and building (or rebuilding) their businesses as a result.[22]

The Changing Perception of Japanese Firms Towards their Suppliers

All except two of the 20 Japanese affiliates buying inputs in the UK in 1983 thought that, over the years, the supply position had improved. This, they believed, was the result of (a) the combined efforts of themselves and their suppliers to improve quality, (b) competitive pressures, i.e. 'needs must', and (c) the depreciation of the £ *vis-à-vis* the yen by 40%.[22] One of the two exceptions – a CTV affiliate – argued that the drastic cut in price cost margins had forced supplying firms to cut quality corners to stay in business; the other asserted that both the quality and price of specialised steel parts had deteriorated. Of the affiliates who thought the quality of their purchases had improved – 35% said they were substantially more satisfied and 65% that they were more satisfied – the corresponding ratios for reliability and promptness of deliveries were 21% and 79%, and for price 15% and 85%.[24]

Several affiliates gave very impressive instances of how their rejection rates for components had fallen – even though they are still above their Japanese equivalents. One colour TV affiliate asserted that its rejection rates of picture tubes had fallen from more than 5% to 0.8%; and that of its cabinets from 10% to 0.5%. Whereas previously it had 100% checks on most of its components, including printed circuit boards, now it makes only sample checks.

It is difficult to quantify the extent to which Japanese affiliates have improved the efficiency of their suppliers or the quality of their products; but it is possible to identify the sectors in which the successes and failures have occurred. Almost unanimously, Group 1 affiliates noted the most marked improvement in plastic mouldings (but not finished mouldings), cabinets, tubes and TV stands. Since the sources of inputs for Group 2 affiliates were rather more widespread, so were the sectors mentioned; they included semi-finished plastic mouldings, upholstery, yarns, polythene, and glass and carbon cloth; by contrast, steel, special chemicals, thread, rubber mouldings, finished plastic and packaging materials came in for more criticism. One Japanese steel-using affiliate which closely investigated a quality problem with a major UK supplier, ascribed a major reason for this, the quality of the raw material i.e. steel supplied by the British Steel Corporation. Failure rates are put at ten times the level encountered in Japan.[25] The affiliate asserted their product quality improved 'a great deal' after collaborative research with the supplier's own engineers, but that no further progress could be made without intrinsic improvements in the quality of steel supplies. Another affiliate found it could not persuade a specialised steel producer to meet its requirements, since it, in turn, could not persuade its supplier of billets to improve its quality. But since the patronage of Japanese affiliates of steel is minute, and British competitors are not so concerned about this difficulty, the Japanese accept that little can be done about it other than to pressurise those suppliers over which they do have influence to try and upgrade the quality of their output.

Conclusions

It appears that, prior to their actual establishment in the UK, most Japanese companies perceived two main disadvantages of operating a factory in the UK, viz. bad industrial relations and poor quality of component supplies. In retrospect, the Japanese have been pleasantly surprised about the first and admit their anxieties were exaggerated. As regards the second, most would assert their fears were initially confirmed, but have since somewhat receded. However, according to the Electronics Industries Association of Japanese companies in Europe, one of the main obstacles to further Japanese investment in the UK – notably in the engineering and electrical industries – remains the concern about supplying facilities.[26] This, in turn, was put down to a mixture of insufficient demand for the standards required by indigenous firms, a casual managerial style – particularly with respect to quality control – inadequate capacity and relaxed attitudes to tudes to deliveries.

Since their arrival in the UK Japanese affiliates have seen a lot of improvements. Yet it is worth noting that the latest arrivals on the colour TV scene are no less critical of their UK suppliers than were their predecessors some years ago. Whether some degree of dissatisfaction of local sourcing capability is inherent in new arrivals from abroad; whether it is a temporary phenomenon which is overcome by a learning process, or more relaxed expectations on its part of both supplier and purchaser; whether it is a bargaining strategy employed by Japanese companies to get even more favourable terms for investing in the UK or whether the parent company expects even higher standards from UK suppliers, to justify it reducing its orders from its Japanese suppliers, we are not sure.[27] But it is worth observing that, 30 years ago, US manufacturing affiliates in the UK were voicing almost identical complaints about their UK suppliers;[28] while the kind of local sourcing problems just described, also appear to be faced by Japanese subsidiaries elsewhere in Europe[29] and in the US. *À propos* the latter, the following quotation from a report published by JETRO (US) (1981) is particularly instructive.

Japanese companies in the US face a number of problems involved with the reliability of local (i.e. US) sources of supply. These include (1) unstable quality of parts, with wide variations, (2) a different attitude than in Japan in regard to standards for parts, (3) delays in delivery, (4) because ordering a small amount of parts at one time results in higher costs and also runs the risk of goods being out of stock, firms tend to keep large stocks of parts on hand in warehouses, (5) if the Japanese affiliate is small or medium sized, it has little bargaining power and is unable to get accommodation on price, delivery dates etc.[30]

At the same time, the report goes on to say

Even in cases where the original rate of procurement from Japan was high, there is a tendency towards gradually increasing local procurement as production gradually becomes stabilized. And in nearly all cases, firms which presently have a high dependence on overseas procurement, have plans to increase local procurement as much as possible.[31]

An interesting suggestion made by one firm is that the suppliers of

Japanese firms should be made a target of an experimental study financed by the government of identifying what is needed and how it may be achieved. The full automation of PCBs was suggested as an example which needed some government backing.

Notes

1. I.e., variable inputs for conversion or assembling into the final product. Other inputs, e.g. heat and light, rates, transport, advertising, telephone, etc., are excluded.

2. Excluding GEC-Hitachi, the proportion for affiliates set up between 1979 and 1982 was 11%.

3. Of a kind similar to influencing the fdi v licensing decision and identified in Chapter 3.

4. And seems likely to be in the future; hence the great interest shown in the investment plans of the Japanese motor vehicle assemblers in the UK.

5. It also appears that the onger established Japanese affiliates buy rather more of their imports from the EEC than those most recently set up, but the age effect is generally less important than the 'industry' or 'firm' effect.

6. We use the world 'direct', as 'indirectly' by controlling quality standards, they were able to influence sourcing origins.

7. One Group 1 affiliate reported that whereas it required to buy 20,000 integrated circuit boards each year, its parent buys 200,000.

8. In each case the main reason given was to reap the economies of bulk purchases.

9. Another example is pre-formed wire which (in 1982) could be imported at 35% below the price quoted by UK suppliers, and carbon chromium steel, the imported price of which was 25% below the UK price.

10. Particularly in the case of the less experienced or smaller affiliates which do not have the necessary inspection or testing equipment.

11. Currently for a TV or radio set to be imported into one EEC country from another without import duty, some 45% of the value of that set must originate from within the EEC. This requirement need not be satisfied for a product to be labelled 'Made in Engand'.

12. See Chapter 7.

13. For example, in the ballbearing industry.

14. European Company Services Ltd (1983).

15. Sometimes the risk to the supplier of not being awarded a contract is considerable. One supplier was asked to produce a batch of 100 loudspeakers for CTV sets for a Japanese affiliate; if they come up to specification, then it would be awarded a one year's contract worth more than £100,000, but if they did not, the design, tooling and other costs already incurred would be lost altogether.

16. In these respect, it is worth emphasising that Japanese firms in Japan have closer and more coordinative vertical relations with their suppliers; and generally much stronger bargaining power. Suppliers are usually treated as satellites, and are often spin-offs of larger hierarchies. One estimate, quoted by Kverneland (1984) suggests that, on average, 80%of the output of small Japanese sub-contractors is sold to their largest customer. For their part, contractors establish a wide network of secondary sub-contractors, each dependent on the other. This structure of vertical/horizontal relationships is very different from that in the UK, where the main manufacturing sub-contractors, at least, are often as large and powerful as their leading customers.

17. In particular how idiosyncratic it is. One major tube company commented 'we supply standard catalogue items, not made to a particular customer's specification'.

18. For further details see Chapter 7.

19. One consumer electronics company claimed the stocks held by its parent company were smaller while its output was 20 times more. That company received containerised deliveries every day, compared with every two weeks in the UK. (NB. This does not seem a volume problem as much as differences in UK and Japanese delivery systems and practices.)

20. An example is given by European Company services (1983); 'If a new model requires a component which is smaller or flatter than its predecessor the components supplier will willingly alter the design in return for their assurance of worthwhile orders. In the UK, dealings are at arms length (p. 81).

21. One small 'other' Japanese affiliate admitted that because of its lack of bargaining power it had given up trying to influence its UK suppliers' behaviour. Instead where it is not satisfied, it simply imports the item from Japan. This same company asserted that when it wrote to suppliers asking them to quote for orders, only three out of five even bothered to reply.

22. Examples include Kenure Plastics (for their success story see an article in the *Financial Times*, 10 October 1983), R.E. Ingham (Cabinet Makers) and GSPK Circuits (integrated circuits). See also Chapter 7.

23. In 1980 the £/yen rate was 552; in 1981 it averaged 448, in 1982 435 and by December 1983 had fallen to 331.

24. One small 'other' affiliate thought that the delivery situation had worsened over the last five years.

25. As described in European Company Services (1983), p. 80.

26. Particularly, in view of the local content requirements laid down by the EEC, and sometimes the UK Government.

27. Another suggestion put to us was that it is likely that, since the recent arrivals may bring with them the latest technology, this will create unfamiliar demands on their suppliers.

28. Dunning (1958), and Dunning (1985).

29. For further details, see Chapter 7.

30. JETRO (US) 1981, p. 30.

31. Op. cit., p. 31.

7 THE IMPACT OF JAPANESE MANUFACTURING AFFILIATES ON THEIR UK SUPPLIERS – PART TWO

The Structure of Suppliers

This chapter presents the perspective of some 20 UK suppliers of Japanese affiliates on some of the issues touched upon in the previous chapter. Altogether, 30 were approached; of these, 21 were visited and/or completed a questionnaire.[1] The names of the suppliers were provided by the purchasing managers or managing directors of 18 affiliates; they included both those from whom affiliates bought raw materials, components and semi-processed goods in 1983, and those whom affiliates had not been able to persuade to meet their purchasing requirements.[2]

Some features of the 20 suppliers are set out in Table 7.1. Their estimated combined output despatched to Japanese affiliates in 1982 was £40 million, some 58% of the total purchases of these affiliates. More than three-fifths of the purchases originated from one firm which supplied six Japanese subsidiaries. In 14 of the 20 cases, however, less than £1 million worth of production were supplied to affiliates, and in eight cases under £200,000. Three of the suppliers sold more than 50% of their output to Japanese customers and six more than 20% The suppliers were of varying size ranging from Shell (UK), British Steel, Plessey, Mullards and Courtaulds, to a small jobbing engineer employing only 25 persons.

Table 7.1: Selected UK Suppliers of Japanese Manufacturing Affiliates

		Number	Output supplied to Japanese affiliates (1982) £m	Estimated number of employees[a]
Group 1 suppliers	Electronic components	3	25.1	767
	Other components	7	8.4	516
		9	33.5	1183
Group 2 suppliers	Materials and parts	10	5.5	185
		20	£39.0	1468

Note: a. Estimate of full-time employee equivalents engaged in supplying output to Japanese affiliates.

120

Like the affiliates, the suppliers also fall neatly into two groups: (i) those supplying the consumer and industrial electronics companies (10), and (ii) those supplying Group 2 affiliates (10). All the suppliers most dependent on Japanese affiliates are of Group 1 variety, and it is they which have been most affected by the Japanese presence.

Some 60% of the suppliers thought that their sales to Japanese affiliates were, at least partly, an addition to their output, and 40% that they replaced output which in any case would have been produced. Six of the suppliers to CTV assemblers asserted that, while output sold to Japanese customers had been partly at the expense of that sold to indigenous competitors, part represented a net increase in output, due *inter alia* to a fall in the share of imported CTV sets from Japan.

In general, suppliers perceived that the output demanded by Japanese affiliates required similar production methods to that produced for other suppliers. However, six of the 20 suppliers (30%) – including four of the ten Group 1 suppliers – thought that as a result of their dealing with Japanese customers, they had upgraded and/or made a greater use of skilled labour; and two had made less use of unskilled labour. The majority of suppliers also accepted that Japanese sourcing methods had had an impact on their productive efficiency, mainly by assisting quality control and testing procedures. Overall, 11 of the suppliers thought their contact with the Japanese affiliates had been beneficial to their company's objectives, *compared with a similar association with UK firms*; six that it had had no effect; and three that the effect had been less beneficial.

In answer to a rather wider question, 'Are you generally satisfied with the results of your dealing with Japanese affiliates in the UK?', 18 of the 20 companies answered 'Yes' and only one plastic moulding firm and one steel tube manufacturer answered 'No'.[3]

The main reasons for the two negative answers, which were also cited by an electronics components and a paper board manufacturer who gave a qualified 'Yes', were that Japanese affiliates insisted on (what they perceived to be) unnecessarily high quality and rigorous standards, were unrealistically tight on their pricing policies, and tended to impose excessive compensation claims for rejects. These criticisms were also voiced in a wider context by suppliers; basically, they reflect the belief that the Japanese managers of affiliates often try and improve on the standards expected by their parent companies, and that they make insufficient allowance for (a) volume differences for orders placed in Japan and the UK and the effect this has on pricing policy, and (b) differences in Japanese and British consumer perception towards quality.[4]

The Initial Approach and Supplying Arrangements

One half of all suppliers first made contact with Japanese affiliates on their own initiative and six (30%) were approached by the affiliates.[5] In one of three remaining cases, a UK chemical firm took over the business of another already supplying a Japanese customer; in a second, to quote the words of the supplier, 'We gained the business as a result of a third party reference based upon a supply position between one Japanese company and its customers in Japan'. In the third instance, the initial contact was made via the parent company in Japan to whom the supplier was already exporting.

Most UK suppliers contacting Japanese affiliates – and especially Group 2 suppliers – did so because of their perception of (a) market trends, (b) the prospective growth of Japanese participation in the UK and (c) their capability in meeting Japanese standards. Two did so as they had supplied the previous owners of the CTV factory now operated by the Japanese. At first, not all approaches were successful. The case of one supplier of plastic mouldings (Kenure Plastics), is particularly instructive.[6] Kenure first attempted to get moulding business from a Japanese affiliate in the UK over a decade ago. It ended in failure when, after numerous discussions and three evaluation visits, the prospective customer decided the company did not have the experience, expertise or quality control of its larger competitors. Kenure only got a second chance as a result of repeated visits to the affiliate and patiently nurturing personal relationships. The first order came in a hurry when a larger supplier had failed to meet the quality requirements of the Japanese. Could Kenure do any better? It could and did – with a lot of help from the Japanese affiliate – and is now one of the major suppliers of plastic mouldings to Japanese companies in the UK.

By contrast, the first approach to a major electronics supplier to supply small TV components initially came from a Japanese affiliate in 1971; since that date, the company has become a specialist in supplying Japanese affiliates in the UK. As the company itself points out

> The Japanese now supply 30% of the TV market; we could not survive without supplying a major share of the components required by these companies; and to be effective we must be prepared to accept the Japanese quality scheme (and in particular the zero defect concept) and delivery dates. In improving our performance, we gained a lot of help from the affiliates we now supply.

There appear to be few major differences between the contractual arrangements concluded between suppliers and their Japanese and UK owned customers, except that it usually takes longer to negotiate and reach agreement with the former. But several affiliates commented on the greater sense of loyalty, responsibility and integrity of their Japanese customers and their painstaking adherence to commitments; they were also widely welcomed as prompt payers. Two suppliers asserted that their agreements with Japanese affiliates were less formal than those with the UK firms, with a letter of intent often being the only form of documentation. The length of time of such agreements varied. In the case of one large producer of electronic components, it was six months for large components and one year for small components; in the case of one of its competitors it was 'an ongoing contract with an annual pricing agreement; monthly schedules with three months firm and two months tentative'. One supplier of plastic mouldings recorded that once an agreement had been made, it normally remained for 'the life of the product'. But the company ruefully observed 'this is always subject to price, quality and service considerations'. Another mouldings manufacturer remarked that its products were normally supplied against a blanket order to monthly schedules; 'A medium term gentleman's agreement with a monthly fixing of volume and prices' seems to sum up the general tenor of the arrangements concluded.

Several UK suppliers noted that, because of the greater coverage period offered by Japanese *vis-à-vis* their UK competitors (one supplier of pressings and turned items cited a 6-9 month period from its main Japanese CTV customer, compared with its main UK customer of 6 weeks), they, in turn, could order larger quantities of materials and gain from the economies of bulk purchase.

The Purchasing Standards of Japanese Affiliates

The following statement was put to each of the UK suppliers

> It is sometimes alleged that the procurement requirements of Japanese affiliates are more demanding than those of UK owned firms buying similar products. Please indicate whether in your experience the requirements are (a) much stricter than, (b) stricter than, (c) about the same as, (d) less strict than those of UK customers.

The results are set out in Table 7.2. Of the indicators set out, the most distinctive characteristic of Japanese affiliates seems to be their insistence on a strict adherence to quality standards laid down, with 13 of the 19 suppliers believing that the affiliates were more demanding in this respect than UK firms. Quality of end product came second and delivery dates third. In price (rather surprisingly) the majority of suppliers thought there was little difference between the requirements of Japanese and UK firms.

Table 7.2: The Perception of Purchasing Standards of Japanese Affiliates Compared with those of UK Owned Customers

| | Number of mentions | | | | | | | | | | | |
| | Group 1 affiliates | | | | Group 2 affiliates | | | | All affiliates | | | |
	a	b	c	d	a	b	c	d	a	b	c	d
Quality of end product	3	6	1	0	2	1	6	0	5	7	7	0
Insistence on quality being adhered to	7	1	2	0	2	3	4	0	9	4	6	0
Price	1	3	6	0	1	2	6	0	2	5	12	0
Delivery dates and adherence to same	4	3	3	0	0	3	5	1	4	6	8	1

Although none of the suppliers identified specific penalties associated with a failure to meet Japanese standards, several mentioned that the slightest deviation (without a really good cause) resulted in a diminution in business: after all, it was said, 'in the last resort the Japanese affiliates can always obtain supplies from their parent companies'.

While nine (45%) of the 20 suppliers asserted that rejection rates for products supplied to Japanese affiliates were higher than for comparable products supplied to UK firms, eight (40%) thought that the former were 'neither more or less stringent' than those of their best British customers; and two (5%) that they were actually less stringent. Another supplier (of a specialised oil) noted that acceptance testing standards are very different in Japanese than in UK firms. The comment was made

The Japanese affiliates adopt novel test methods and require more rigorous failure analysis reports than those normally required by UK firms. At the same time, they are very cautious in disclosing the test and control methods they expect you to meet.

On the whole, these standards were accepted by the suppliers. In the words of one electronic component firm

> The quality standards are by mutual agreement, but they are considerably higher than those of most of our existing customers, and therefore we are at the limits of our technology to meet the Japanese customer requirements. This is good for us; it keeps us on our toes.

On quality control, the biggest innovation, emphasised by one large electronics firm, was the PPM system favoured by the Japanese. *Inter alia*, this suggests an iterative process in the reduction of reject rates of components supplied. As a result of participating in the scheme, this supplier acknowledged its own 'better quality and fitness for purpose, and hence lower rejection rates'. As we have already indicated, the system is predicated on the belief that *no* faulty components should be produced; whereas, it was claimed that European firms adopt a policy of supplying components which are just good enough to just pass inspection and keep the customer happy.[7]

The same electronics firm asserted that the main benefits it had derived from its contact with Japanese affiliates were

(1)   the need to record exactly what was happening on the production line and to identify precisely and thoroughly why faults occurred;
(2)   to promote a philosophy of 'things should get better every year' and to pay attention to detail; and
(3)   to inculcate the worker on the shop floor with a sense of responsibility not to accept anything less than the best.

Another cabinet maker reinforced these comments

> The Japanese do not hesitate to reject a whole consignment of our product. In addition they expect a high level of quality and are absolutely insistent on delivery dates to meet their sales targets.

Ten of the nineteen suppliers indicated that Japanese affiliates were more demanding in their delivery requirements than their UK competitors. This, it was argued, partly reflects the fact that, as supplies must be quality approved and Japanese firms value long-term relationships with their suppliers, they do not engage (as much as UK firms) in dual sourcing; hence the paramount concern for schedules to be met. Not always did UK suppliers think the Japanese customers reasonable in their delvery expectations. Quoting from one, 'No matter how much you tell them material is not available they still push for impossible delivery dates'.

The opinion of suppliers about pricing was mixed. Much of it seems to depend on the nature of the product and how well known (and regarded) the Japanese affiliate is and how long it has been dealing with the supplier. Two of three suppliers of electronic components thought there was no difference in pricing policy between UK and Japanese customers, and one thought the latter more rigorous. The suppliers of plastic mouldings and wooden products also observed that the price demands of Japanese customers were 'very keen' and that they insisted on a detailed cost structure breakdown before agreeing to any price.

In several cases, the suppliers thought Japanese customers unrealistic in their pricing policies. One specific criticism was that the Japanese customers expected their UK suppliers to match the prices of the suppliers of their parent companies. In the words of a supplier of electronic components

One Japanese affiliate rejected our product on price and specification grounds as we were not able to match those of their Japanese supplier. It is very difficult to meet these standards against the Japanese supplier around whose component the specification has probably been written and the system actually designed. The prime supplier will also enjoy volume supply to the parent company in Japan and therefore be more price competitive.

Assistance Provided by Japanese Firms to their Suppliers

On Specifications

Having set the procurement standards, how far do Japanese firms assist UK suppliers to meet them?

Again a statement was put to each supplier:

It is sometimes alleged that Japanese affiliates (a) provide more detailed specifications of the materials or components they purchase from their UK suppliers than do UK owned firms and (b) go to a lot more trouble, e.g. by obtaining samples or by direct technical *et al.* assistance to ensure that UK suppliers can meet such specifications. Do you agree?

Rather surprisingly, only nine of the 19 suppliers answered 'Yes' to both questions – two integrated circuit, three plastic moulding, one steel, one zinc alloy, one dyestuffs, and one specialised oil producer. To quote from one of the plastic firms

The Japanese affiliates have been very helpful; samples are available and a discussion on production methods always takes place before an order is placed.

and from another

The average UK enquiry is usually by post and responded to similarly with, perhaps, a follow-up visit by salesman. There is rarely a query over our manufacturing or technical capability. If we say we can do it, that is generally accepted. Japanese affiliates always make their own analysis of a potential supplier's capabilities. They insist on seeing our facilities and talking to our key personnel prior to granting us a contract. Thereafter, they keep in closest possible touch with us.

and the third

We were asked to mould a part for a Japanese affiliate which by British standards required crazy specifications. But we agreed, providing that the affiliates would arrange for us to visit the Japanese subcontractors to find out how it was done. We not only discovered major differences in moulding between our two countries, but that Japanese firms placed greater emphasis on advanced mechanical handling techniques and a rigid time scale imposed on the tool makers.

More generally Japanese affiliates provide samples and full specifications, and insist on regular technical meetings with our production engineers to ensure everyone understands exactly what is required.

One of the integrated circuit manufacturers commented

We get more help from the Japanese in terms of technical assistance and drawings. They see us as an extension of their own factory; therefore it is essential we have a mutual understanding of requirements. If we have any problems, they will always send specialists to help or advise us and do anything they can to enable us to be a successful supplier.

One of the cabinet makers presented a different view

Very often Japanese affiliates provide us no detailed documents; merely the end specification required. However, we found that their examination and testing of proposals and offerings is more extensive.

A large producer of steel tubes agrees

Japanese affiliates specify the most stringent of test requirements and are more insistent than UK firms on being provided with detailed results of these tests.

By contrast, another manufacturer of electronic components was rather more critical

The contract and specifications for one product supplied to a major Japanese CTV affiliate took nearly a year, and the quality and specifications were stricter than normal. We did not receive samples from Japan, but invariably our samples were sent to Japan HQ for investigation, with a consequent loss of time (up to six months) and difficulty in communication during the product qualification phase.

In the case of a large tube supplier it was claimed that the company supplied 'standard catalogue items', and did not make to a particular customer's specification.

On Production Efficiency

Table 7.3 sets out the opinion of the 20 suppliers about the ways they believe Japanese affiliates may have influenced their productive efficiency. Each supplier was first asked to rank on a scale 0-5 the influence they perceived Japanese affiliates had had in helping them to produce more efficiently, and second (where comparisons were possible), and on a scale 0-3, how this influence compared with that exerted by UK suppliers.

The data set out reveal that the major Japanese influence has been felt in three areas: (1) details of product design and specifications (which the previous section dealt with), (2) materials specifications and

Table 7.3: Impact of Japanese Affiliates and Efficiency of UK Suppliers

		A			B		
		Group 1	Group 2	Total	Group 1	Group 2	Total
1	Product design, formulae, specifications, etc.	2.4	1.9	2.2	2.1	1.8	1.9
2	Procurement of materials and/or advice on materials specification	2.1	1.4	1.8	1.8	1.7	1.7
3	Processing methods	1.7	1.6	1.7	2.4	1.6	2.0
4	Machinery and equipment for production and/or product fabrication	1.7	1.4	1.6	2.2	1.6	1.9
5	Advice on plant layout and work organisation	0.3	0.8	0.6	1.7	1.7	1.6
6	Managerial and/or general technical assistance	0.6	1.1	0.9	1.9	1.4	1.7
7	Quality control and/or testing procedures	3.2	2.5	2.9	2.7	1.9	2.3
8	Training of operatives	0.7	1.0	0.9	2.3	1.7	2.0
9	Information assistance, e.g. on sourcing of inputs or market trends	0.9	1.1	1.0	1.8	1.8	1.8

A = Influence exerted by Japanese affiliates on 0-5 scale (0 = no influence).
B = How the influence compared with that exerted by UK suppliers (1 = UK firms have greater influence, 2 = no difference, 3 = Japanese firms have greater influence).

sourcing, and (3) quality control and/or testing procedures. Influence appears to be least in respect of work organisation, managerial and organisational methods and the training of operatives.

Generally speaking, the suppliers of Group 1 Japanese customers appear to have been more influenced than those supplying Group 2 customers. Suppliers selling more than 20% of their output to Japanese customers record significantly higher indices of influence than other suppliers. There is also a negative correlation between size of supplier and influence felt — except in the sphere of quality control and inspection procedures.

In connection with (1) above, one producer of electronics components opined that Japanese affiliates were much more forthcoming about the information provided. To quote from the firm's own words

we get printed specifications on raw materials in great detail, specifications on all drawings to the product, a lot of information as to where the product is used and the estimated volume used and the market place the product goes into. Coupled with this, we receive visits from and make visits to Japan.

This appears to be another example of a practice which is common in Japanese affiliates, viz. the exchange of information being extended to firms with whom they have dealings.

Although specific examples of technical assistance given by Japanese affiliates were cited — these included auto-insertion equipment for electronic components, colouring of ink, colour shade of paper, processing of specialised oils, and so on — most comments were more general. One electronics component supplier observed

> Our main Japanese customers maintain much more consistent and effective pressure on us to maintain standards of quality and delivery than do our UK customers. They also insist on detailed engineering reports of all device failures and regular and effective progress chasing.

Among the other comments we might record.

> Japanese firms are aware of every design variable and its effect on price and performance and they share this knowledge with us (a cabinet maker);

> We are directed towards suppliers in which our customer has both confidence and experience of (a supplier of loudspeaker systems);

> We learnt a great deal from both the Japanese affiliate and the supplier of the parent company about moulding and mechanical handling techniques (a plastic moulding firm).

On quality control and testing procedures, a number of suppliers confirmed the assertion of Japanese affiliates that their products were often sent to Japan for testing and final approval. But in the case of one large electronics company, help and advice was given by its Japanese customers in improving its own quality control procedures by setting up quality circles and by the introduction of the PPM scheme.

Some suppliers emphasised the meticulous attention to detail paid by Japanese affiliates, coupled with a willingness to provide managerial and/or organisation assistance to help the supplier if he ran into difficulties. On the other hand, the view was frequently stated that, beyond a point, quality standards could only be raised at the expense of productivity and/or an increase in reworked goods. One firm also claimed that Japanese specifications were often written up to a different format than those submitted by UK customers, and that this necessitated lengthy negotiations, and often some compromise on production yields or testing techniques; while another asserted the frequent revisions to its modes of working demanded by the new standards raised its overhead costs. Though generally suppliers felt that their productivity had been raised as a result of their contact with Japanese affiliates, several asserted that this was only achieved at the cost of lower all-round efficiency during the initial stages of production.

Apart from information, technical and managerial assistance, the 'greater assurance of where we stand in the future, which aids our forward planning' provided by Japanese customers was welcomed by many UK suppliers. Only one of the suppliers indicated that financial aid (e.g. long-term loans at reduced rates of interest, extended credit, advance payments for goods, etc.) was provided by a Japanese customer; in this instance it was to do with tooling costs. On the other hand, several subcontractors mentioned that Japanese firms either provided them with specialised tools and equipment, or bought them on their behalf. One supplier was given financial assistance towards a visit to its counterpart supplier in Japan.

To what extent are suppliers able and willing to meet Japanese purchasing standards? Most suppliers assert that from a technical standpoint they have no great difficulty in reaching these even if they were not initially familiar with the product or the production process required. The main problem seems to be, first, that such standards are not normally demanded by UK firms and second that, because of the low volume of orders, it is uneconomic to invest in the new machinery and training of workers needed to meet them. As suggested in an earlier chapter, further appreciation of the yen and increased investment by Japanese companies in the UK may make this kind of component production more viable in the future.

To quote again from one firm

For one particular job we were unable to provide the appropriate product at a price competitive with our customers Japanese supplier. It did not suit our long-term plans to invest in the type of equipment; however, were demand much higher (and guaranteed) we might reappraise the situation.

On the other hand, one plastic moulding company regarded its own workforce's attitude towards improving quality as a limiting factor. In its words

> There is no doubt that quality is the key word in our dealings with Japanese affiliates, and our unwillingness or inability to supply on occasion is connected with the daunting prospect of changing workforce attitudes towards quality. The 'quality is not my job' attitude is particularly prevalent in larger old established companies, where any change in job definition is often linked to pay.

Conditions Attached to Contracts Concluded with Japanese Affiliates

It is often alleged, and indeed in some cases shown to be the case, that multinational companies (or their affiliates) impose restrictions on the use of technology transferred to their subcontractors. We asked UK suppliers whether this was so in their dealings with Japanese affiliates.

The general answer is, there are few important covenants placed on subcontractors. Of the 20 firms, 15 indicated there were none at all. Three of the remainder, producing cabinets, plastic mouldings and specialised oils, asserted they were not allowed to (or agreed not to) sell their output to competitors or to penetrate certain export markets; two of the same firms and one electronics component supplier indicated they had agreed not to use some of the knowledge provided to produce competitive products; one – a specialised oil producer – agreed to sell its product only to the contracting firm; and five, including all the above and another electronics firm, said their own sourcing policy was influenced by that of their Japanese customers – partly it seems, to ensure quality, and partly to conform to rules of origin requirements.[8]

The Spillover Effects of Supplying Products to Japanese Affiliates

How far have the benefits gained from producing for Japanese affiliates spilt over to the rest of the suppliers production programme? In the case of six suppliers the answer is apparently not at all. As one chemical firm put it

> There have been no spillover effects; we have a number of UK customers who have standards at least equal to those of our Japanese customer.

Another seven suppliers thought their general attitude and approach to solving production problems had improved as a result of their contacts with Japanese firms; and that being required to produce at a lower profit margin forced them to be more cost conscious. Other suppliers were more specific in their remarks. One – Kenure Plastics – is on record in asserting that, as a direct result of dealing with Japanese affiliates, it has completely revolutionised its production methods and management philosophy,[9] and as a result is now premier supplier of high-quality precision mouldings. A supplier of electronics components asserted

> The spillover effect has ensured our quality control and process control has developed rapidly. Because of this pressure, it has enabled us to supply high-quality products to our other customers. We have also benefited from discussions on raw material usage and various other areas that have improved our overall business.

Another said that

> Because of a change in our quality philosophy to PPM, the control of production has improved and all our customers have benefited from this. We are now more aware of certain aspects of quality control based on specific customer requirements.

One supplier claimed that the Japanese approach to purchasing had spilled over to its own sourcing methods: 'We make higher demands on ourselves and our suppliers for better quality and delivery'. Another supplier to CTV set assemblers pointed to a more indirect effect of the Japanese presence.

> The influence of Japanese affiliates on the UK market place has not been directly on our firm as a supplier, but has been more significant in the commercial pressure applied to other CTV manufacturers who, in turn, have placed more stringent quality requirements on their suppliers – including ourselves.

Exchange of Visits

Visits by Suppliers

Japanese firms in Japan believe in keeping in close touch with and regularly visiting their suppliers. This philosophy also extends to their affiliates in the UK. But also they like to enourage visits by their more important suppliers in the UK either to their parent company in Japan or to the suppliers of the parent company.

Of the 19 suppliers providing us with data, nine had visited the parent company of one or more Japanese affiliates and eight their counterpart suppliers in Japan. Another six suppliers had visited 'related' Japanese companies, including competitors and plant and machinery manufacturers. Most of these visits were by Group 1 suppliers (i.e. those predominantly supplying products to the consumer electronics industry) and by those who supplied more than 20% of their output to Japanese affiliates. Usually the visits were once a year or more than once a year.

The benefits from visiting parent companies of their UK customers were mainly a better understanding of the Japanese mentality and working practices or, in the words of one supplier, 'of their good housekeeping and methodical working'. 'To help our understanding of the forward planning and thinking of our Japanese customers' was given as another reason for visiting the affiliate's parent company. Suppliers approaching their counterparts in Japan seem to feel their visits had been particularly worthwhile in acquiring new technical and process information, gaining an insight into specialised plant and, to quote from one supplier, 'The ability to compare our operation with similar Japanese operations

A large tube manufacturer was more specific

> As a result of our past visits to Japan, we have gained insight into integrated circuits designed into colour TV sets intended for the UK; and support for technical release of other components.

This company and others also expressed the value of 'empathy and understanding' gained through such visits, which were usually undertaken by the chief executives, senior technical managers, production and plant managers.

Visits to Suppliers

All but one of the 20 suppliers had been visited by one or more of their Japanese customers. Apart from the normal courtesy visits and those related to contract negotiations, most were of a technical character and usually involved senior production, design and quality control engineers and back-up personnel from the Japanese affiliate. In some cases, visits were paid specifically to assess the capability of a supplier in undertaking work; in others to monitor progress on existing contracts. The main benefits identified by suppliers were of three kinds: first, a better appreciation of the sourcing philosophy and needs of the Japanese customers; second, detailed help in production methods and work organisation; and third (and most important), assistance with quality control procedures.

The technical visits were often quite frequent, particularly in the case of suppliers who supplied a large proportion of their output to Japanese affiliates. Mullards, for example, had visits from the liaison engineers of their customers four times a year, and separate visits from management and quality engineers once a year.

Twelve of the affiliates, which had been visited by their Japanese customers, indicated this was usual practice in their experience and there was nothing distinctive about the Japanese interest in their operations. The balance, again exclusively supplying consumer electronics companies, thought there was a definite difference between the UK and Japanese customers in this respect. Our impression is that the answer may lie in (a) the extent to which the Japanese customers require higher standards than their UK competitors, and (b) the efficiency of the suppliers. One of the most frequent complaints voiced by Japanese affiliates concerns the quality of the non-electrical parts of a CTV or radio set; and it is the suppliers of these products which emphasise the distinctiveness of the interest by the Japanese in their operations. Size of supplier also seems to be relevant. None of the larger suppliers saw any difference between the interest shown by the UK and Japanese customer; most of the smaller ones did!

Several suppliers of Group 2 affiliates mentioned that their Japanese customers had organised seminars to assist employees to better understand their requirements. The message at these seminars was 'If you follow these steps, you will learn to meet our requirements'. Given the long-term relationships which some suppliers wish to establish with their Japanese customers, it is not surprising that some cannot refuse or take lightly such assistance and advice.[10]

A European Comparison

The JETRO survey on Japanese companies in Europe (JETRO, 1983) came to the following broad conclusions about the ability of UK, relative to other European suppliers to meet their procurement standards.

(1)   Problems faced by Japanese companies in the procurement of parts and materials in Europe were greatest in Italy, Ireland, and least in the Netherlands and West Germany. The UK was ranked 6th out of 8 countries as a problem-free country.

(2)   Local sourcing of raw materials, parts and machinery by all European affiliates of Japanese firms averaged 50%, 45% and 47%, respectively; the corresponding percentages for UK affiliates were 37%, 49% and 38%. Of the countries which recorded the highest percentages for local sourcing, Spain (75%, 53% and 50%) and Italy (71%, 68%, 61%) stand out; by contrast, the percentages for Ireland were very low (4%, 13% and 11%).

(3)   There was little difference in the reasons given for the percentage of outside procurement by companies according to their European location; failure to meet Japanese quality standards, unavailability of local supplies, and price being the main reasons mentioned by all affiliates.

(4)   Japanese affiliates in the UK are likely to give rather more help and guidance to their suppliers than are those in other European countries. It also appears that the technical problems of suppliers are less likely to be resolved in the UK than in other countries apart from in Spain and Ireland; and that, where solutions are possible, they need fairly drastic measures.

Conclusions

The experience and opinion of suppliers of Japanese affiliates seem to confirm those of the affiliates themselves. As one would expect, the suppliers believe they have good reasons for their occasional inability or unwillingness to supply items at the price and quality required; and several feel that the standards asked for are unnecessarily meticulous and not always appreciative of local supply constraints. Indeed, in some cases it appears that procurements demanded by the affiliate are even higher than those normally required in Japan – possibly so that the local managing director can impress his opposite number at home or justify to the UK authorities, continuing imports from Japan.

Several suppliers also thought that the UK government ought to do more to assist them to meet the demands of their Japanese customers. One suggested that the government might help to subsidise travel trips to Japanese factories to study Japanese methods; another to give cash grants to Japanese subsidiaries only on condition that they bought a certain proportion of their components and materials from UK (or EEC) sources. Two argued for import controls on competitive products; a reduction in energy costs was mentioned by one supplier, and better depreciation allowances and low interest loans for new plants by two others. One electronic components company echoed the feelings of most affiliates

> The government should continue to apply pressure on Japanese companies to source their supplies in the UK and urge targets for domestic sourcing as a condition for granting government aid; and also to step up protection against unfair competition from European suppliers, e.g. in the form of export subsidies.

One plastics moulding company thought the best contribution the government could make would be to

> educate the consumer that the perfection he expects when he buys a one off consumer durable will only be achieved if he plays his part at his workplace.

But at least two suppliers did not think the government ought to do anything. 'It's up to us' was the terse comment made.

This leads us into our final point which will be taken up again in Chapter 12. In our discussions with both Japanese affiliates and UK suppliers, it seems clear that a proportion – and perhaps a sizeable proportion – of the total purchases of CTV affiliates is unlikely to be provided by UK suppliers in the near future. This is because, whatever their technical capability, as long as the design of the final product (or, in the case of CTVs, of the chassis) is determined by the Japanese parent company, and the components are geared to that design, and unless UK competitors to, or suppliers, of Japanese affiliates are able to penetrate the Japanese market and influence these designs, it will not be possible for UK suppliers to secure the volume of output necessary to meet the prices of their Japanese counterparts.

However, while in part agreeing with this sentiment, one of the largest UK electronics companies was strongly of the view that the only way for UK companies to break into the Japanese market was for them to develop a particular ownership advantage of their own. To quote

> We believe that if British suppliers could offer the Japanese set manufacturers a new and viable system of integrated circuitry for CTV

chassis, they would be the first to buy it, but they need persuasion as, in Japan, most of the process innovation in this field is undertaken not by the component suppliers but by the CTV set assemblers.

One electronic components producer believed that the main problem lay in the inability of the UK suppliers effectively to penetrate the Japanese market and influence the design of integrated circuits for CTV production. In its words, the UK government should do everything possible

> to encourage Japanese affiliates to design their television chassis using European components. It is extremely difficult for European manufacturers to supply the affiliate if the design only uses Japanese integrated circuits.

The same company also felt that inter-government negotiations should focus more strongly on reducing non-tariff barriers which currently restricted European integrated circuit producers from selling to the major Japanese CTV companies. In its words:

> without selling our designs directly to major Japanese producers and benefiting from large volume business, we cannot hope to compete with our Japanese competitors, even on our own ground.

Notes

1. One of the suppliers only partially completed the questionnaire, so is not included in our statistical analysis.

2. In other words, we wanted to consider both successful and unsuccessful stores.

3. However, one other electronics supplier, though satisfied with its associations with the Japanese affiliates in the UK, was most dissatisfied with its dealings with their parent companies. The reason was cited earlier in Chapter 6.

4. One example cited by a producer of packaging materials was that Japanese purchasers expect (unrealistically in its eyes) the printing on cartons containing TV sets to be of the same standard as might be expected by a consumer buying a box of high-class chocolates. But this view was countered by a large UK motor car manufacturer who asserted the Japanese were entirely realistic in the standards they set.

5. NB. This refers to the first contact. Increasingly, it would seem contacts originate from both directions.

6. See also 'The Management Page', *Financial Times*, 10 October 1983.

7. Also asserted to be the case in the US. See JETRO (US), 1981, p. 30.

8. The case of one affiliate was particularly interesting. While its parent company drew its supplies from all over the world, it was required to source from approved factories of origin sited in Europe.

9. *Financial Times*, 10 October 1983.

10. Hayes (1982).

8 THE IMPACT OF JAPANESE AFFILIATES ON THEIR COMPETITORS

Introduction

We now briefly consider some of the possible ways in which Japanese manufacturing affiliates may have impinged on their indigenous competitors. In doing so we drew upon data provided by the affiliates and ten of their UK competitors.

Market Structure

Between them, the six Japanese affiliates producing colour TV sets accounted for 30% of the UK market in 1982 with individual shares ranging from 2% to 10%. By the middle of 1984 this share had risen to nearly 40%. Each regarded its main competitors as another Japanese affiliate, Thorn-EMI, Philips or Standard Telephones and Cables. Since none of the affiliates had a share of the market exceeding 10%, it may be reasonably assumed that they compete within a monopolistic competitive, veering towards an oligopolistic, market structure.[1] The one specialist producer of audio equipment asserted it had only one UK competitor, but many from overseas. The three suppliers of video recorders were the first to produce the product in the UK; they mainly compete with each other, Japanese and European imports, and other UK firms producing under Japanese licence.

At the time of their initial entry into the UK, Japanese CTV producers — apart from GEC-Hitachi — had about 7% of the UK market. GEC was already a major producer in its own right. It is then clear that the Japanese companies have quite dramatically increased their market share — especially since 1976 — but how much this is *specifically* due to their presence in the UK, it is impossible to say. It might be reasonably speculated however, that in the absence of any tariff or non-tariff barriers, the market penetration by the Japanese would unlikely to have been less and could have been more.

The position of one of the industrial electronics firms (NEC Semiconductors Ltd) which began manufacturing in 1982, is that its main competitors are either US subsidiaries in the UK, or Japanese-based companies. It is expected that this additional manufacturing facility — and that of Shin-Etsu in 1985 — will lead to more, rather than less, competition in the semiconductors and integrated circuit industry; at the same time, because the design of most components originate in Japan, the presence of Japanese affiliates *could* make it more difficult to develop an indigenous design capability in this important new industry.[2]

The market structure in which Group 2 affiliates operate varies a great deal. In the case of four affiliates, their share of the UK market was over 50%, and in seven others they were one of the three largest suppliers of their product range. In 11 out of 13 cases competition was oligopolistic veering towards monopolistic; and usually the affiliate was the first UK supplier of its product.

The reason for this more concentrated market structure is to do with the uniqueness of the product being supplied: although, interpreted more widely, the product may have its competitors. To take one example, Merlin Aerials is the largest producer of automatic (i.e. motorised) car aerials in the UK and sells to upmarket car producers, e.g. Rolls-Royce, Rover, Jaguar, etc.; but there are many producers of non-motorised aerials, and even the replacement market for motorised aerials is partly met from Far Eastern imports. Similarly, there is one Japanese firm which has the major share of the sale of ultraviolet curing inks, but it does not supply other types of inks. The sealed lead-acid batteries produced by Yuasa Battery is another example; they are mainly sold to industrial users and the company does not compete in the mass market for car batteries.[3]

The increase in the market share of most Group 2 affiliates since their establishment has been hardly less dramatic than that of Group 1 affiliates, the unweighted mean of market share rising from 15% to 34%. However, in the case of one light engineering, one chemical, and one 'other' affiliate, the market share has fallen due to new entrants and increased competition, both from UK and foreign based firms.[4] Excluding these three affiliates the shares quoted above would have been 6% and 43%.

We have shown (in Chapter 2) that, until the Sumitomo involvement in Dunlop, only one affiliate, viz. GEC-Hitachi, originated by way of a take-over or merger with an existing UK company. To this extent, then, the initial impact of Japanese direct investment had either helped to introduce a new range of products or to increase the number of competitive firms. Subsequently, however, such additional competition might lead to the rationalisation of a sector and an eventual decrease in the number of firms. This certainly occurred, as a result of the presence of US affiliates in the automobile industry in the interwar years and early postwar period; and it has happened more recently in the CTV, fire detector and zip fastener industries as a result of Japanese competition. However, as far as one can tell, most mergers and exits occurred prior to the start of Japanese *manufacturing* in the UK; one can therefore conclude their impact on market structure has not been a decisive one.

This does not mean the competitors of Japanese affiliates have been unaffected by their presence. Thorn-EMI has gone on record as saying that their whole approach to production and quality control has been revolutionised in the 1970s; and that the activities of Sony and Matsushita in the UK provided a major stimulus for this new approach. Austin Rover, however, assert that their association with Honda has had only a marginal (albeit a positive) affect on their management philosophy and techniques. They do, however, admit that competition from Japanese car manufacturers by creating a 'needs must' or 'change or bust' situation has dramatically affected 'every aspect of our organisation from research and development to after sales servicing'. More generally, when the Japanese affiliates were asked to give their assessment of the way in which they believed they had impacted on UK market structure, the responses given in respect of 27 major products can be seen in Table 8.1.

Table 8.1: Changes in Market Structure as Perceived by Japanese Affiliates

| | Group 1 affiliates | | Group 2 affiliates | |
	More concentration[a]	Less concentration	More concentration	Less concentration
More competition[b]	—	10	8	5
Less competition	1[c]	—	3[d]	—

NB; One Group 2 firm has remained the sole supplier of the goods being produced throughout its UK operations.
Notes: a. Defined as the share of three largest UK based firms of total of UK output.
b. Defined as more intensive or effective competition (as perceived by the affiliates). It is possible that increased concentration may result in more effective competition.
c. But more competition from imports.
d. One of which cited more competition from foreign sources.

Clearly, the great majority of affiliates thought their presence had enhanced competition within the UK; moreover, of the four which perceived this had been reduced as a result of rationalisation, three argued that, since their arrival they had been faced with ever more intensive competition from Far Eastern imports; fishing rods, spectacle lenses and radio sets were quoted as examples.

Only one thought the market for its products was genuinely less competitive than it was prior to its arrival in the UK.

Response of Competitors

The Perception of the Affiliates

How did Japanese firms consider their UK competitors had reacted to their presence? The most common perception, mentioned by two-thirds of affiliates, was that their competition has engaged in more intensive price or non-price competition; one firm specifically identified a price cutting programme on the part of its major (foreign) competitor; another cited the example of its main UK competitor pursuing a 'Buy goods from UK firms' policy; and a third, a policy of trade discounts to industrial buyers.

There were also some suggestions that competitors had reacted by improving product quality or diversifying their product range; or by providing better after sales servicing, and more reliable and speedier delivery dates. One affiliate, supplying motor car components, asserted that its major competitors responded to its presence by trying to conclude to a licensing agreement with one of its Japanese competitors. All of the main competitors of the Japanese CTV affiliates appear to have visited one of the latter's plants, and as a result (so it is asserted) have implemented some Japanese work methods. In three instances, it was claimed that competitors had been forced further to differentiate their products or the kind of markets they served. It also seems quite clear that, in the great majority of cases, the affiliates serve the top end of the market, and, in the case of industrial products, e.g. smoke detection equipment, circuit breakers, etc., prefer to sell to specialised, knowledgeable and trained buyers rather than to the trade in general.

It would also appear that Japanese firms perceive the quality of their competitors' products to have improved as a result of their presence in the UK. Three-fifths of firms suggested this was the most important outcome of competition which, in turn, 'constantly keeps us on our toes'. In the CTV sector, the affiliates also believed that there had been marked changes in their competitors' management style while the majority of Group 2 affiliates placed more emphasis on pricing policy and product innovation. Indeed, two or three affiliates thought that this was their major impact on their competitors; only rarely did they perceive marketing and distribution or production methods as being noticeably affected.

In both the CTV and the motor vehicle sectors, the Japanese penetration of the UK market, whether by imports or the presence of UK affiliates, has forced their major competitors — Thorn-EMI and British Leyland — to reappraise their sourcing production management, quality control and inspection procedures. Both companies strongly assert that the main thing they have learnt from the Japanese presence in the UK is 'an awareness of what can be done rather than any new technology or management philosophy'. Both, however, further allege that it is one thing to know what is needed, another to put this into practice in an established, cf. a greenfield operation — and a third, and altogether different proposition, for this to be imposed on a management and labour force familiar and comfortable with traditional and often unproductive working methods.

The Perception of the Competitors

We interviewed and/or received information from ten UK competitors of 12 Japanese affiliates; the following paragraphs summarise our overall impressions.

(1) The three competitors to Group 1 affiliates agreed that the impact of the latter on their behaviour was greater than that of other competitors; but little more than it would have been had the UK market been served by direct imports from Japan. Of the seven competitors to Group 2 affiliates, two thought their behaviour had been more affected, and two (both producing ophthalmic lenses) that it had been less affected. It should be recalled that Group 2 affiliates are subject to more import competition than are Group 1 affiliates.

(2) Both Group 1 and Group 2 competitors were unanimous in their perception that the main impact of Japanese affiliates in the UK had been in two main functional areas: (a) product design and (b) cost and quality control. One optical lens manufacturer thought the Japanese had 'taken an early lead in the introduction of a new range of lens'; while Group 2 competitors noted that they had forced price reductions in the industry — partly by making their competitors more cost conscious and partly by their attempts to capture a larger share of

the UK market.

(3) When asked about the areas in which Japanese affiliates were perceived to have a competitive edge, those most frequently mentioned were

(i)   purchasing techniques;
(ii)   access to technology, information and advice of parent company;
(iii) management style;
(iv)   in-house quality control; and
(v)   ability to take advantage of bulk buying of components and parts by the Japanese parent company.

It was also asserted, particularly by CTV competitors, that the greenfield investments by Japanese affiliates in regions of above average unemployment had provided an additional benefit in the form of regional incentives, and assisted them in concluding no strike and one union agreements. The 'more efficient computer systems for controlling material flows of our main Japanese competitor' was mentioned by one ballbearing company; while a producer of circuit breakers summed it up as follows: 'they are better organisers of people, machines and methods than we are'.

On the other hand, it was clear that most UK companies thought they had the edge over their Japanese competitors in marketing; all but one company believed this to be the weakest functional area of the affiliates. Views on production methods were mixed; the three CTV companies − one British, one Dutch and one American − thought that, as of the end of 1983, their production methods matched those of the Japanese. But one of the firms went on to say 'mind you, we have learnt a lot from the Japanese, particularly with respect to chassis design, quality control and testing procedures'. Another thought the real test would come if and when the affiliates undertook more design and development work in the UK. The CTV companies also agreed that Japanese affiliates had the edge on industrial relations, though this view was not shared by competitors to Group 2 affiliates. Opinions were also mixed on inventory control and product policy.

(4) As might be expected, the response to competition from Japanese affiliates had been varied. At the one extreme, we have the example of IMI choosing to leave the zip fastener business altogether, rather than

retaliate to the presence of **YKK** — the world's leading producer of zip fasteners.[5] At the other — as typified by the response of Thorn-EMI — UK companies have fought Japanese competition by improving their own product designs, production methods and quality control procedures; and by devoting a higher proportion of their resources to product and marketing development. When asked to rank (on a scale 0-5) their reaction to the Japanese presence the following average scores were recorded.

(1)	To improve product quality	3.25
(2)	To diversity into new product areas	2.88
(3)	To look for ways to reduce costs	2.75*
(4)	To be more price competitive	2.38
(5)	To improve inventory control	1.50
(6)	To tighten up quality control, testing and inspection procedures	1.38
(7)	To advertise or market more aggressively	1.63
(8)	To seek new markets	1.50*
(9)	To upgrade and better control purchasing standards	0.88
(10)	To conclude licensing arrangements with other freight companies	0.25

Those scores marked with an asterisk were ranked particularly highly by the CTV companies.

(5) All except one of the UK competitors thought the presence of Japanese affiliates in the UK had been beneficial to their motivation and efficiency. The exception was in the CTV industry, where it was felt that, since most Japanese affiliates in the UK were still 'offshore assemblers', the real competition continued to emanate from the Japanese parent companies.

(6) The general opinion among competitors was that Japanese direct investment in UK industry was good for the UK economy, in so far as it showed that the advantages commonly ascribed to Japanese firms could be successfully transferred to a UK culture. More specifically, mention was made of 'improved standard of product and product specification'. One firm argued the main benefit was 'good for our drive for quality and efficiency; and good for management in forcing them to be closer to the "coal face"'. At the same time, two important disadvantages were perceived. The first was the tendency of some

Japanese affiliates to engage in aggressive penetration pricing (in some cases by dumping,[6] and this may have destroyed some capacity in UK industry which cannot easily be replaced. The second was the concern, expressed most forcibly by the CTV companies, that, as a result of the Japanese gaining a larger share of the CTV market the UK might lose some of its design capability as the majority of the R & D capability of Japanese companies is still located in Japan.

In conversations with Austin Rover, it is clear that the main advantage it perceives to have resulted from its agreement with Honda to produce the Triumph Acclaim is the improvement brought about in Austin Rover's quality control and testing methods, from the point of purchasing right through to the inspection of the end product. Austin Rover accepts that there was some transfer of design knowledge derived from the agreement,[7] particularly in respect of interior trim and finish of the vehicle, but they believe the real gain has been in the assistance given by Japanese engineers and technicians towards achieving the kind of quality and productivity standards normally accepted in Japanese factories.[8] To quote

The Japanese have given us a heightened sense of awareness of what must be done to improve our performance standards and have helped demonstrate that it can be done; they have not so much helped improve our knowledge about standards as on ways to achieve and stick to the standards which we know can be obtained.

An Additional Note on the CTV Sector

A decade ago there were no Japanese affiliates producing CTV sets in the UK. Thorn-EMI, Rediffusion, Rank, Pye, GEC, Decca, Philips, Jankeig and ITT (the last two being wholly or partly foreign owned) accounted for the entire market. In 1983, 53% of the market was served by Sanyo, Toshiba, GEC/Hitachi, Tatung (a Taiwaian firm), Mitsubishi, Matsushita, Sony, ITT, Amstrad and Binatone; and the balance by Philips, Thorn, Fidelity and Rediffusion. The change has been particularly dramatic since 1979, as illustrated in Figure 8.1.

While the increasing share of Far Eastern companies is partly in place of direct imports from Japan and elsewhere, it is widely accepted that the quality and reliability of Japanese CTV sets (wherever they were produced) was very much higher than that of their European competitors in the mid and late 1970s. For example, surveys by the Consumers

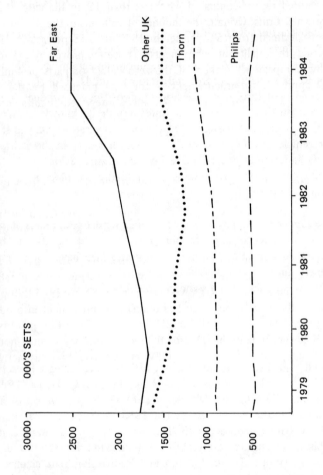

Figure 8.1: UK Colour Television Production, 1979-84

000'S SETS

Far East

Other UK

Thorn

Philips

30000

2500

200

1500

1000

500

1979   1980   1981   1982   1983   1984

Association showed that whereas in 1975/6, some 58% of CTV sets produced by UK owned companies needed repairs wthin a year of purchase, the relevant percentage for sets produced by Japanese-owned companies was 10%. By 1982, however, the gap had been greatly narrowed; in that year, only 7% of CTV sets produced by UK-owned firms needed repair, compared with less than 1% in the case of Japanese-owned firms. Overall, the number of call-outs in the first year on UK sets declined from 5% per set in 1977 to 0.58 per set in 1982.

Second, the quality of components has been improved by the adoption by European set makers of the zero defect or parts per million (PPM) approach to procurement – for long practised by the Japanese. In 1977, the failure rate of UK-made integrated circuits used in CTVs was 37,000 per million; by 1982 the rate on more complicated circuits was down to 1,500 per million – a 25-fold improvement. In tuners there has been a 37-fold improvement. The failure rate on the cathode ray tube is now down to 6,000 per million; while among low volume components, that of British made diodes has fallen from 1,740 per million in 1977 to 15 per million in 1982.

Third, within UK CTV plants production rejects have fallen. In 1977 an average of 2.5 faults per set were found on UK production lines; by 1982, this had been reduced to 0.4.

How far these improvements can be attributed *specifically* to the Japanese presence in the UK is difficult to say. However, one telling fact is that in the case of CTV sets produced by Continental European producers there has been much less dramatic improvement in product reliability. For example, in 1982, 25% of sets made in Europe outside the UK needed repairs in the first 12 months. It may or may not be coincidental that the Japanese CTV affiliates are not as actively involved on the Continent as in the UK.

Conclusions

Our findings suggest that the presence of Japanese manufacturing affiliates has been generally beneficial to both market structure and the performance of UK competitors. Perhaps even more important is the fact that, had the Japanese CTV companies decided to locate their plants elsewhere in Europe than in the UK, there would be both fewer TV sets produced in the UK and less competition among the indigenous manufacturers (which include other foreign affiliates). While rationalisation and closure of plants has most certainly occurred, it seems likely this is less the result of the Japanese presence *per se*, as that the growth in international competition — particularly from other parts of Europe and the Far East. What the presence of the Japanese affiliates has demonstrated, however, is that it is possible efficiently to produce and sell CTV sets in the UK; and most certainly this has spilled over and affected (mostly to the good) the major competitors.

While the data for UK firms are insufficiently disaggregated to allow a precise comparison to be made, our impression is that Japanese affiliates are not noticeably concentrated in sectors with above average concentration ratios, although both Group 1 and Group 2 affiliates do tend to favour sectors which produce branded goods and spend above the average on advertising.

Notes

1. The concentration index (measured by the output of the five largest enterprises as a % of all UK output) in the colour TV industry was 55%, only slightly above the average for all quoted minimum list headings in 1979.

2. We take up this point later in Chapter 11.

3. Indeed because of excess capacity in the UK battery industry, Yuasa agreed not to compete with UK indigenous firms in the products they produced for a period of ten years.

4. That is to say, although the sales of the Japanese affiliate are more than they used to be prior to its presence, those of competitor firms have risen even faster.

5. Withdrawals have also occurred in other sectors, notably audio equipment, car aerials, fishing rods, optical lens and no-fuse circuit breakers.

6. For the most part this has been successfully counteracted by the EEC anti-dumping duties.

7. As perceived by the manager most closely associated with the project.

8. As part of the deal, Honda provided the engine and the gear box and the basic design of the car. But about 70% of the ex-factory price of the Honda Acclaim is local (i.e. European) value added.

THE IMPACT OF JAPANESE AFFILIATES ON
THEIR CUSTOMERS

The Destination of Sales

About one half of Japanese affiliates sell their output direct to their
own sales and/or marketing affiliates. Of the balance, seven sell mainly
to industrial customers and five to wholesalers, retailers or mail order
houses.

The form of the sales varies with the nature of the product. Most
consumer goods and standardised industrial products are sold on the
spot market, and most industrial and a few idiosyncratic consumer products by way of 6 month-1 year contracts or gentlemen's agreements.
As a rough estimate, about 60% of the output of affiliates in 1983 was
sold to their own marketing subsidiaries, 15% on external contract and
the balance on the spot market.

Sales and Marketing Techniques

Chapter 4 showed that Japanese affiliates are only moderately influenced by Japanese marketing and sales methods, and that in the case of
only one company was there a strong degree of centralised control over
such methods. However, the same work application and company
philosophy which motivates production management and factory
workers extends into the sales and marketing area; and so one finds no
less intensive and dedicated efforts directed both to providing the
appropriate technical back-up service to customers and to after sales
service.

In answer to the question, 'What if anything distinguishes marketing
and distribution methods among Japanese affiliates compared to UK
companies?', there were two recurring perceptions voiced by the
Japanese affiliates. The first, is that the marketing function is completely different from the manufacturing function and should be
regarded as a very special skill to be nurtured by training; the second
was that the salesman were 'out of their office getting business' very
much more than their UK counterparts.

Several affiliates endorsed the importance of providing full technical advice to industrial users (particularly on the installation of equipment, and, in one case, on safety standards), information on new products and market trends, arranging group conferences for customers to exchange information and ideas, and closely working together with clients on any problems they may face. Most also stressed their speed, reliability and frequency of delivery *vis-à-vis* their UK competitors.

Our general understanding, however, is that there is nothing distinctively Japanese about these and other practices; and that for the most part, neither in the terms of selling (e.g. with respect to discounts to wholesalers and retailers or other dealing arrangements)[1] nor in their marketing, e.g. distributing or advertising techniques, do they have much (if anything) to teach their UK competitors. Apart from the top sales personnel in Group 1 affiliates, it is not normal for training to be given in Japan; although regular international conferences or seminars are held in which a certain amount of Japanese philosophy is inculcated. The only difference is, perhaps, a greater emphasis given in marketing to *quality and reliability* of the end product; and the provision of rather more technical data. Generally speaking, the sales literature of Japanese affiliates is attractive, articulate and comprehensive.

Because of the separation of the marketing from the production function of Japanese affiliates and because the sales office also markets products imported from Japan, the number of personnel engaged in marketing activities is not very meaningful. It is not our impression, however, that the Japanese affiliates allocate proportionately more resources to the sales function.

Note

1. The Japanese colour TV producers mostly operate through authorised dealers and accept discounting in the way other UK based firms do. They do not, however, normally supply the rental market which is largely dominated by Thorn-EMI and related companies. This marketing decision has indirectly helped to raise product quality, in that it has eliminated one of the criticisms of rented sets, viz. product unreliability. Moreover, as noted earlier, although Japanese made CTV sets rarely need repairing, where they do, the cost involved is usually very considerable indeed. Hence the preference of rental companies for UK designed sets.

10 LABOUR RELATED QUESTIONS

Introduction

A good deal of attention has already been given to the personnel policy of, and industrial relations, within Japanese affiliates in the UK.[1] In this chapter, we shall concentrate on the Japanese impact on a number of labour-related issues; and the extent to which Japanese style personnel practices have been successfully translated into a UK environment.

Some Background Statistics

Employment Data

Table 10.1 presents details on the structure of employment in Japanese affiliates at the end of 1982. Of the 4,857 employees, just over 56% were women; this proportion ranged from 64% for 'other' affiliates and 61% for Group 1 affiliates to 17% for chemical affiliates and 29% for light engineering affiliates. The proportion of factory operatives to all workers in Group 1 affiliates averaged 75%, and in Group 2 affiliates 67%.

The structure of the labour force reflects both industry and Japanese-specific characteristics. The colour TV set industry, for example, employs a higher proportion of female workers, and the chemical industry a lower proportion. The ratio of non-operatives tends to be higher in Group 2 affiliates, which are generally smaller and less automated than Group 1 affiliates. The significance of supervisory (foreman and above) and office personnel fluctuates wildly among the affiliates and we were unable to draw any useful conclusions.

What does seem clear, however, is that the age structure of factory workers employed by Japanese affiliates is very different to that of their UK competitors. It seems to be a policy of most affiliates to recruit their labour – particularly female labour – directly from school, and inculcate them with the Japanese 'way of doing things' right from the start. This is the practice in Japan, and it has been applied with much vigour and determination in the UK. Because, too, the Japanese affiliates are generally located in areas of above average unemployment,

153

they have been able to be very selective in their hiring policies. Several affiliates emphasised that they look particularly for applicants likely to work hard and as part of a team, and to take pride in themselves, their work and their company.

Table 10.1: Structure of Workforce in Japanese Manufacturing Affiliates, end 1982

| | Group 1 | | Group 2 | | | Total | % |
	Eng.	Chem.	Other	All			
Male	1,501	445	88	83	616	2,117	43.6
Female	2,388	185	18	149	352	2,740	56.4
	3,889	630	106	232	968	4,857	100.0
Operative	2,924	436	62	143	641	3,565	73.5
Non-operative	965	194	14	89	327	1,292	26.5
	3,889	630	106	232	968	4,857	100.0
Japanese nationals	92	36	5	9	50	142	
(% of all employees)	(2.4)	(5.7)	(4.7)	(3.9)	(5.2)	(2.9)	

Because of their branch plant status, foreign affiliates usually employ a lower percentage of administrative and sales workers. Except in the CTV sector, this was not so in the case of the Japanese affiliates, possibly because most of them were fairly new and small. However, compared with an average of 37.4% of non-operative to total workers in all UK establishments producing electrical appliances for domestic use in 1979, the corresponding ratio for Japanese affiliates was 20.5%.

Research and Development in Japanese Affiliates

Perhaps the area of greatest difference in the number of personnel employed by Japanese affiliates, compared with both their parent companies and UK competitors, is in pre-production activities. In 1982, only four Group 1 and three Group 2 affiliates did any genuine research and development and design work, although several others did a limited amount of testing and quality inspection and product and process adaptation. At a rough estimate, in December 1982 about 50 or 0.9% of the total workforce in Japanese affiliates were engaged on R & D related activities. In Japan, the average *expenditure* on R & D as a percentage of total sales was 4.0% for Group 1 affiliates and 2.0% for

Group 2 affiliates. In the UK, the major indigenous competitor to the Japanese CTV affiliates — Thorn EMI — is thought to allocate about 3.5% of its sales to R & D. Only in the case of one light engineering affiliates was the R & D done in the UK an important proportion of the total R & D budget of the Japanese enterprise of which it was part, viz. 28%. Among Group 1 affiliates, both the longest established ventures and the joint ventures, viz. GEC-Hitachi and J2T, undertake some R & D. It is also worth mentioning that only four of the Japanese MNEs with UK manufacturing affiliates undertake R & D elsewhere in the world.[2]

As in other functional areas, strategies towards R & D in their UK affiliates vary among Japanese affiliates. At the one end of the scale, GEC-Hitachi has its own product design department employing over a score of people; Sony is aiming to set up a European design centre for CTV production; and Matsushita is actively developing computer control tuning systems and new chassis designs (using the PAL system) in conjunction with Mullard and Plessey. Indeed, as new communications and media technologies develop in Japan, these companies may well relocate some of their more traditional R & D activities in Europe.[3]

At the other end of the scale, it would seem that the Mitsubushi plant is unlikely to be more than an offshore assembly operation for the foreseeable future. Sanyo comes somewhere in between, while so far up to the middle of 1984 at any rate, Toshiba (UK) had not got the management resources to engage in serious development work.

The Role of Japanese Expatriates

There were 142 Japanese nationals employed by the 23 affiliates, just 2.9% of the total workforce. Apart from one affiliate employing only two people — both Japanese — the proportions varied from 20% in the case of one chemical firm to zero in the case of one engineering and one other affiliate. At least 90% of the Japanese were employed in a managerial, professional, supervisory or advisory capacity; so, as a proportion of non-operative labour force, they accounted for 11.6%. As indicated in Chapter 4, in 20 of the affiliates the managing director was a Japanese national; there were also 57 other Japanese directors or heads of sections.

Almost all Japanese expatriate appointments — including that of the chief executive — are short-term appointments, usually 3-5 years. The propensity to employ such personnel varies with the philosophy and management style of the parent company. Affiliates most strongly controlled by their parent companies tend to employ rather more Japanese than those who are not. The age of the affiliate is also relevant — older affiliates employ fewer Japanese than younger affiliates (although both Sony and YKK are exceptions);[4] as is the nature of the product and production process — the more important the human component in assuring quality control, the more Japanese personnel seem to be present. All the affiliates assert their ultimate aim is to completely indigenise the labour force and eight have come near to achieving this objective;[5] however, even in these affiliates, there are frequent visits to and from Japan for the exchange of ideas, re-training and technical guidance.

Labour Quality and Motivation

The perception of the parent companies of Japanese affiliates of labour conditions in the UK in the late 1960s and early 1970s was, generally, a very unfavourable one.[6] Most affiliates state quite categorically that, had it not been for language difficulties, and a feeling of cultural affinity between Japan and the UK, the Low Countries and Germany would have been the preferred location for their initial investment. In the mid 1980s, for reasons outlined in Chapter 3, the situation in the UK is viewed more optimistically, though as is evident in the current discussions with intending Japanese investors, industrial relations remain a key concern.[7]

The facts — for one reason or another — are very different from the expectations. In only one Japanese affiliate — GEC-Hitachi — has there been a single day lost from strikes or disruptive action. In all but two affiliates, there is either no formal union representation (in eight affiliates) or just one union; and in all but two the managing director of the affiliate asserted that he was either 'very pleased' or 'pleased' with the relations established with his workforce.

Each affiliate was asked the question

How satisfied are you with (a) the quality, (b) the motivation of (1) shopfloor workers, (2) other workers, (3) line management. Rank your answers 1-5, 5 representing the highest degree of satisfaction.

The results are set out in Table 10.2.[8] Taking Group 1 affiliates first, all companies except one ranked the *quality* of UK workers of 4 or 5;

but two affiliates thought slightly less highly of UK line managers. Rankings for *motivation* were slightly lower, with that of supervisory and line management scoring the best.[9, 10]

Table 10.2: The Quality and Motivation of Labour and Management in Japanese Affiliates (as perceived by the Chief Executive in Japanese Affiliates)

| | Group 1 | | Group 2 | | | Total |
	Engineering	Chemical	Other	All	
Quality of:						
Shopfloor workers	4.3	3.3	4.5	4.3	3.9	4.0
Other workers	4.2	3.3	4.3	4.3	3.8	3.9
Supervisory and management	4.0	3.6	4.5	3.8	3.8	3.9
Motivation of:						
Shopfloor workers	3.5	3.5	3.8	3.5	3.7	3.6
Other workers	3.5	3.5	4.0	4.0	3.5	3.6
Supervisory and management	4.0	3.6	3.8	4.3	4.0	3.9

Worker and management quality scored slightly less well for Group 2 affiliates, although most of the '3s' — there were no scores below this figure — were in the light engineering sector. Worker and management motivation were ranked 3 or 4, except in one chemical affiliate and one 'other' affiliate where operator motivation was ranked 2.

One of the main causes of satisfaction among Japanese affiliates has been the willingness of workers to undertake more than one job. Work flexibility and the absence of job demarcation is a particular feature of Japanese industry; it goes alongside job security and worker involvement in decision-making. In 20 of the 23 affiliates, workers are trained for more than one job; the usual number given was two or three, but one affiliate said 'many' and another 'several'. Though, initially, it appears there was some reluctance or hesitation in accepting the principle of job flexibility, the great majority of affiliates claim the attitude of workers is now very favourable.

Which of the Japanese style practices have the Japanese affiliates found least desirable or the most difficult to introduce into the UK? Here a general point should be made. Our perception of the Japanese management style in the UK is that the Japanese wish to accept as many of the local personnel policies and industrial relations procedures as they possibly can. To this extent, they delegate a great deal of responsibility to British personnel managers. The main concern of the Japanese is twofold; first to produce the right quality of product at the right price; and second to acknowledge the value of each worker in contributing to this goal. To this end, they are concerned with ensuring that each individual (1) understands the work standards expected of him or her (these include timekeeping and cleanliness, as well as quality control), and (2) is properly looked after and encouraged to share in the company's goals and aspirations, e.g. by being kept informed about its progress and problems, identifying with its goals and participating in decision-taking.

The first priority perceived by the Japanese is then to get the philosophy of personnel policy right; to this end, and as quoted by the managing director of one large CTV company,

> The responsibility for our employees starts and ends with me. My personnel manager is responsible for administering a policy which is part and parcel of our company's overall product and production strategy.

Other statements about the philosophy of Japanese management speak for themselves

> Being a Japanese affiliate has meant that our workforce has been willing to try new ideas; however, the novelty of any new idea is all too frequently attributed to the Japanese influence, even if it comes from the UK (a CTV set producer).

> Japanese management style is an open one, and relies upon a participative and co-operative workforce; the British, however, tend to prefer a clearer direction and emphasise management responsibility. But the most important part of our philosophy is caring for people; we put this above everything else (a CTV set producer).

> The most perceived Japanese style of management is inimitable as far as it relates to managing people. The major aspect of our case refers to production methods and control. Both are highly systemised and, in effect, regulate all working patterns and habits (a CTV set producer).

It seems quite clear, however, that all labour-related questions are a means to this end. Many detailed examples might be given of the way the practices seem to differ between affiliates and UK firms, and between the affiliates themselves. Certainly not all the affiliates — particularly in Group 2 — were influenced by Japanese management styles. But let us now detail several areas in which they were practised, and two (wage negotiation and wage determination) in which they were not.

Work Flexibility

We have already indicated that Japanese factories favour work flexibility and that, in many factories, workers are trained to do several tasks. This goes alongside the distaste of the Japanese for having to lay off employees in times of falling demand or structural change. However, in the Japanese context, work flexibility needs to be interpreted very broadly; it may include not only a different job in the same factory, but a job in a different factory of the same company, even if this is overseas. It is also usual for workers to be given general titles for their work, e.g. shop floor worker. Demarcation by craft or seniority tends to be discouraged; and although there is grading, e.g. by age, experience or skill, discrimination is kept to the very minimum and everyone is expected to 'muck in as necessary'.

Japanese companies are used to flexible manufacturing systems in their domestic factories; they stress the importance of this even more in the UK because of the smaller size of factories and the greater unreliability of suppliers. It is made easier by the fact that many affiliates are not unionised or only operate with one union. But Japanese managers are not afraid to argue the case for work flexibility to their employees as they believe it is to the latter's advantage; it is often mentioned at the time of recruitment, and the principle is sometimes enshrined in work agreements. As one company put it,[11]

> We work as a team to let employees know about company objectives and their relations to them. We want to get a feeling of involvement by our employees, coupled with work flexibility and no demarcation. This means no discrimination.

Some affiliates observed that there was some initial resistance to work flexibility, mainly because of traditional working practices; and this was particularly noticeable among Group 2 affiliates. One radio set producer said that women workers were not enthusiastic because they were happy with repetitive tasks and 'to be near their friends'. Another CTV affiliate commented

Most of our workers prefer to move their jobs around providing that they are consulted about the moves and they are not redeployed simply to give job satisfaction. Many people prefer a predictable job at which they are competent, rather than change.

Recruitment Policies

In Japan it is usual for companies to recruit directly from school leavers rather than the labour market; and very rarely from other firms. This is also part of the lifelong employment philosophy of the companies.[12] Moreover, the manner of recruitment is laid down. Applicants are first sifted out (from detailed school and other reports) on the basis of their character and attitude to work. Those thought appropriate are then interviewed to test their technical or professional capabilities.

Most Group 1 affiliates and a few of Group 2 affiliates try and implement this policy in the UK – particularly in the recruitment of female labour. *Inter alia* this has meant little poaching by Japanese affiliates of local labour. In five cases – Toshiba, GEC-Hitachi, Mitsubishi, Sanyo and J2T – there was a factory on site, and the new owners were able to choose from the workforce previously employed: otherwise 80% of the factory workforce has been hired from schools. More recently some Group 1 affiliates have modified this recruitment policy. In the words of one Welsh affiliate

We started off by recruiting female school leavers but found them undisciplined, bad timekeepers and lacking in motivation. In Japan they would have been trained to be housekeepers. Nowadays we prefer to employ 20-25 aged married women. They often need the money, have learnt to manage their own homes and have a greater sense of responsibility.

Managers and professional staff are usually recruited through the national press, often with the help of an executive search company.

In the 14 Group 2 affiliates, there were fewer discernible Japanese influences on hiring policy; the one most frequently cited was the preferred recruitment of school leavers.

The average age of employees in all affiliates in the UK was 27.5 years compared with around 30.0 for Japanese affiliates in Europe. Recruitment is mainly undertaken via newspaper advertisements and both public and private employment agencies, and the pattern is similar in most parts of Europe (JETRO, 1983).

Work Discipline

There is no doubt that the Japanese do make particular and unique demands on their workers, which some commentators have criticised as being authoritarian and paternalistic. The Japanese argue that they are necessary to achieve their production goals. First, is the importance paid to timekeeping. In Japan, hours of work mean the hours at the work bench; in the UK (so it is asserted) the time is interpreted as the time of arrival at to the time of departure from the factory gates. Some Japanese affiliates have attempted to encourage a sense of punctuality in their workers by timekeeping bonuses or penalties, but most try and achieve this by verbal persuasion. This has met with some success as reflected in the much better timekeeping and lower absenteeism ratio in Japanese affiliates. For example, absenteeism rates among Group 1 affiliates ranged from 50 to 75% of the average in the region in which they are situated in the years 1981-2; and for Group 2 affiliates 85-95% of the average.

Japanese affiliates are also particularly strict on cleanliness. Operatives, rather than specially employed cleaners, are usually responsible for clearing up their work areas after the day's work; this responsibility may extend to social facilities and washrooms as well. The timing of lunch and other breaks is rigorously monitored and chattering at the work benches or in the office is discouraged. This all gives the impression of a somewhat military regime. But again, as the affiliates are at pains to emphasise, it is just one aspect of a holistic approach to management. As one managing director of a CTV affiliate put it

> We are strong as our weakest link. We are determined that undisciplined labour should not be that weakest link.

Employee Compensation and Working Conditions

Wage Negotiation. At least one half of the Japanese affiliates assert they do not negotiate about wages and working conditions. They — and usually this means the managing director of the affiliate sometimes with the advice of the personnel manager — discuss with the appropriate employee representatives or a joint consultative panel of workers and management, proposed wage increase and/or wage relativities. In such cases it is normal for data to be obtained on wages paid by other Japanese affiliates in the region and other firms in the industry. Detailed information about the affiliate's performance is usually (but not always) laid on the table alongside the proposed wage settlement. At this point, it appears that the workers will normally agree to the settlement, although it may be it is left to them to decide on how exactly the increase is allocated between differnt grades of employees, or between different forms of payment, e.g. incentives, improved working conditions, etc. It also seems that the joint committees help fix the structure of wages between different grades of labour.[13]

In the area of wage negotiation, the Japanese prefer to leave the bargaining to UK personnel; if anything – and this point was made by several UK personnel managers of Japanese affiliates – because of their dislike of adversary industrial relations, they tend to give in to the demand of workers more easily than their UK counterparts.[14] If it is not peace at any price, the Japanese try their very hardest to avoid anything which may interfere with the smooth running of their operations.

Wage Determination. Wages are mainly determined by similar criteria to those used by UK firms. There are some differences between affiliates, but in the main, given the age, experience and skill mix, they are based upon rates paid in the region by other Japanese affiliates (this is especially so in Wales), other firms in the same industry, and internal performance. The offer then made is usually slightly above average or average for the industry and/or region.[15] The Japanese are especially sensitive to being accused of poaching from local firms through high wage offers.[16]

The method of assessing individual achievement and responsibility varies between affiliates, but most employ some kind of job-evaluation scheme. As Appendix A to the chapter we include a scheme currently employed by one Group 2 affiliate. It is not untypical of those in use by other Japanese affiliates.

Incentives. It is also the policy of most Japanese affiliates not to offer many monetary incentives. In Japan, it is thought neither necessary nor desirable; Japanese workers work out of loyalty, pride and sometimes fear of not being seen to offer their best. Incentives, then, are not part of the bargaining process but often 'gratitude' payments (e.g. Christmas bonuses, free holidays, food hampers, etc.) are made to workers who have excelled,[17] while achievements are publicised, e.g. by way of certificates, plaques and the like. In the words of one CTV affiliate

> We offer no monetary incentives. We believe that high recruitment standards make this unnecessary. On the other hand, we take care to inform and praise when good performance is achieved. Also we pay

special attention to providing good social facilities.

We came across only one major exception to this major principle. One assembler of hairdressing chairs indicated that since the top position in the affiliate would always be held by Japanese nationals, UK employees needed 'good incentives to compensate for lack of promotion possibilities'.

In the UK, incentives are deeply ingrained in the rewards system. The UK worker feels he should be remunerated for doing over and above what he considers to be 'the normal course of duty'; and this includes timekeeping!

The Japanese also argue that one of the best incentives for workers is for everyone to be treated equally and for there to be the freest possible communications upwards from the shopfloor. 'We believe the only real incentive is that provided by a management style which combines commercial reality and firmness with a caring attitude' was the way in which one CTV affiliate expressed it.

'A contented worker is likely to be a good worker' is the philosophy to which most companies would give lip service; the Japanese treat it very seriously. Almost every affiliate has lines of communication between management and workforce clearly laid down; compared with most UK companies, the sharing of information, opinions and ideas is less vertically and more horizontally structured.[18]

The Role of TUs

Trades unions are represented in 15 of the 23 manufacturing affiliates. All of the rest except one have agreed sole negotiating rights with a single union,[19] and in at least three cases there are closed shop agreements. In a few cases, the exclusion of trade unions is deliberate management policy; in others, the workers were offered the chance to belong to a union but they refused. Most of the smaller Group 2 affiliates claim that their size and family atmosphere make trade union involvement irrelevant. In the great majority of affiliates, there are ample opportunities for the representation of workers' views on almost every issue.

We have indicated that most wage negotiations are conducted through consultative committees. But most of the time of such committees, and others like them, are spent on production and allied issues. Like others who have written on this subject,[20] we have been impressed at the frequency and extent of discussions between workers and management. This extends from a short daily get-together, in which information is shared on matters of mutual interest, to detailed discussions, e.g. in quality circles, about very specific work problems. Again the Japanese philosophy is to encourage a family atmosphere, in which workers and management each have their distinctive role to play, but each is working for the company's (i.e. family's) good. Although differences of views and perspectives will inevitably occur, underlying such differences, as one UK personnel manager put it, 'we are all in the same boat and we sink or swim together'.

In their dealings with UK TUs – mainly the EETPU, TGWU, AUEW and GMWU – the Japanese have nothing but praise. Six companies have now signed, or are in the process of negotiating, no strike agreements with the EETPU. This union, which is one of the most progressive of all unions in the UK, has also assisted Japanese companies in their recruitment; and its representatives have visited Japan to study industrial relations issues there. How far this reflects a 'honeymoon' relationship it is too early to say; but it would appear that the Japanese approach has much to offer (at least on paper!) and that the unions are willing to put it to the test.[21]

Other Practices

Much play is made in the popular press about Japanese practices such as wearing of company overalls or jackets, morning exercises, communal dining facilities and the like. But, once again, to take any of these in isolation misses the point. It is true that the majority of factories require all personnel to wear similar clothing. But this is less to promote an atmosphere of equality or conformity as to encourage the workforce to identify itself with the common objective and philosophy of the company.[22] Most workers, and particularly younger ones, seem to like this idea and, in several cases, have enthusiastically designed the outfits. We came across no case of 'early morning exercises' and the like; on the other hand, a 10-15 minute morning assembly, post-shift discussions and divisional meetings (once a week) to exchange views on company progress, targets, quality, etc. are commonplace. Group discussions are kept as informal as possible and aimed at achieving the maximum amount of personal contact. The communal dining room is also liked; again it is accepted as a sign of a non-discriminatory policy of management towards different grades of workers; and the fact that rank and authority, though respected, confer their holder no special social privileges.

How Far are Japanese Personnel Practices Transferable to the UK?

In general, Japanese affiliates have not had much difficulty in introducing their personnel policies. One reason may be that over the last ten years the industrial relations climate has, for the most part, improved; another is that to survive, Japanese companies (particularly in the CTV industry) have had to be efficient. But undoubtedly the main reason is that, in almost every case, their entry has been through a greenfield venture. The general view was expressed by one CTV producer

A new company can establish its operating philosophy from day one and select employees who are willing to accept the 'ground rules'. To engineer change is far more difficult as employee attitudes have been established by a history of ingrained habits.

Again, as has already been mentioned, the recruitment efforts of Japanese affiliates are usually directed to school leavers or from the general labour market rather than from other firms. One Japanese affiliate opined it was as important for employees to be trained in attitudes and motivation as in technical skills. This same firm − one of the newcomers − also favoured in-house promotion and expected that in ten years time all its senior people will be recruited internally.

Hiring policy has been eased by above rates of unemployment. In addition, in some areas, notably parts of South Wales, conciliatory style of Japanese management has proved a welcoming change from the traditional adversary and often embittered industrial relations. Several Scottish and South Wales companies spoke of eight applicants for every job, and in Plymouth where Toshiba recruited 200 people, after the Rank-Toshiba venture closed, the ratio was 20 to 1. Up to June 1985, Nissan had received over 5,000 applications for 450 jobs in its Washington (Tyne and Wear) factory. Companies were unanimous in their requirements:

All our staff have to accept the Japanese way − be punctual, tidy, acceptable and prepared for hard work. (an industrial electronics affiliate).

Sometimes such requirements are spelled out in writing; in advertising for jobs at their new Telford factory, Hitachi Maxell management specifically indicated that their management would be Japanese styled. Their company reported 2,000 applicants for 170 jobs. By following a similar policy, Sanyo recruited 30% of the workers who earlier worked in its factory under Pye ownership. Workers now being recruited for Nissan are in no doubt of what is expected of them.

What working practices did affiliates think it difficult to transfer from Japan? There was a strong feeling among both Japanese and UK managing directors and personnel managers that while most Japanese style personnel practices could be satisfactorily introduced into the UK environment ('after all,' quipped one UK personnel director, 'they are only common sense') there remained a fundamental difference between the attitudes to work by Japanese and UK workers. Fairly typical of the views expressed is that of a Group 2 affiliate.

By their nature, the Japanese are more co-operative and less individualistic in their approach to work; and they have a far greater commitment to their company. They are more anxious to solve problems whatever the cost in time to themselves. Indeed their pride of achievement or fear of failure drives them to do this — and their families understand. Moreover, they are also more conducive to suggestions and respectful of authority. A certain amount of indiscipline and individuality among UK workers means that, in repetitive factory operations UK companies can never hope to reach Japanese productivity levels.

This view was challenged by a UK motor vehicle assembler, who asserted that Japanese workers had been conditioned to behave in the way they do; and that in due course, as they become exposed to Western ways, they will become less devoted to their work and more to leading a balanced life between work, leisure and family needs.

How far these differences in Anglo-Japanese culture and work ethic, which we believe are the most significant non-transferable reasons for differences in the performance of Japanese affiliates and their parent companies, will last, as the Japanese enterprises become more multinational, remains to be seen. Neither should it be assumed that one culture or ethic is preferable to the other. But for the moment, the Japanese example is something to be studied and learnt from — even though institutional and other rigidities in the UK industry may sometimes make it difficult to assimilate.[23]

To What Extent Can Work Practices be Applied in UK Industry?

Nevertheless, within institutional constraints, Japanese affiliates believed that the worker-related practices could be successfully applied by UK industry. Among the most commonly stated were:

1. No status-related differences, in employment, hours of work, holidays, working conditions, social facilities, etc.
2. Open plan space usage; no separate offices, except, perhaps, for most senior executives and meeting rooms.
3. Open door attitude; the willingness for discussions and consultations between people at all levels.
4. Good communication; tell the people all the time the facts of industrial life.
5. Reduction of job grades to the absolute minimum.
6. Incorporate flexibility of work clauses into contracts.
7. Pay special attention to recruitment and selection methods and criteria.
8. Increase attention to encouraging workforce to give of their best, without always expecting an immediate financial reward.
9. Try and do without formal incentives, but, through promotion and gifts, reward good workmanship.
10. Encourage promotion of single company, rather than several crafts unions.

Other Issues

There appeared to be only a limited impact on the work practices of other firms in the region in which Japanese firms were located, except perhaps in South Wales. One CTV company said, 'Our conditions have raised the standards of the physical environment of many local companies'. Another asserted

> Our main impact has been to show other ways to run a company than by autocracy; that it is possible to practise worker participation without surrendering managerial responsibility and control.

It was also reported by several affiliates they had been visited by major UK companies; and that the most interest was shown in quality control practices and industrial relations. However, they believed the difficulty of putting these into practice in established hierarchies remained the main obstacle to their wider dissemination.

One Scottish affiliate believed it had had some impact on the way in which its local Engineering Training Board operated but only because 'we are at the forefront of integrated circuit technology'. Another CTV affiliate established an information network with other local employers in order to monitor and advise on wage levels and working conditions. One large Welsh CTV company believes that its example of good industrial relations − in an area where the history is one of 'constant battle between employer and employed' − helped to bring the Ford Motor Company to Bridgend. This same company also claimed that

> Our factory conditions have raised the standards of the physical environment of many local companies. Our style has been investigated by major UK companies. e.g. Lucas, British Steel and Plessey.

The GEC-Hitachi Story

In March 1984, Hitachi purchased the 50% GEC stake in GEC-Hitachi. Had it not done so the company would most probably have gone bankrupt, as would the GEC TV division had not Hitachi purchased its interest in 1979.

Over the years of the joint venture, the numbers employed fell from over 2,100 to 1,250. Following the Hitachi takeover, the labour force was cut by another 500. Of the total reduction in the labour force, about one-half has represented voluntary redundancies and the rest enforced dismissals. The history of GEC-Hitachi has been fraught with management problems and bad industrial relations. Within 18 months of the joint venture, nearly 30% of supervisors and line management had left the company disillusioned by the management style and lack of vision of the company. In 1983, there were two strikes and morale in the plant was at its lowest ebb. Throughout the joint venture it had been expected that Hitachi would eventually buy out GEC, and this would have been acclaimed by the workforce. As it was, while Hitachi provided technical support for the venture, and invested nearly £3 million in new plant and equipment, GEC continued to manage the plant on traditional lines with an industrial relations style, described as the 'opposite of progressive and autocratic in the extreme'.

By July 1982, it was clear there was gross overmanning at the plant. In addition to a reduction in the labour force of 600 (from 2,100 to 1,500) a wage and salary freeze was enforced. An attempt to repeat this freeze in April 1983 led to a six-day strike which was only quelled by the threat of wholesale sackings. Another six-day strike occurred in the following November, when feelings were so high there was some sabotage at the plant.

Plans for a Hitachi takeover began to be made in December 1983. By then, the joint venture had accumulated a deficit of over £10m and the choice was taken to withdraw from Hirwaun altogether. By that time only 25% of the CTV sets being produced at Hirwaun were for the GEC market, and it was clear that GEC was much more interested in the industrial/defence side of the business than the consumer side.

Immediately after the takeover, Hitachi began to introduce quite dramatic changes to personnel policies, which are detailed in a document 'A new future at Hirwaun'. Foremost among these changes are

(1)   A reduction in the number of unions from 6 to 1 (EETPU).
(2)   The institution of a company members board to ensure that there is a 'full and meaningful involvement of all company members in the activities and plans of the Company'.
(3)   The introduction of single-status conditions of employment, coupled with acceptance by employees of 'the complete flexibility of jobs and duties within and between the various company functions and departments'.
(4)   Much stricter control on hours of work, start and finish times and lunch breaks; the introduction of company work clothes.
(5)   The introduction of new negotiating procedures over wage and salary claims and work conditions; and of grievance procedures.

Redundancies were agreed mainly on a 'last in first out basis', although originally there were plans for more selective shedding of the workforce.

When we paid our second visit to the plant in July 1984, it was in the process of modernisation and automation; and there were plans to produce 14" CTV sets from the late autumn. Senior Japanese industrial engineering staff from the head office at Yokohama helped to plan the new layout, and all departments were in the charge of a Japanese national (including personnel and purchasing). The redundancies necessitated were determined in three stages:

(i)   by estimating new standard times for factory operatives, based upon the new equipment being installed and new work methods (due allowance being made for the cleaning time required);
(ii)   by rehauling purchasing methods and reducing the number of

components from 6,000 to 2,500;
(iii)   by reducing employment in other departments.

As regards improving worker productivity Hitachi has initially concentrated its attention in two directions. First it is training team leaders (foremen and above), shop stewards and worker members of the management board in the Japanese way of doing things. Second it has attempted to tighten up control procedures, from the maintenance of tools and equipment supplied to subcontractors, through timekeeping on lunch and cleaning up time, to the final inspection of the finished product. Hitachi contends that this lack of control in monitoring of materials, goods and people was the biggest single reason for the losses suffered by the joint venture.

As a measure of good faith, Hitachi paid all workers a 7% backdated pay rise (in spite of a £3 million loss in the preceding year); it also incorporated all bonus payments into basic wages. We understand it plans no incentive payments. As a further measure of new goodwill a £100,000 restaurant was installed.

Some European and American Comparisons

Rest of Europe

There is some evidence to suggest that the Japanese managerial style and pattern of labour relations has been transferred more completely to the UK than to other parts of Europe (JETRO, 1983). The reasons for this are mainly two-fold; first the greater ease at which the Japanese can communicate in English as compared with other European languages; and second, the fact that Japanese manufacturing actually in the UK is much more concentrated in the type of sector the success of which has been particularly associated with the adoption of Japanese management practices.

For example, in almost every area of management there are proportionately more Japanese expatriates employed in the UK than elsewhere in Europe; the introduction of quality control circles, consultation systems, meetings with employees (including regular morning get-togethers) is more widespread in the UK;[24] Japanese style labour policies such as stabilisation of employment, more flexibility, personnel development, welfare benefits, hiring methods, the publication of house journals, are all more in evidence in British (and Irish) factories than in other parts of the EEC; and the evaluation of worker productivity in the UK compares favourably with that of other Western European countries, apart from Belgium and the Netherlands. In 1982, labour turnover was marginally higher in the UK than in other parts of Europe except Ireland, but layoffs and/or dismissals were proportionately lower, except in France. Labour disputes were relatively fewer in the UK than in France, Italy, Belgium, Ireland and Spain but greater than in Germany and the Netherlands. Compared with their European counterparts, a considerably higher proportion of UK managers and technical workers (engineers, chemists, etc.) had received training in Japan; otherwise educational and training schemes offered by Japanese affiliates in the UK broadly corresponded to those in the rest of Europe.

The US

In general, Japanese style labour practices are less in evidence in US than in European factories. For example, the introduction of work flexibility and job rotation has proved less acceptable to US workers; plans and policies regarding layoffs are much less specific;[25] US style incentive systems differ very considerably from the Japanese counterparts, while bonuses and the like account for a much larger part of the pay packet of a US worker than that of his European equivalent; only one-fourth of Japanese affiliates negotiated with unions; and in nearly every subsidiary, the method of determining wages (at least for blue collar workers) followed the American system.

On the other hand, many Japanese style recreational activities had been introduced into American factories; educational and training schemes similar to those adopted by European affiliates; and the philosophy of Japanese management in respect of promoting employee loyalty, disseminating information, and the introduction of quality circles was widely acclaimed.

Few Japanese affiliates in the US reported labour-management disputes in 1980; US workers were thought better than their Japanese equivalents when 'they used their time to the fullest';[26] but they were not considered as flexible, they lacked initiative in devising new methods and improvements in their work, and were weak in team play and co-operative work.

Our general reading of the labour-management situation of Japanese affiliates in the US is then, that, because of the more individualistic nature of the US (*vis-à-vis* the European) worker, the introduction of the Japanese management style *in toto* is unlikely to be as successful; and that a more patient and gradual wooing process with American workers is necessary to gain their understanding, acceptance and loyalty. It may well be that as Japanese participation grows in UK industry, Japanese personnel policies will need to be more carefully and selectively applied to take account of the idiosyncrasies of the individual UK worker and the macro-economic labour environment than has been necessary up to now.

Notes

1. See especially Thurley, Nangaku and Uragami (1976), Thurley, Reitsperger, Trevor and Worm (1980), Kidd and Teramoto (1981), Trevor (1983).

2. One chemical affiliate indicated that 30% of its R & D was done outside Japan, mainly in the US and Europe.

3. Matsushita has announced plans to set up an R & D laboratory in the UK – its third overseas research base after the US and Taiwan. Potential fields of research include: cable and satellite CTV, office automation and computer software. It is hoped that a UK scientist will head the proposed centre.

4. In the case of Sony, the setting up of a new tube making plant in 1982 brought in a fresh contingent of Japanese engineers to get the plant operating and to help train local personnel.

5. The policy of one CTV affiliate is to employ Japanese nationals as departmental managers for the first three years of the affiliate's life; then for a 'junior' UK manager to be appointed and finally, after six years for all departments to be headed by UK nationals but assisted by Japanese liaison officers.

6. For a Japanese view on such conditions, see Oba (1983).

7. As demonstrated, for example by the strenuous efforts of the Nissan and the Hitachi management to conclude no-strike agreements with a single trade union. For details of the agreement finally made with the Amalgamated Union of Engineering Workers in April 1985, see *Financial Times* 23 April 1985.

8. Based upon data supplied by 20 affiliates.

9. Eight of the 20 affiliates gave a rank of 3 or less to the motivation of shop-floor workers.

10. In the case of GEC-Hitachi the main reason for their difficult industrial relations is put down to the reaction to new management policies which themselves have been necessitated by the failure of previous policies. These past policies were unsuccessful because of the inability of the two parent companies – GEC and Hitachi – to agree on a common managerial philosophy.

11. And quoted by European Company Services (1983), p. 63.

12. Lifetime employment should not be interpreted too literally. Often the age of retirement is 55 and in most contracts there are various caveats under which employment may be terminated. The fact that these have not been greatly used is thought by some observers a testimony to the buoyancy of the Japanese economy as much as anything else. In times of recession Japanese companies tend to reduce their subcontracting and do as much of the production in-house as possible.

13. Although the number of grades is kept to the very absolute minimum, and in the case of at least two CTV affiliates to one only (i.e. in the factory).

14. One illustration of this was the way in which the redundancies at Hitachi were handled in 1984. While the company had originally preferred a structured redundancy (based *inter alia* on the work record of employees) they were persuaded by the workers to accept a 'last in-first out' formula.

15. One exception is that of a textile affiliate which pays above the national

average, and by way of time rather than piece rates.

16. For example, one large employer in South Wales has a general ruling not to recruit more than three persons per year from any other firm in the region in which it is situated.

17. One motor components affiliate, for example, offered a present (details not forthcoming) to its employees every five years 'as a token of our appreciation for their efforts on our behalf'.

18. Several affiliates referred to the 'nemawaki' process of negotiation and discussion, whereby there is a great deal of informal communication between the individual negotiators and discussions prior to any formal meeting. It appears wage settlements are often agreed to in this way.

19. In July 1984 Hitachi announced single negotiating rights with one union. Previously GEC-Hitachi had dealt with six unions. In the earlier joint venture Rank Toshiba was obliged to deal with seven unions; these it has now cut down to one. Another affiliate – Merlin Aerials – has recently become unionised. The management claim that 'it has not made the slightest difference'.

20. Notably Dore (1973) and Trevor (1982).

21. Note also that the economic climate for negotiating with foreign MNEs is very difficult than in the 1970s. Several unions, for example, vied for the sole bargaining rights with the Nissan Motor Company.

22 One company silenced one of its Welsh critics by referring to the fact that it would look odd if the Welsh rugby 15 turned out in different colours!

23. It will be interesting to follow through the efforts to do so by Hitachi and Sumitomo, both of who have acquired existing UK (or in the case of Hitachi an Anglo-Japanese) ventures.

24. Though management briefs to all employees in corporate policies are less widely practised.

25. For example, such plans seldom take the form of a promise which a company makes to its employees and even firms that do commit themselves apply such conditions as 'to the extent that the employee works conscientiously or barring unforeseen circumstances', JETRO (US), 1981, p. 44.

26. JETRO (US), 1981, p. 57.

Appendix A to Chapter 10
Evaluating Worker Performance: One Affiliate's Profile

Evaluating worker performance (an example of a scheme operated by one Japanese affiliate, in mid-1983).

At the request of staff members, and in pursuance of good company policy, a Personal Assessment Card is being actioned.

A Evaluation

In order to arrive at the Points Evaluation Total, it is essential that all personnel be assessed by Managerial Team, consisting of Departmental Manager, and General Manager – Final points assessment agreed by Managing Director.

B   Evaluation Areas

One: Attitude

This covers the behaviour pattern of the employee in many areas, and these can be defined as:

(1)   Attitude towards company objectives.
(2)   Attitude towards other company employees.
(3)   Attitude in general.
(4)   Attitude towards customers.

Two: Accountability

Accountability is associated with Job or Task area, and therefore the employee is answerable for their task performance geared to Cost Productivity Areas, i.e. Job Completion is executed with minimum of time, therefore, fulfilling the company's Cost Effective Programme.

Three: Responsibility

This is a clearly defined area and a very important one; however, it has many areas such as:

(1)   Job responsibility.
(2)   Section responsibility.
(3)   Departmental responsibility.

Four: Adaptability

The evaluation will take into account the employee's adaptability in Job Change Function.

Job Evaluation

Evaluation Content	Attitude	Account-ability	Responsi-bility	Adapt-ability	TOTAL
Standard					
1st Evaluator Signature:					
2nd Evaluator Signature:					
Final Evaluation Signature:					

The points awarded on Job Evaluation can be easily assessed by the evaluator as follows:

Attitude and Accountability

50   Dedicated.
40   Above average.
30   Average.
20   Below average.
10   Bottom range.

Responsibility and Adaptability

30   High responsibility.
25   High adaptability.
20   Average responsibility.
15   Average adaptability.
10   Both if pushed.

(i.e.) Should a person be totally dedicated in attitude, then 50 points.

Accountability Average	30 points
Responsibility High	30 points
Adaptability Average	15 points
Total	125 points

Appendix B to Chapter 10
The Nissan Agreement with the AUEW

Nissan Motor Co. (UK) Ltd, and the Amalgamated Union of Engineering Workers announced on 22 April 1985 a labour agreement, which in the words of the Nissan personnel director Peter Wickens aims to 'eliminate the need for industrial action'. The agreement is designed to promote both common employment conditions for all members of staff and full labour flexibility; *inter alia* it outlaws industrial action while negotiation, arbitration and conciliation procedures take their course. The following four aspects of the agreement are path-breaking in the motor vehicles industry; as already described in this Chapter they are more common in the CTV sector.

One: Single Union

Nissan negotiated with several UK unions (includng the transport workers and the general municipal workers), but finally chose AUEW as the sole negotiating body, to represent every member of staff, up to, and including, senior manufacturing staff, technicians, administrators, supervisors and engineers. One reason for this choice was it believed that most of its staff in the North East would feel happiest in belonging to that Union. Nissan will not have a closed shop, but the company will encourage its employees to take up AUEW membership and actively participate in the union. Nissan did consider having no union at all but the Personnel Director gave two reasons for the decision taken; first he said it was the 'right' thing to do; and second the company did not want to spend the next 5-10 years fighting off attempts of the unions to gain recognition.

Some 10 employee representatives will be elected to a company council on which they will sit with management, as a consultative forum and negotiating body, reporting twice yearly to all employees on the current state of the company.

Two: No Industrial Action

The company council will formulate and negotiate all salary claims and on matters to do with working conditions. If, in exceptional circumstances, and where the two sides cannot agree, then the issue will be put to the Advisory, Conciliation and Arbitration Service (ACAS) for a conciliated solution. If this fails, there is a provision for the issue to go to pendulum arbitration where the arbitrator would decide in favour of the company or the union with a previous commitment on both sides to accept it.

During this whole process, the agreement stipulates there should be no industrial action. (N.B. this is not a no-strike agreement *per se*).

Three: Flexibility

Complete flexibility and mobility of workers is a further keynote of the agreement, not just with respect of current work organisation, but of future changes in technology processes and practices. The company recognises such flexibility will not be possible at the start of production in the UK; but it intends to train staff in multi-skills, and UK supervisors will spend some time at Nissan's Oppama plant at Yokasuka (south of Tokyo) learning the Japanese way of work organisation.

There will be only two job descriptions for manual staff – technical and manufacturing staff, with no detailed job description and no grade, multiplicity supervisors will have an expanded role and keep in close contact with 'team leaders' who will work directly to them, and deputise for them and with the staff in their section.

Four: Common Conditions

As in other Japanese-owned factories in the UK, there will be one canteen and one overall worn by staff. All hours of work, holidays, shift and overtime premiums will be the same for all staff. All employees will be salaried and paid monthly directly into their bank accounts. Pay rates will be the subject of detailed negotiation with the AUEW, but salary ranges will be established for each occupation with individuals moving through the range based on their own performances. The company has agreed to pay its supervisors somewhat above the normal, but asserts this is partly because of their higher status and responsibility, and partly because most were already working in the area for other companies.

11 SOME OTHER FEATURES OF JAPANESE DIRECT INVESTMENT IN UK MANUFACTURING INDUSTRY

Introduction

In the course of our survey, we obtained a lot of data which might be used to answer a variety of questions, but which our terms of reference did not require us to consider. We briefly deal with four such issues — viz. balance of payments, the level of employment, technological capacity and profitability.

Balance of Payments

In the Steuer report on the impact of foreign direct investment in the UK economy,[1] the authors attempted to make some assessment of its balance of payments consequences. Whatever way one wishes to look at it, the impact of the Japanese affiliates is bound to be extremely small. In Chapter 2 we estimated the total exports of such affiliates in 1982 to be £74m and the total imports due mainly to their UK production to be £93m. Goods imported for resale by either the manufacturing affiliates or their sales companies were however very much more — probably in the order of £400m. What proportion of this latter figure is directly due to the presence of Japanese affiliates in the UK it is impossible to say.

At the end of the 1982/3 financial year, Japanese manufacturing affiliates owned net assets worth £74m. Over the previous year they spent about £20m on new plant and equipment. This included about £13m of imported machinery, parts and equipment, of which £10m was bought from Japan. In the future, this is likely to rise considerably. Nissan alone are reported to be planning to spend £50m on their Washington factory, 80% of which will be within the UK.

The payment of dividends, royalties and fees by Japanese affiliates to their parent companies is very small: in 1983, it was little more than £1m. Capital growth has been financed from additional capital imports from Japan (particularly in the case of Sony and Group 2 affiliates), loan capital from the UK or international capital markets, and ploughed back profits. On a transactions basis, then, and excluding new capital imports from Japan, Japanese affiliates recorded a net deficit on their balance of payments of £33m (£74m – (£93m + £13m + £1m)). However, if one assumes that in their absence, everything produced in the UK would have been imported, then clearly the contribution would have been strongly positive. If, alternatively, one assumes the output gap would have been filled by UK competitors (a somewhat dubious assumption), it would have been even more negative. The most likely scenario is somewhere between these two extremes, but veering towards the former, for the simple reason that had the Japanese companies not invested in the UK, they would have done so elsewhere in the EEC, and penetrated the British market from that base.

It is also important to take the indirect effects of the Japanese into consideration. By stimulating competitors and suppliers to be more efficient, e.g. as in the CTV sector, this may lead to additional UK exports and fewer imports. However, where production by UK firms which relies on higher local value added content is replaced by output by Japanese affiliates which has a higher import component, then the balance of payments could be worsened. This is exactly what is claimed to happen as a result of YKK's penetration of the zip fastener market; and what some fear might transpire in the Nissan case. In the CTV sector, there is some evidence that, in the initial years of the operation of Japanese affiliates, their reliance on non-UK, and particularly Japanese, components and parts is greater than that of their indigenous competitors; however, in the case of the more well established affiliates, their domestic sourcing ratio is about the same as their competitors. Moreover, it is worth observing that in this industry, as in the motor vehicle sector, the sourcing of components and parts is becoming increasingly international, with the options to source from the cheapest and most reliable outlet widening for all firms – both UK and foreign owned.

All CTV affiliates, especially the most recent arrivals, expect to increase the share of their output going to exports by the mid-1980s; compared with a 1982 ratio of 29%, the ratio is likely to be 40-45% by 1986. By contrast, the import ratio (especially from Japan) (especially of video recorders) is likely to fall; in consequence, the balance of payments contribution of Group 1 affiliates will improve considerably. It seems fairly clear that in the CTV and video sectors, at least, the UK is destined to become the major supplying base for the European market; there are also signs that in the electronic components sector, the UK is – and Scotland in particular – a greater attraction (for example relative to Germany) for Japanese investors.

The Level of Employment

Evaluating the employment effect of the Japanese presence in the UK poses the same difficulties as assessing the balance of payments effects. Much depends on the 'alternative' position or counter factual situation assumed. It is true that, within the sectors in which Japanese affiliates are most strongly represented, their capital/labour ratio tends to be above that of their indigenous competitors; but it is also the case that in recent years this ratio has risen faster among UK-owned firms and other (non-Japanese) foreign affiliates.

Indirectly, too, as we have seen, in the first years of their UK production, Japanese affiliates tend to import a higher proportion of their imports than their (established) UK competitors; hence their consequences for employment in supplying industries may be negative. On the other hand, the fact that most Japanese investments are greenfield operations, that they record higher levels of efficiency than their competitors, and that they have had a favourable impact on their suppliers' costs and product quality, would suggest they make possible an increase in output, and hence employment levels. But much more important to the estimated employment effects is what one assumes would have happened in the absence of Japanese participation in the UK. Take Nissan as an example. It is quite possible that if, as a result of its presence in the UK, Nissan takes markets away from existing UK vehicle producers, and if the capital/labour ratio of Nissan and the percentage of imported parts and components are both higher than those of these same competitors, the effect on UK jobs could be negative. If, on the other hand, the UK vehicles industry is made more efficient as a result of the Nissan investment, then UK exports of cars might well rise and UK imports of cars might fall. Add to this the dramatically adverse consequences on employment if Nissan were to produce elsewhere in Europe, and continue to supply the UK markets from that location, then the impact of UK employment, resulting from its presence, might be substantially positive.

The above scenario we believe realistically describes what, in fact, has happened in the CTV sector over the last decade, and is likely to occur in the video recorder sector in the mid and later 1980s. As long as there is a free trade between Europe and the UK (at least within the EEC countries) and there are few or no restrictions on the conditions for Japanese companies to invest in Europe, then the presence of Japanese affiliates in the UK is likely to be beneficial for the level of UK employment.[2] It is possible it may have rather less welcome effects on the *structure* of employment.[3] This possibility is briefly considered in the following section.

Technological Capacity

To date, Japanese manufacturing affiliates have made little direct difference to the technological capacity of the UK economy. There has been a limited amount of product development, design and adaptation in a few of the subsidiaries, but only in three is there any genuine R and D.[4] Moreover, few companies expect there to be much innovatory activity in the UK in the foreseeable future.[5] One exception was a chemical affiliate who asserted

> We anticipate a centralised European R and D strategy and policy will be established in the near future. Our UK operation will enjoy the results of the centralised R and D.

And another Group 2 affiliate stated

> We believe that in the next few years it will be necessary for us to develop new products specifically for the European market. If this comes about, we are likely to establish a research centre to meet this need in Europe.

It was also generally felt that if and when R and D is done in Europe, it is likely to be located in the UK.

There appear to be some examples of a reverse feedback in knowledge, especially in the colour TV industry and the more established Group 2 affiliates. In the CTV sector, the UK content of sets currently exported from the UK has increased as a result of the Japanese manufacturing presence. Included in the kits of parts exported by affiliates to their parent companies are tuners, aerial sockets, capacitors and plastic mouldings. If successful, the joint development programme of Matsushita and Mullards on tuning systems may have far-reaching implications for the former's parent company. Another example was given by a zip fastener affiliate

> We make monthly reports on our UK operations to Japan. These sometimes include information on R and D related matters, e.g. ways in which machinery or processes require adaptation to meet safety

standards, new marketing methods, innovations by competitors, information on raw materials and so on. This knowledge is also obtained from our other 38 plants throughout the world and is distilled, interpreted and recirculated to all subsidiaries in the form of an information newssheet. In this way, the Japanese parent company acts as a clearing house for new ideas and information coming from all over the world.

This was confirmed by a light engineering affiliate:

> We are continuously passing back technical knowhow because of our understanding of the market and closeness to competitors. This has often resulted in modifications being made in products by our Japanese parent company which have then been exported to other foreign subsidiaries.

and a chemical affiliate:

> Particularly in the field of engineering our improvements in, and modification of equipment is followed by our Japanese factory.

One general concern about the impact of Japanese affiliates on UK technological capability is the extent to which their presence might inhibit or adversely influence the innovating ability of UK companies. This anxiety has so far been directed to the involvement of the Japanese in the high technology sectors of the electronics industry, and the argument runs as follows. The key determinant of the future of the UK electronics component industry rests on the extent to which the manufacturers can influence the design of the final product, e.g. CTV sets, into which the components are inserted. If, for example, the design of integrated circuits becomes dominated by Japanese assemblers or component suppliers with the needs of their own CTV industry in mind, there is a danger that the UK components industry may not be able to match these designs, because, if they are excluded from the Japanese markets it may be uneconomic for them to do so. This would suggest that as the Japanese CTV assemblers increase their output in Europe, there will be an increasing incentive for Japanese component suppliers to establish UK (or other European) affiliates. In its turn, this could lead to UK component suppliers being outcompeted in international markets, with the consequential erosion of their R and D base. The subsequent effects could extend far beyond the consumer electronics industry; as these same suppliers also supply components to industrial electronics – notably telecommunication companies. As telecommunications is acknowledged to be one of the critical infrastructure sectors of any advanced industrialised economy, the consequences of letting control slip out of UK hands could be very serious.

To be fair, Japanese affiliates are very conscious of the anxieties outlined. Moreover, the need to take account of differences in the availability of local materials and of customer requirements, together with the incentive to reduce lead times for imports, encourages the promotion of local design capability. In the CTV sector there are two aspects of product design. The first is to do with the function of a TV set (colour, brightness, quality of sound, etc.), improvements in which are likely to be accepted worldwide, and the R and D for which may be very costly to decentralise. The second is the layout of the chassis to meet these needs and the special requirements of different systems, e.g. PAL in Europe, of customers, e.g. teletext, cable TV, etc., and of materials availability. It is these which can best be decentralised, and in which the R and D departments of GEC-Hitachi are already actively engaged,[6] and Sony and Matsushita are in the process of setting up.

Profitability

The interpretation of the balance sheets or profit and loss accounts of foreign subsidiaries is fraught with difficulties. In the case of Japanese manufacturing affiliates, these difficulties are compounded, as sometimes the marketing operations of the companies are included (which in sales terms are often as important, or more important, than the manufacturing operations), and sometimes they are not. It is also well known that Japanese companies gauge performance in a very different light than do their European counterparts. Moreover, since only three Japanese affiliates have been manufacturing more than ten years, only the most limited credence can be given to profitability data as a measure of efficiency. The Japanese themselves look upon their UK investments as a part of a long-term strategy to capture a sizeable share of the European market, *and only one of the 23 companies regards its UK operations as a failure.*

With these reservations in mind, we observe that of the 23 manufacturing affiliates, only 14 were making any trading profit[7] in the financial year 1982/3. Seven of these were Group 1 affiliates;[8] as a whole, these affiliates made losses of £5m in that financial year, with only one CTV company (Matsushita) recording profits. Group 2 affiliates did much better. Twelve of the 14 made profits, and four of the affiliates, Sansetu, YKK Fasteners, Nittan and NSK Bearings, did very well indeed.[9]

In all, Group 2 affiliates recorded profits before tax of just under £5m in 1982/3, just about balancing out the losses of Group 1 affiliates. The light engineering affiliates did best; the rest did little better than break even.

Most of the affiliates have received sizeable government grants over their lifetime in the UK. Regional development grants have probably exceeded £5 million,[10] interest relief grants a further £1.5 million and other capital and training grants at least £2 million.

Only two companies reported remitting any profits to their parent companies in 1982/3; one of which recorded a 12% dividend. Five Group 2 affiliates paid corporation tax totalling £2.5m. Prior to taxation, 17 subsidiaries paid out interest on bank or long-term (including intra company) loans amounting to £7.5 million;[11] and another eight affiliates paid royalties and fees to their parent companies totalling £1.3m. Depreciation amounted to £7.6m in 1982.

The reconciliation between high productivity and low profitability cannot easily be made from published accounts; but there can be little doubt that a major part of the losses of Japanese affiliates reflect substantial initial start up costs (net of regional and interest relief grants and capital allowances) and the accumulation of stocks and work in progress. Most Group 1 affiliates have not reached their 'break-even' volume of output. Sony, Mitsubishi and Matsushita are exceptions. It is impossible on the basis of published data to assess whether or not there are transfer price manipulations between the parent and subsidiary companies; only one affiliate we interviewed admitted to this, but no Group 1 affiliate, at least, would deny that it was possible to transfer funds back to Japan in this way.

What does seem to be the case, however, is that Japanese parent companies do charge for handling, packaging,[12] invoicing, etc., of items exported from Japan to their UK subsidiaries, and that this is contained in the transfer price.

Further details of the profitability of Japanese affiliates, before and after depreciation, interest payments, directors' emoluments and taxation since 1975, or the date of their establishment in the UK, are set out in Tables 11.1 and 11.2. The combined years of manufacturing operations of Group 1 affiliates were 34; before tax profits were earned in 12 of these years, and post tax profits in 15. Of the 63 combined years of Group 2 affiliates before tax profits were earned in 42. In the

Table 11.1: Trading Profit (before tax) Net Asset Ratio of Japanese Affiliates in UK, 1975-82

	1975/77	1978/80	1981	1982	1975/82	Years of profit
Group 1 Affiliates						
1 Sony[a] (1973)[b]	18.4	26.8	33.4	−56.1	14.1	7/8
2 Matsushita (1976)	−32.7	−3.6	9.9	14.7	−6.9	3/7
3 Mitsubishi (1979)	−22.4	4.0	−80.4	−71.6	−26.4	1/4
4 GEC/Hitachi (1979)	—	—	−4.8	negative	n.a.	0/3
5 Aiwa[a] (1971)	54.1	−58.8	−41.0	−48.3	−53.3	2/5
6 Toshiba (1971)	—	—	—	−13.0	−13.0	0/1
7 Sanyo (1982)	—	—	—	−11.6	−11.6	0/1
8 NEC Electronic (1982)	—	—	—	−232.9	−232.9	0/1
9 J2T (1982)	—	—	—	−130.7	130.7	0/1
Group 2 Affiliates						
(a) Light Engineering						
10 Nittan (1972)	20.7	4.5	20.4	39.0	16.0	7/8
11 YKK (1972)	35.0	15.3	17.4	n.a.	24.1	7/7
12 Takara Belmont (1974)	n.a.	n.a.	26.1	18.3	22.2	2/2
13 NSK Bearings (1978)	−4.2	11.1	14.8	12.6	7.2	5/8
14 Terasaki Europe (1978)	—	12.8[c]	39.2	n.a.	22.0	3/3
15 Yuasa Battery (1982)	—	—	—	—	—	—
(b) Chemicals						
16 Takiron (1973)	−262.2[d]	−24.1	0.7	n.a.	−99.8	2/6
17 Sekisui (1978)	2.9[e]	−0.7	−13.5	1.2	−1.9	3/6
18 Sansetu (1979)	—	108.2	74.9	65.6	82.9	3/3
19 Tamura Kahen (1980)	—	n.a.	n.a.	−26.3	−26.3	0/1
(c) Other						
20 Merlin Aerials (1975)	−518.0[f]	74.3	11.1	n.a.	−133.8	4/6
21 Daiwa Sports (1978)	−19.6[g]	−11.0	−56.7	3.5	−17.7	1/6
22 Paddox Fine Worsted (1978)	—	11.2	21.1	n.a.	14.2	4/4
23 Hoya Lens (1980)	—	..	17.0	22.7	19.9	2/2

Notes: a. Figures in brackets represent date of establishment of manufacturing venture.
b. Accounts include those of sales and marketing company.
c. 1980 only.
d. 1975 and 1976 only.
e. 1977.
f. 1980 only.
g. 1976 and 1977 only.
Source: Company accounts.

Table 11.2. Profit (after tax) Net Asset Ratio of Japanese Affiliates in UK 1975-82

	1975/77	1978/80	1981	1982	1975/82	Years of profit
Group 1 Affiliates						
1 Sony	9.3	11.5	21.3	−83.7	0.0	6/8
2 Matsushita	−31.0	−4.2	10.9	16.3	−5.9	4/7
3 Mitsubishi	15.6	6.5	22.8	6.4	11.4	3/4
4 GEC/Hitachi	—	n.a.	−4.8	neg net assets	n.a.	0/3
5 Aiwa	47.2	−58.8	−41.0	−48.3	−54.4	2/5
6 Toshiba	—	—	—	−13.0	−13.0	0/1
7 Sanyo	—	—	—	−11.6	−11.6	0/1
8 NEC Electronic	—	—	—	−232.9	−232.9	0/1
9 J2T	—	—	—	−130.7	130.7	0/1
Group 2 Affiliates						
(a) Light Engineering						
10 Nittan	10.0	0.9	18.6	32.3	10.5	7/8
11 YKK	29.0	15.8	13.2	n.a.	21.1	7/7
12 Takara Belmont	n.a.	n.a.	15.1	9.8	12.5	2/2
13 NSK Bearings	−10.4	1.2	14.8	12.6	7.8	3/8
14 Terasaki Europe	n.a.	39.5	21.0	n.a.	30.3	3/3
15 Yuasa Battery	—	—	—	began manufacturing in 1982		
(b) Chemicals						
16 Takiron	−262.2[a]	−24.1	0.7	n.a.	−99.8	2/6
17 Sekisui	2.9[b]	−0.7	−13.5	1.2	−1.9	3/6
18 Sansetu	—	108.2	62.5	38.3	69.7	3/3
19 Tamura Kahen	—	n.a.	n.a.	−26.3	−26.3	0/1
(c) Other						
20 Merlin Aerials	−518.0[c]	74.3	11.1	n.a.	−133.8	4/6
21 Daiwa Sports	−19.6[d]	−11.0	−56.7	3.5	−17.7	1/6
22 Paddox Fine Worsted	—	10.2	18.8	n.a.	12.4	4/4
23 Hoya Lens	—	—	0.9	6.4	3.7	2/2

Notes: a. 1975 and 1976 only.
b. 1977.
c. 1980 only.
d. 1976 and 1977 only.

case of the CTV assemblers, Matsushita took four years to break even. Apart from Sony, whose huge loss in 1982 is explained by a large capital investment (paid for out of past and current year profits) in a new CTV tube plant, none of the other Group 1 affiliates have yet recorded profits. Of Group 2 affiliates, YKK, Nittan, Paddox, Hoya Lens and Terasaki have been profitable from the start. Of the rest, Takiron broke even after seven years, NSK Bearings and Daiwa Sports after four years, Sekisui and Merlin Aerials after three years and Sansetsu after one year.

A comparison with other European affiliates of Japanese manufacturing firms suggests that the performance of UK affiliates is in line with those in Germany, Belgium and the Netherlands, and rather better than those in Spain, Ireland and France.

The Structure of Assets and Financing of Capital Employed

At the end of the financial year 1982/3, the 23 Japanese affiliates recorded gross assets of £164m, of which fixed assets accounted for £41m and current assets £115m. Net of current liabilities, assets (capital employed) were £74m. Further details are set out in Table 11.3.

The shareholders' interest in the capital employed fluctuated a great deal from 100% to only 25% around an average of 47.9%. Some companies like Sony, YKK, Takara Belmont, Merlin Aerials and Paddox Fine Worsted recorded very high gearing ratios (loan capital as a % of net assets), but in several cases the entire long-term finance of the affiliate was provided by the shareholders' capital and reinvested profits.

As might be expected, in the early years of any manufacturing venture, the ratio of current liabilities to total liabilities is high. In Group 1 affiliates it ranged from over 100% to 32.8% around a mean of 79.3%; in Group 2 affiliates the dispersion was between 76.6% and a positive figure of 12.0% around a mean of 30.6%. About one-third of the current liabilities were accounted for by short-term loans, including bank overdrafts, about two-fifths, amounts due to creditors, and the balance amounts due to related (mainly parent) companies.

The JETRO survey on Japanese companies in Europe found that Japanese affiliates in the UK financed their capital expenditure 'in major facilities' predominantly through reinvested profits and funding from their parent companies. Unlike their German and Belgium counterparts they made little use of Japanese banks in Europe; considerably less use (compared with their Italian, Belgian and Irish counterparts) of local banks. On average, European manufacturing affiliates of Japanese affiliates secured 29% of their funding from their parent companies and 37% from reinvested profits; the corresponding figures for UK affiliates were 41% and 32%. Central government helped fund 8% of expenditure in UK affiliates, somewhat less than the European average, and well below

Table 11.3: Assets of and Shareholders' Interest in Japanese Affiliates, End 1982

	Fixed	Current	Total	Net[c]	Share capital	As % of net assets	Current	As % of total assets
Group 1 Affiliates								
1 Sony[a]	12.5	9.7	22.2	17.8	2.1	11.8	4.2	18.9
2 Matsushita	2.7	3.5	6.2	5.7	5.0	87.7	2.4	38.7
3 Mitsubishi[b]	1.6	16.0	17.6	3.5	2.0	57.1	26.3	94.3
4 GEC/Hitachi	6.2	25.6	31.8	5.0	5.0	100.0	28.8	90.6
5 Aiwa	0.4	6.4	6.8	(4.1)	0.6	n.a.	9.2	134.9
6 Toshiba	2.0	7.9	9.9	5.3	3.0	56.6	4.7	47.5
7 Sanyo	2.6	3.2	5.8	3.9	3.8	97.4	1.9	32.8
8 NEC Electronics	0.1	3.0	3.1	(0.2)	0.2	n.a.	3.2	103.2
9 J2T	1.5	6.9	8.4	0.9	0.9	100.0	7.5	89.3
	29.6	82.2	111.8	37.0	22.6	61.1	88.2	79.3
Group 2 Affiliates								
(a) Light Engineering								
10 Nittan	0.1	1.1	1.2	0.6	0.3	50.0	0.7	58.3
11 YKK	7.1	11.1	18.2	14.6	1.0	6.8	3.7	20.3
12 Takara Belmont	0.1	1.4	1.5	0.6	0.03	5.0	0.9	60.0
13 NSK Bearings	5.6	9.1	14.7	12.3	7.6	61.8	2.5	17.0
14 Terasaki Europe	0.4	3.2	3.6	1.3	1.3	100.0	2.6	113.0
15 Yuasa Battery	1.8	0.5	2.3	1.5	0.8	53.3	(0.3)	(12.0)
	15.1	26.4	41.5	30.9	9.8	31.7	10.1	24.3
(b) Chemicals								
16 Takiron	0.8	0.8	1.6	1.0	1.0	100.0	0.5	33.8
17 Sekisui	1.8	1.3	3.1	2.0	0.6	40.0	2.0	64.2
18 Sansetsu	0.3	0.2	0.6	0.2	0.04	20.0	0.4	65.7
19 Tamura Kahen	0.04	0.1	0.2	0.05	0.05	100.0	0.1	73.8
	3.0	2.5	5.6	3.3	1.7	51.5	3.0	53.5
(c) Other								
20 Merlin Aerials	0.01	0.4	0.5	0.2	0.03	15.0	0.3	57.2
21 Daiwa Sports	0.2	1.7	1.9	1.5	1.0	66.7	1.5	76.6
22 Paddox Fine Worsted	0.2	0.6	0.8	0.4	0.01	2.5	0.4	51.8
23 Hoya Lens	0.5	1.2	1.7	1.1	0.5	45.5	0.6	35.2
	0.9	3.0	4.9	3.2	1.6	50.0	2.8	57.1
Total	48.6	115.2	163.8	74.4	35.7	47.9	104.1	63.5

Notes: a. Manufacturing venture only.
b. Or nearest financial year.
c. Less current liability.
Source. Company accounts.

that recorded by the French affiliates and Italian affiliates (17% and 20%, respectively).

Notes

1. Steuer (1973).
2. Of course, by a variety of policy measures, it might be possible to increase the employment impact of inward investment even further, but unless other European countries also adopted such measures, the danger (if these measures are unacceptable to Japanese investors) is that they would switch their investments (or at least their new investments) to the Continent.
3. We have no evidence about the impact of Japanese investment on the *stability* of UK employment. However, the various surveys undertaken by JETRO (US) suggest that lay-offs by Japanese affiliates in the US recession of 1980-2 compared very favourably with those of indigenous American companies.
4. E.g. in teletext and remote control in the CTV industry.
5. The advantages of centralising and concentrating R and D activities in Japan were stressed by several affiliates.
6. When the joint venture was formed, Hitachi became associated with the development and design department which was already servicing GEC. Coupled with new knowledge imported from Japan, GEC-Hitachi was able to market a new and substantially European designed CTV in 1980.
7. Prior to depreciation, payment of interest, directors' emoluments and taxation.
8. By the end of the 1982/3 tax year, these companies were recording accumulated losses of more than £45m.
9. Earning profits before tax, as a % of net assets in 1982/3 of 65.6%, 39.0% and 17.4% and 12.6% respectively.
10. The loans made to Group 1 affiliates include one by the Scottish Economic Planning Department to Mitsubishi, one by the EEC (of £5.6m) to Sony, and one by the ICFC to Aiwa Ltd.
11. Calculated on the basis of data supplied by six large affiliates eligible for such grants.
12. Particularly where kits of parts obtained from other Japanese companies are packed and shipped to the affiliate, etc.

12 THE FUTURE OF JAPANESE PARTICIPATION IN UK INDUSTRY

The Statistical Picture

How do the existing Japanese manufacturing affiliates in the UK see the future of their operations? We asked each company to estimate its sales (at constant value terms) and employment in 1985 and 1990. Of the 20 affiliates providing data, 18 were planning for a sizeable increase in the volume of their UK output by the end of 1985. The average expected growth of output of CTV sets between the end of 1982 and the end of 1985 was 114% (ranging from 25 to 328%); that of video recorders 306%; that of audio equipment 120%, that of video cassettes (from 1983 to 1985) 33%; and that of semiconductors 428%. Overall, the nine Group 1 affiliates expected to increase their numbers employed from 3,889 in December 1982 to 6,100 in December 1985, i.e. by 57%.

Most Group 1 affiliates expected their growth to occur through further penetration of the European market and an increase in vertical integration in their UK plants. Some product diversification was also anticipated, especially by audio producers and the four CTV affiliates. One CTV producer expects to diversify into VDUs for home computers and cable TV terminal equipment, and another into video discs and microwave ovens. Group 1 affiliates also anticipated a marked rise in their European sourcing of components and parts between 1982 and 1985. Sony, for example, is now manufacturing its Triniton tubes from funnel glass imported from the Continent, rather than importing complete tubes from Japan.

All CTV affiliates expect to increase the share of their output going to exports, especially the most recent arrivals, by the mid 1980s; compared with a 1982 export ratio of 29%, the ratio by the end of 1985 is likely to be over 40%. By contrast, the import ratio (especially from Japan) is likely to fall (especially of video recorders); in consequence, the balance of payments contribution of Group 1 affiliates will improve considerably. It seems fairly clear that in the CTV and video sectors at least, the UK is destined to become the major supplying base for the European market; there are also signs that in the electronic components sector, the UK — and Scotland in particular — is increasing her attraction (for example relative to Germany) for Japanese investors.

Looking further ahead to 1990, the six Group 1 affiliates who were willing to speculate, envisaged a further 25% increase in output. One colour TV set manufacturer – Matsushita – is on record as planning for a five-fold expansion in Europe by 1990, with an increase in the share of European production from 18 to 33%. To achieve this and allowing for productivity improvement, it would need to increase its UK labour force by two and a half times. Of the more recently established CTV producers, Sanyo and J2T have ambitious expansion plans.

The anticipated and/or planned expansion of Group 2 affiliates is less dramatic. Of the 12 affiliates providing data, eight expected sales to rise by 10-25% between December 1982 and December 1985, three by 50% or more, and one anticipated no change in output. Employment was expected to rise from 948 to 1,150, i.e. by 19%, with one firm anticipating a reduction in its labour force and three firms no, or virtually no, change.

The expected modality of growth of these affiliates varied; however, there was a general consensus of opinion that there would be a gradual shift towards more high value production; six affiliates specifically mentioned a greater degree of vertical integration and four a wider variety of end products. The proportion of imported raw materials and components was expected to fall, but not as dramatically as in the case of Group 1 affiliates.

The comments by one light engineering affiliate are instructive:

By 1986, we hope to double our factory accommodation and expect to supply 90% of our UK sales from this factory. We expect to increase sales by 2½ times and double our workforce. We also expect our new plant will be more capital intensive and make use of the latest production methods; so productivity should rise by 25% or more. We expect to produce a wider range of products, although much will depend on whether Nissan comes to the UK.

Evaluation

A doubling of sales between 1983 and the end of 1985 and an increase of employment by 2,200-2,500 suggests that existing Japanese affiliates have a great deal of faith about their future in Europe, and in the UK in particular. It seems that while several anticipate setting up or expanding their Continental European plants,[1] most of the thrust of Japanese growth (at least of affiliates already in the UK) will be within the UK.

However, no less impressive — in sales and employment terms — are the new investments detailed in Chapter 2. Apart from Sumitomo's acquisition of Dunlop, by the end of 1985 another 2,000 jobs are likely to be created; and by the late 1980s another 7,000. In particular we anticipate major new involvements by Japanese companies in the electronics components industry; and a diversification of consumer electronics companies into new product areas. We also believe that as Japan seeks to build up its international reputation in sectors in which it currently does not have a comparative advantage, e.g. chemicals, pharmaceuticals and food products, it breaks into the European market by way of merger with or acquisition of established European companies. Assuming that new manufacturing affiliates enter the UK at least at the rate they have been doing over the last three years, and taking account of the Sumitomo takeover, our best guestimate is that *the numbers employed in Japanese affiliates will rise to around 22,000 by the end of the 1980s; and their sales (at current prices) to over £1 billion.*

But the really significant impact of Japanese direct investment on UK employment may not occur until the 1990s, when the currently planned projects and those of the later 1980s are likely to be fully operational. It is a feature of all advanced industrial economies that a sizeable proportion of the output of their firms is produced outside their national boundaries; and the majority of this within other industrialised countries. Even in the mid-1980s, Japan is in the infancy of the internationalisation of her industries. If, to take just one possible scenario, we were to assume that by the turn of the century their companies produced in the UK an amount equal to that *currently* exported to the UK, then employment in Japanese affiliates would be ten times its present level. If the ratio of subsidiary sales to imports were to reach that of US subsidiaries in the UK — a not impossible situation, in view of the high export propensity of Japanese affiliates — the number employed by such affiliates would exceed 250,000. It is, perhaps, with this scenario in mind, that the Japanese presence can be seen to make a very real contribution to the manufacturing aspirations of the UK.

As the local value component of Japanese participation increases, its effects on UK employment and the balance of payments are likely to become more favourable. The impact on technological capacity is a little more difficult to estimate for reasons cited in the previous chapter. It could become more beneficial, but much depends on the extent to which the design facilities of Group 1 companies are relocated in European and/or UK electronics companies are able to gain a larger share of the Japanese domestic market.

There is no reason to expect that either the reasons for growth in Japanese participation or the distinctive attributes of such participation are likely to change over the next few years, although the ownership advantages arising from being part of an integrated European strategy are likely to become more important. The emphasis on the kind of management philosophy set out in this volume and its consequences for quality control, work organisation and industrial relations, is here to stay: the interesting question is how far it will be taken up by indigenous companies and competitors — including American affiliates — through the effect which Japanese direct investment is having on the American economy.[2] For the Japanese challenge is an international one. Our research into Japanese manufacturing affiliates suggests quite strongly there is no Japanese miracle as such. What is unique is the ability of Japanese companies to supply the consumer with an (almost!) fault-free product and to co-ordinate their quality control procedures by the appropriate management philosophy and work organisation. If this philosophy and attitude cannot or will not be translated into the UK economy, this is not because of our ignorance of what needs to be done; but rather because of outdated traditions and values, institutional rigidities or a lack of motivation. It is this, rather than anything else, which is the real British disease!

A Policy Footnote

We believe that the evidence marshalled in this study strongly supports the continuation of a liberal policy towards Japanese participation in UK industry; and, indeed, of attempts by the Invest in Britain Bureau and other government agencies to attract a larger share of Japanese investment destined for Europe.

At the same time, governments should be aware of the possible conflicts of interest which may arise between what is perceived to be in the private interests of a foreign multinational enterprise and the social interests of the host economy. These are well documented in the literature[3] but two are of particular significance in so far as the presence of Japanese affiliates in UK manufacturing is concerned. These are

(1) The extent to which the affiliates, both directly and indirectly, contribute to local value added and domestic employment. Here much rests both on the ability of UK suppliers to meet the needs of Japanese affiliates, and on the international sourcing and market

servicing policy of the Japanese parent companies.

(2) The extent to which Japanese participation may be of a 'Trojan horse' kind, and that the UK may become regulated as an offshore assembly house for Japanese MNEs, whose main innovatory and technological capability remains in Japan. By fair (or unfair) competitive tactics, it is possible to envisage a situation of Japanese affiliates gaining dominance over key industries. If this should mean a diminution of indigenous R and D, then the UK would be in danger of becoming increasingly dependent on the R and D strategy of companies whose UK activities are only a small part of their worldwide interests, and therefore not necessarily those which determine that strategy.

We have seen these two anxieties most vociferously expressed in the electronics industry, and we believe they will become more, rather than less vocal with the passing of time. If Nissan and Honda should have the same impact on the UK domestic car industry as Sony and Matsushita have had on the CTV sector and NEC and Shin-Etsu are likely to have on the industrial electronics sector, then this concern is likely to be a major factor fashioning future attitudes towards Japanese investment in the UK.

In this connection it may be useful to refer to some guidelines towards (all) inward investment by the electronic components working party of NEDC in 1980.[4] Since that date Japanese involvement has very considerably increased and rather more attention is being paid to ensuring that, when Japanese component manufacturers set up plants in the UK, they should be encouraged to transfer as much of the high-value activity associated with these components as they possibly can.[5]

However, no less important, some would argue, is that if Japanese (and other kinds of inward investment) is to make its fullest contribution to UK economic and social goods, then the UK government, for its part, must create the right kind of economic environment and provide the appropriate technological and educational infrastructure. This does not necessarily mean giving large subsidies or investment allowances to foreign investors (and indeed in the long run this could be counter productive); much more important in this modern technological age is the provision of the necessary transport and communications infrastructure so essential to the speedy transmission of information and knowledge; and also an entrepreneurial climate which can tempt firms (and particularly small firms) to supply the foreign investors with the components and parts they need.[6] Such facilities are, of course, no less important for indigenous producers; indeed, if there is to be effective competition by domestic firms to foreign affiliates, governments may have to assist both in rationalisation programmes and doing their best to counteract restrictive trade practices of other governments which make it difficult for UK firms to gain the markets they need to compete effectively on an international scale.

Notes

1. The JETRO study suggests that of 90 Japanese affiliates with factories in Continental Europe, 78 expected some future growth in their activities.
2. E.g. the effect the presence of Nissan (US) may have on Ford and General Motors and, through them, on their affiliates in the UK.
3. See, for example, Brech and Sharp (1984).
4. Reproduced as Appendix to Chapter 12.
5. In the case of a computer product such as integrated circuits, the stages of production are five-fold: (i) initial design; (ii) mask design; (iii) diffusion of the silicon chip; (iv) assembly; (v) test, marking and packing. If the UK activity was limited to the last two operations the resource investment would be low. A relatively few operators could operate highly automated machinery. An investment in the first three stages is the key to long-term creation of a high technology base and the development of a highly skilled personnel pool in the UK.
6. For further comments on the possible directions the UK consumer electronics industry might take and the conditions necessary for a thriving domestic industry, see Brech and Sharp (1984), pp. 67ff.

Appendix to Chapter 12
Inward Investment: Guidelines Suggested by the Electronic Components Working Party of NEDC (prepared in May 1980)

1. Britain's electronic components industry is an international industry and it will inevitably remain so. Some of the major companies producing in Britain are foreign-owned, such as STC, with its parentage in ITT; and Mullard, owned by Philips.
2. Furthermore, to achieve economies of scale, much of the industry's output requires production runs that are too large to serve the British market alone. This leads to specialisation, and to the growth of both imports and exports. Indeed, the extent of specialisation in research, development and production, provides both the opportunity for exports and the necessity of tapping technology developed abroad.

3. Any policy towards inward investment, therefore, must start from the observation that in its best forms it is not just desirable, but

essential. Yet there are forms in which it can be damaging. The basic objective of any inward investment policy should be to ensure the best long-term interests for the UK in terms of availability of electronic components; research, development and manufacturing capability; and long-term employment prospects, and export growth and import substitution.

4. No set of guidelines can cover every contingency. Yet it should normally be possible to assess each proposal for inward investment against various criteria. These should include:

(a) *Capacity*: Does spare or sufficient capacity already exist in the UK for the component(s) proposed? If so, is it likely that overall UK production will be increased, or merely redistributed among more plants? Where spare capacity does exist, but the argument for allowing the inward investment rests on the prospect of using newer technology, preference should be given to proposals directed towards the acquisition and modernisation of existing plants, and/or on joint ventures with existing companies operating in the UK.

(b) *Employment*: How many new jobs will be created? Will these exceed any jobs lost in competing electronic component plants and where will they be located? What are the implications for security of employment (a) on workers already in existing plants, (b) on workers newly hired to operate the new plant? Encouragement should be given to creating new jobs on a long-term basis, wherever possible in high unemployment areas. It is important that this should occur without exacerbating skilled labour or other shortages within existing plants.

(c) *Product range and development*: Will the personnel extend the range of electronic components manufactured in the UK? Will these components be designed, developed and fully manufactured or only assembled, in this country? Proposals that seek to extend the range of UK manufactured components and add to the UK's technological base should be encouraged.

(d) *Use of local suppliers*: To what extent will the proposal generate work and opportunities for other UK plants by placing orders with UK suppliers? Inward investment should be encouraged in such a way as to extend the benefits into other sectors of the economy.

(e) *Balance of trade*: Will the proposal lead to the reduction of imports? Will it lead to the creation of a supply centre for world markets, and so increase exports? A positive contribution to both sides of the trade balance should be regarded as an important criterion when judging the merits of an inward investment proposal.

(f) *Commitment*: Will the company commit itself to maintain production over a number of years? Assurances should be sought that each proposal brings long-term benefits to the UK.

(g) *OECD guidelines*: Will the company commit itself to adhere to the guidelines drawn up by the OECD? Assurances on this should be sought from the company.

(h) *Inward investment in equipment industries*: Where inward investment in equipment industries is concerned, will this lead to an expansion of UK component output? Assurances should be sought that such inward investment projects would employ a majority of UK made components in value terms.

APPENDIX: JAPANESE DIRECT PARTICIPATION IN UK MANUFACTURING INDUSTRY
Terms of reference for a research project conducted for the Department of Industry, 1982/4

Scope of Project

1. The study will include an analysis of the growth and sectoral composition of such participation as compared with (i) other forms of Japanese economic penetration (imports, licensing, etc.) and (ii) investment by other foreign and UK companies. It will attempt to present as detailed a picture as possible on the finance, organisation, ownership and management structure of Japanese affiliates in the UK, their trading patterns with the rest of the world (including their parent companies), the location of their activities in the UK, their sales, net output, employment and capital expenditure and their sourcing of inputs.

2. The study will also attempt to assess (using a variety of measures) the performance of Japanese manufacturing affiliates; and, where possible, compare this performance with 'paired' US (and/or other foreign) and UK owned plants. Where differences in productivity, profitability, export performance, etc., are revealed, the main causes of such differences will be identified.

3. The study will examine some of the economic effects of Japanese direct investment in the UK and pay particular attention to the spin-off benefits of such investment, e.g. new or improved management and organisational styles, product and process technology, and marketing and distribution techniques. Some attention will also be paid to industrial relation practices within Japanese affiliates, but since 'in depth' research on this subject is currently being pursued by the Department of Industrial Relations at the London School of Economics, it will not attempt to obtain new data in this area.

4. In evaluating these effects, we propose to interview all Japanese manufacturing affiliates and a selection of their suppliers, customers and competitors. We intend to give special attention to the various

linkages formed by Japanese affiliates with indigenous UK firms and to provide as detailed an appraisal as possible of the distinctive way in which such affiliates (cf. their US and other counterparts) create and/or maintain new quality control and/or dissemination of new product and process technology. Wherever possible, we shall provide quantitative supporting evidence to our findings.

5. We shall also seek to relate our conclusions to the particular management and organisational style of the parent company and/or the Japanese affiliates. For example, with respect to the functional areas of decision-taking (e.g. those to do with product and process strategy, procurement policy, the location of research and development, etc.), how far are decisions on these delegated to the management of the Japanese affiliates and how far are they centrally conducted? Special attention will be paid to the locational attractions of the UK compared with other European countries as a base for supplying the European markets.

6. A final section of the study will deal briefly with policy issues. After reviewing the effect which UK policies have had on influencing Japanese foreign direct investment in the UK and broadly evaluating some of the main costs and benefits of such investment, the implications for future UK policy towards Japanese investment will be considered.

7. In the course of the study, many questions and issues not explicitly set out in the previous paragraphs will be examined. These include the interaction (if any) between Japanese investment in the UK and UK investment in Japan; the dynamics of Japanese involvement in the UK; the form of entry of Japanese companies (take over v. greenfield venture); the cases in which joint ventures cf. 100% owned affiliates are preferred; the main obstacles to further Japanese investment in the UK; and so on.

8. A final section will speculate on the future course of Japanese involvement in the UK in the light of the empirical findings of the study and the kind of predictions suggested by recent theories of foreign direct investment.

Methods of Working

1. Because of the relatively small number of Japanese companies operating in the UK at the moment (Department of Industry data reveal that in 1978 there were 94 Japanese affiliates in all sectors of UK industry, and current (1982) estimates suggest that there are 20-25 manufacturing affiliates), it is intended to collect a large part of the data for the study from interviews with the affiliates in question. From preliminary investigations made, it would seem likely that Japanese companies are willing to co-operate in such investigations (particularly if they are conducted by researchers with an established reputation); we have also secured the endorsement of the Japanese Embassy and the Japanese Chamber of Commerce for our project. Another set of interviews will be conducted with selected suppliers, customers and competitors of Japanese affiliates, with UK firms producing under licence to Japanese companies and also to central and local government officials dealing with applications by Japanese companies to set up affiliates in the UK.

2. In addition to the field data, all relevant macro-production trade and employment statistics will be examined and interpreted. These are mainly contained in UK and international, e.g. OECD and UN, publications.

REFERENCES

ACM Executive Seminar (1983) *Business Survival: Learning from Japanese*, ACM, Chelmsford

Aliber R.Z. (1971) 'A theory of foreign direct investment', in Kindleberger, C.P., *The International Corporation*, MIT Press, Cambridge

Anglo-Japanese Economic Institute (1981) *The Japanese Presence in Britain*, London

Beresford M.D. (1982) 'Japan's Euro-investments: threat or opportunity', *McKinsey Quarterly*, Spring

Brech M. and Sharp M. (1984) *Inward Investment: Policy Options for the United Kingdom*, Chatham House Popes No. 21, Routledge and Kegan Paul, London

Buckley P. and Casson M.C. (1985) *Economic Theory and the Multinational Enterprise*, Macmillan, London

Burton F.N. and Saelens F. (1980) 'The structure and characteristics of Japanese foreign direct investment in West Germany', *Management International, 20*, No. 4, pp. 7-16

Calvet L. (1982) 'A synthesis of foreign direct investment, theories and theories of the multinational firm', *Journal of International Business, 12*, pp. 43-60

Caves R. (1982) *Multinational Enterprises and Economic Analysis*, Cambridge University Press, Cambridge

Dicken P. (1983) 'Japanese manufacturing investment in the UK: a flood or mere trickle', *Area, 15*, No. 4

Dore R. (1973) *British Factory – Japanese Factory*, Allen and Unwin, London

Dunning J.H. (1981) *International Production and the Multinational Enterprise*, Allen and Unwin, London

—— (1983) 'Changes in the level and structure of international production; the last one hundred years', in Casson, M.C. (ed.), *The Growth of International Business*, George Allen and Unwin, London

—— (1984) 'Japanese investment in UK industry: Trojan horse or new catalyst for growth', *Multinational Business, No. 4*, pp. 1-6

—— (1985) *US and Japanese Manufacturing Affiliates in the UK: Some Similarities and Contrasts*, University of Reading Discussion Papers in International Investment and Business Studies, No. 90, October

European Company Services (1983) *Japan Direct Investment in UK Manufacturing*, London

Franko L.G. (1983) *The Threat of Japanese Multinationals*, John Wiley, Chichester

Hayes R.H. (1982) 'Why Japanese factories work', *The McKinsey Quarterly*, Autumn

Hood N. and Young S. (1982) *A Comparative Study of Corporate Strategies of Manufacturing MNEs operating in Areas of High Levels of Regional Assistance in the UK and Northern Ireland*, A report prepared for the Department of Industry, the Scottish Office, the Welsh Office and the Department of Commerce Northern Ireland

JETRO (1983) *Japanese Manufacturing Companies in Europe*, London JETRO

JETRO (US) (1981) *Japanese Manufacturing Operations in the United States*, New York, September

JETRO (US) (1982) *Japanese Manufacturing Operations in the United States: A Follow Up Study*, New York, June

JETRO (US) (1984) *Japanese Manufacturing Operations in the United States: A Third Follow up Study*, New York, June

Kidd J.B. and Teramato Y. (1981) *Japanese Production Subsidiaries in the United Kingdom: A Study of Managerial Decision Making*, University of Aston Management Centre Working Paper, No. 203 (May)

Knickerbocker F. (1973) *Oligopolistic Reaction and Multinational Enterprise*, Boston, Mass. Graduate School of Business Administration, Harvard University

Kverneland A. (1984) *Japan's Industry Structure – Barriers to Global Competition*, Stockholm, mimeo, November

Lake A. (1976) 'Foreign Competition and the UK Pharmaceutical Industry', NBER working paper No. 15

Marsh F. (1983) *Japanese Overseas Investment*, London Economist Intelligence Unit, April

Ministry of Trade and Industry (1982) *Direct Overseas Investment from Japanese Companies in Fiscal Year 1981*, Tokyo

Oba S. (1983) *Japanese Views on British Business & Industry*, Mimeo

Reitsperger W. (1982) *Japanese Manufacturing in Europe: Myths and Realities*, Paper presented to European International Business Association, 8th Annual Conference, Fontainbleau, France, December

Rugman A.M. (1979) *International Diversification and the Multinational Enterprise*, Lexington Books, Lexington

Sekiguchi S. (1979) *Japanese Direct Foreign Investment*, Macmillan, London

Steuer M. (1973) *The Impact of Foreign Direct Investment with UK Economy*, HMSO, London

Teece D.J. (1981) 'The market for knowledge and the efficient international transfer of technology', *The Annals of the American Academy of Political and Social Science*, 458, November

—— (1983) 'Technological and organisational factors in the theory of multinational entprise' in Casson, M.C. (ed.), *The Growth of International Business*, George Allen & Unwin, London

—— (1985) 'Transaction Cost Economics and the Multinational Enterprise: An Assessment' (mimeo)

Thurley K.E., Nangaku M. and Uragami K. (1976) 'Employment Relations of Japanese companies in the UK. A preliminary report', in *Production of the British Association for Japanese Studies*, Vol. 1, University of Sheffield

Thurley K.E., Reitsperger N.D., Trevor M.H. and Worm, P. (1980) *The Development of Personnel Management in Japanese Enterprises in Great Britain*, International Centre for Economics and Related Disciplines, LSE, London

Thurley K.E., Trevor M.H. and Worm P. (1981) *Japanese Management in Western Europe*, London International Centre for Economics and Related Disciplines, LSE, London

Trevor M.H. (1983) *Japan's Reluctant Multinationals*, Frances Pinter, London

Tsurumi Y. (1984) *Japan and European Multinationals in America: A Case of Flexible Corporate System*, mimeo, City University of New York, June

Vernon R. (1966) 'International investment and international trade in the product cycle', *Quarterly Journal of Economics*, 80, May

—— (1979) 'The product cycle hypothesis in a new international environment', *Oxford Bulletin of Economics and Statistics*, 41, November

White M. and Trevor M.H. (1981) *Under Japanese Management*, Heinemann, London

INDEX